The African Novel
and the Modernist Tradition

Studies in African and African-American Culture

James L. Hill
General Editor

Vol. 12

PETER LANG
New York • Washington, D.C./Baltimore
Bern • Frankfurt am Main • Berlin • Vienna • Paris

David I. Ker

The African Novel and the Modernist Tradition

PETER LANG
New York • Washington, D.C./Baltimore
Bern • Frankfurt am Main • Berlin • Vienna • Paris

Library of Congress Cataloging-in-Publication Data

Ker, David I.
The African novel and the modernist tradition / David I. Ker.
p. cm. — (Studies in African and African-American culture; vol. 12)
Includes bibliographical references and index.
1. African fiction (English)—History and criticism. 2. Literature,
Comparative—African and English. 3. Literature, Comparative—African and
American. 4. Literature, Comparative—American and African. 5. Literature,
Comparative—English and African. 6. Modernism (Literature)—Africa.
I. Title. II. Series.
PR9344.K47   823—dc20   95-51801
ISBN 0-8204-2648-2 (hardcover)
ISBN 0-8204-4084-1 (paperback)
ISSN 0890-4847

Die Deutsche Bibliothek-CIP-Einheitsaufnahme

Ker, David I.:
The African novel and the modernist tradition / David I. Ker.
–New York; Washington, D.C./Baltimore; Bern; Frankfurt am Main;
Berlin; Vienna; Paris: Lang.
(Studies in African and African American culture; Vol. 12)
ISBN 0-8204-2648-2 (hardcover)
ISBN 0-8204-4084-1 (paperback)
NE: GT

The paper in this book meets the guidelines for permanence and durability
of the Committee on Production Guidelines for Book Longevity
of the Council of Library Resources.

∞

Printed in the United States of America.

TO BEATRICE

TABLE OF CONTENTS

Acknowledgments ix

1. Introduction: Modernism and the African Novel 1

2. The Dramatised Perspective: Henry James, *The Tragic Muse;*
   Wole Soyinka, *The Interpreters* 16

3. The Inward Perspective: James Joyce, *A Portrait of the Artist as a
   Young Man;* Virginia Woolf, *The Waves;* Kofi Awoonor, *This
   Earth, My Brother* 40

4. The Multiple Perspective I: Joseph Conrad, *Nostromo;*
   Ngugi Wa Thiong'o, *Petals of Blood* 75

5. The Multiple Perspective II: William Faulkner, *Absalom,
   Absalom!;* Ayi Kwei Armah, *Why Are We So Blest?* 103

6. The Communal Perspective: Chinua Achebe, *Things Fall Apart
   and Arrow of God;* Ayi Kwei Armah, *Two Thousand Seasons;*
   Gabriel Okara, *The Voice* 125

7. Conclusion 182

Notes 186

Bibliography 197

Index 216

ACKNOWLEDGEMENTS

I have been lucky in my interaction over the years with several people who have given me the courage and inspiration that made this book possible. In its early stages Professor Norman Jeffares proved to be a most helpful teacher. I went to Stirling overawed by his reputation but was amazed by his humility. He taught me a lot about writing and about developing confidence. At Stirling too I met Angela Smith whose kindness and commitment saw me through the early drafts of the manuscript. I am also glad to acknowledge the contributions of Felicity and John Riddy and of Lance St. John Butler.

While in the United States on a Fulbright grant I worked with Edward Griffin of the University of Minnesota, a most useful senior colleague and friend. In the United States too I had the benefit of incisive comments from Neil Lazarus of Brown University while the University of South Carolina gave me an opportunity to present parts of the book at a seminar on Africa. Several colleagues in Nigeria have also been helpful. I can only mention a few: Sam Asein, Olu Obafemi, Yakubu Nasidi and Tyohdzuah Akosu. My brothers, Aondover, Igbawase, and Tarhemen have always stood by me. I thank them for their faith and warmth of family.

I owe debts to the Benue State Government and the Fulbright Commission without whose generous grants this work would not have been completed. Ahmadu Bello University also gave a lot of support and I wish to thank Professor D.I. Saror, the Vice

Chancellor for his interest in my work. I am happy to acknowledge that it took the tranquillity of the Rockefeller Foundation's Villa Serbelloni at Bellagio, Italy to complete this book.

My wife, Beatrice, to whom the book is dedicated remains the best friend I have. Without her faith in me and her tireless and meticulous care this book could not have been written. Our children, Terrumun, Tavershima, Erdoo and David Ker Jr. have developed an admirable understanding for a dad who keeps disappearing. I know they will grow to understand more.

CHAPTER ONE

INTRODUCTION: MODERNISM AND THE AFRICAN NOVEL

Chinua Achebe's *Things Fall Apart* (1958), one of the first African novels to gain international acclaim, appropriated its title from the spirit of the modernist age. Yet discussions of the African novel, novels that were published in quick succession after Achebe's debut, tend to ignore the significance of his choice of title. Nor did critics take the cue when Achebe also chose the title of his second novel, *No Longer at Ease* (1960) from T.S. Eliot's 'The Journey of the Magi.' Surely, the insistence on these themes suggests a conscious attempt by Achebe to respond to the scenario of chaos caused by colonialism which for him and for other African writers bore resemblance 'to the horror,' 'the nightmare of history' that modernist writers in Europe and America were writing about. Modernism provided the African novelist with an art that could adequately express his view of history.

My purpose in this book is to show the manner in which several African novelists have taken full advantage of the experimentation that modernism offers to tackle their own 'crisis of culture'. I shall show how modernism's consciousness of disorder, despair and anarchy is the perfect medium for the African novelist for conveying on the one hand his nostalgia for the past, with all its imperfections and on the other hand his bitterly ironic indictments of the present.[1] In doing so I accept the definition of Bradbury and Macfarlane who see modernism as 'the movement toward sophistication and mannerism, towards introspection, technical display and internal self-scepticism.' Bradbury and Macfarlane show quite correctly that modernism's experimentation does not simply suggest the presence of sophistication, difficulty and novelty as their definition above implies. It also suggests bleakness, darkness, alienation and disintegration.[2] The modernist artist is not simply an artist set free in the Joycean sense but the artist under a specific historical strain. For the African novelist, colonialism is the strain that brought him into the international literary modernist scene.

That this entry of the African novelist into the modernist stream has been glossed over is obviously a problem that African literary criticism needs to address. It is common to assume as many critics and writers have done that the African novel is not yet ready for the modern. In condemning Ayi Kwei Armah's fine novel *The Beautyful Ones Are Not Yet Born* (1968) Chinua Achebe observed caustically that Ghana is not a modern existentialist country[3] and up till 1979 Kole Omotoso, another novelist, could still say that:

> Very few African novelists, if any, have bothered to keep up in their novel writing with the technical development in the novel form in the respective language of their writing, being as it were satisfied with the conventional form of the European novel.[4]

Theo Vincent also ends an otherwise brilliant essay on the issue of black aesthetics by lamenting that it is quite possible that the African writers will add some new dimension to the novel form, but we have to wait for that.[5]

This study hopes to show that these observations have been made a bit too hastily and cannot account for the novels by Africans that are examined here.[6] In examining these African novels side by side with British and American modernist novels, I hope to demonstrate that there are striking similarities between them much as there are some clear differences. The African novelists equally make conscious attempts at experimentation much of which have not been identified preoccupied as critics have been with endless quarrels over the different approaches to African literary criticism.[7]

I have not ignored the debate over standards of criticism but I have chosen to take part by means of this comparative study which argues that the African novel is part of a larger fictional universe. I have shown that the novelists participate in this universe in a mature, path-breathing way by appropriating the most innovative techniques of modernist fiction the ones we associate with James, Conrad, Woolf, Joyce and Faulkner.[8] In doing so they contribute to the modern novel by providing a special way of handling point of view.

Point of view is not used here in Lubbock's older, more formalist sense, rather I employ it in Genette's sense of a pronominal vertigo which thus allows us to think about other fictional features than the relationship of the narrator to the story.[9] In these highly experimental novels I find that the novelists establish what Genette discusses in a related context, as a variable and floating relationship in tune with a freer logic and a more complex conception of personality. Genette further observes that the type of emancipation these modernist novelists achieve is not perceptible because the 'classical attributes of character have disappeared along with the signs that direct pronominal traffic.[10] The arguments against the classical attributes of character and the primacy of the narrator with regard to management of point of view are supported in this book by a category which I have described as the COMMUNAL PERSPECTIVE. In Ayi Kwei Armah's *Two Thousand Seasons* (1977), for example, pronominal usage is dominated by the collective 'we' but the reader soon discovers that such a sign is not helpful in determining the point of view of the narrator in the story.

The attention of the reader is drawn instead to a unique characterisation which is worked through an inventive use of language and setting. The novel's use of a simple language is meant to be read as a hall-mark of the community's uncomplicated way of life but such word as 'discombolulation' reveal another narrator who clearly supervises the performance of the communal narrators; one who tries to control the reader's judgement on the central concerns of the novel. Moreover in the case of Achebe's *Things Fall Apart* and *Arrow of God* (1964) and Gabriel Okara's *The Voice* (1964) this communal perspective or voice of the community is achieved without the benefit of the collective pronoun.

Point of view for the modernist may thus be manifested at many levels in a novel; it initiates and develops the devices which convey the presence and the attitudes of a textual voice; it is, as Susan Lanser observes, the 'stylistic philosophic centre of a novel.'[11] My aim in this book, however, is not to establish point of view as a blue print of literary theory and criticism, nor is it claimed as the only 'sensible' way through which criticism of the modern African novel may be conducted. I have used point of view to show how modernist tendencies manifest themselves in the novel irrespective of its specific cultural background.

The novels I have discussed in detail are classified into four broad divisions inspired by the theories of Uspensky, Genette and Susan Lanser which I have modified to serve the comparative designs of the book.[12] The question of emphasis and relative weight has determined which of these modernist novels are considered as deploying the dramatised, the inward, the multiple and the communal perspectives.

In Chapter two I examine the novels of Henry James and Wole Soyinka using the dramatised perspective as a guiding concept to provide a useful approach towards technique and thematic definition in the novels. I am not implying by this method that the dramatised perspective is peculiar to the two novelists. On the contrary it can be successfully argued that every modernist novelist integrates dramatic elements in his novels. Few people, however, will dispute James's claim to the title of the modern master of the dramatised perspective. James not only wrote his novels from a dramatised point of view but also left a rich legacy of critical terms for evaluating his novels in particular, and the art of the novel in general.

In the preface to *The Tragic Muse* (1890), for example, he refers to 'scenic conditions which are as near an approach to the dramatic as the novel may permit.'[13] The material of *The*

Ambassadors (1903) is taken, James asserts, 'absolutely from the stuff of drama; emphasising that the novel displays a 'scenic consistency.'[14] Percy Lubbock and other critics of James have added a great deal to our understanding of his novels explaining and supplementing the numerous terms such as 'scene and summary,' 'foreshortening,' 'pictorial fusion,' 'the ficelles,' James's 'scene a faire' and 'coups de theatres.'[15] It is sometimes difficult to say whether drama, and not the novel, is the subject-matter of most of the critical studies of James's novels.

Wole Soyinka is the reverse side of the same Jamesian coin. Soyinka is, unlike James, a successful dramatist, and can perhaps be called an amateur novelist. Like James, however, Soyinka seems to believe that the novelist should show events in the act of happening, indeed, the intended title for his first novel was *The Happening*.[16] For both writers each event that is crucial to the story must be presented in action. In their novels action and characters interact to the point of fusion. A close study of the novels reveals further similarities in structural and thematic concerns. Many critics of James's novels emphasise what they see as 'renunciation and repudiation' in them. Sallie Sears, for example, insists that we view James's vision as negative because of what she describes as his inability to assert positive values with any degree of success.[17] Similarly, Wole Soyinka has been accused by many of a negative vision and several critics are frustrated by what they see as his aimless virtuosity.[18] The modernist sensibility often involves an unhappy view of history which is what critics of both novelists are worried about, indeed Soyinka has talked about the cannibalistic nature of human civilization.[19] In the novels I have examined here a toughened modernist irony is seen at work as the main characters who are mainly artists find ways of coping with the tyranny of their time.

James's *The Tragic Muse* represents the story of the artistic life and it bustles with characters as well as with scenes and actions. There are, in fact, two stories in the novel but as Ernest Baker observes, James manages to give a good general picture of life going vigorously on.[20] Similarly, Soyinka's *The Interpreters* dramatises 'stories' of the artistic life. The novel is also crowded with characters and with scenes and much activity and, as in *The Tragic Muse*, the major characters are faced with choices which prove 'tyrannical.' The characters in both novels are in every sense modernist interpreters. What Gabriel Nash feels in *The Tragic Muse* about his role might well apply to Egbo and his friends in *The Interpreters*:

> He was so accustomed to living upon irony and the interpretation of things that it was strange to him to be himself interpreted.[21]

To examine the workings of point of view in these two modernist novels is thus to examine the characterisation, the way the characters are linked by numerous dramatic scenes and actions in which relationships are entangled, such scene or action being structured by the conflicting world view of the characters, a world view expressed largely through the novelist's copious use of dialogue. Dialogue is the essence of drama and consequently the dominant feature of the novels of James and Soyinka. Time too plays a significant role in the development of character and relationships and there are significant differences between James's and Soyinka's use of time, all of which are examined in this chapter.

The INWARD PERSPECTIVE, a term I prefer to the more familiar stream-of-consciousness, is used in chapter three to examine the novels of James Joyce, Virginia Woolf and the Ghanaian poet-novelist, Kofi Awoonor. Joyce's name has become synonymous with the technique which is described as the inward perspective. Readers of Virginia Woolf have also found a kinship in method between some of her novels and those of Joyce and the pair can be regarded as the quintessential stream-of-consciousness novelists. Through their novels 'the very folds and creases of the individual mind' are unravelled. The reader's interest is drawn from the outer to the inner world of the character and in these writers the modernists's search for a style is made manifest. Both writers are engaged in a profound and ceaseless journey through the means and integrity of art.

In this chapter I show that the Ghanaian, Kofi Awoonor, employs similar devices to those of James Joyce in *A Portrait of the Artist as a Young Man* (1916) and Virginia Woolf in *The Waves*

(1931). *This Earth, My Brother*...(1972) has quite correctly been described as 'a prose-poem' and Awoonor himself has acknowledged a debt to Joyce.[22] Yet in examining the novels, Richard Priebe describes it as a work which thoroughly defies conventional Western criticism.[23] The purpose of the comparison in this chapter is to show that these three modernist novels have a lot more in common than would appear. 'The details of language, culture, history;' as Awoonor himself observes in a related situation, 'may define the variations.' But they are all variations upon the same theme: MAN.[24] Indeed, there are striking similarities in thematic concerns which match the similar techniques used by all three novelists. The reader notices in these novels a kinship of search and pilgrimage. All their protagonists are modernists who embark on adventure in real and metaphoric terms. George Moore, one of the earlier exponents of the inward perspective provides an accurate metaphor for these adventures:

> There is a lake in every man's heart.... And every man must ungird his loins for the crossing.[25]

Stephen crosses into exile, Bernard into eternity and Amamu joins his ancestors. Each of these characters has a fertile imagination which allows him to maintain the balance between symbol and action; in many ways symbol is action in the novels.

An examination of the way the inward perspective works involves ripping apart the means by which a character's inner mind is exposed to the reader. Such a task entails a closer look at symbolism which is largely conjured through memory and an analysis of the way the question of time is affected by, and affects the point of view which the novels represent.

I have used the MULTIPLE PERSPECTIVE in chapter four and five to examine the novels of Joseph Conrad, William Faulkner, Ngugi Wa Thiong'o and Ayi Kwei Armah. "A work of art" Conrad once said, 'is very seldom limited to one exclusive meaning and not necessarily tending to a definite conclusion.'[26] Conrad's observation could be seen as a blue print of modernist writing and is applicable, to a large extent, to all the novels in this study. The difference though lies in the fact that Conrad's aim in his own novels seems to have been to test the full implications of his observations. Consequently, the novels highlight the difficulty of understanding human nature and motivation in general. The novels are usually the confessions of witnesses who are given ample opportunity to speak and who pass the narrative back and forth to one another so that the same story acquires different shades and forms. In Conrad's novels, the reader like the detective, weighs the evidence and analyzes action by studying the surface as well as the psychological states of the characters in order to arrive at conclusions which may differ from those of other observers of the situation. This pluralization of world view is a common feature of modernism and William Faulkner used it with interesting variations which are considered in chapter five.

The Kenyan, Ngugi Wa Thiong'o, also adopts Conrad's modernism which he describes as 'the questioning technique.' 'This kind of questioning, Ngugi admits, 'has impressed me a lot because with Conrad I have felt I have come into contact with another whose questioning to me is much more important than the answers which he gives.[27] Ngugi's *Petals of Blood* (1977) deploys similar devices to those used by Conrad in *Nostromo* (1904). The former like the latter presents a complex of interfused confessions emanating from the dramatic actions of characters who are caught in a crucial historical moment. In both novels, that moment is the advent of capitalism; of 'material interests' and the impact this event brings to bear on individual characters and of the societies depicted. What Thomas Moser says of *Nostromo* could well be said of *Petals of Blood*. Both novels, 'literally annihilate the reader with a surfeit of sounds, sights, names, facts and complicated information imperfectly apprehended.' Moser suggests with regard to *Nostromo*, that this is a deliberate way of enabling the reader to experience some of the emotional chaos of the characters....[28] This is equally true of *Petals of Blood*. The two novels show a modernist's obsession with pluralization. Each of the major characters in the novels, like Munira in *Petals of Blood*, imagines that he has found a key which opens up, 'once and for all time the true universal connection between things, events, persons, places and time," but Munira's conviction only results in the arson which leads to the murders under investigation in the novel and is as mistaken and as disastrous as Nostromo's decision to get rich slowly. In these novels as all but a few of the characters learn, things are not what they seem. What appears as a clue to one character becomes a fresh question to another.

Much of what has been said of the novels of Conrad and Ngugi could also be said of the novels of William Faulkner and the Ghanaian Ayi Kwei Armah, although there are significant variations in their use of the multiple perspective which I have tried to highlight. Studies of Faulkner's narrative techniques generate some useful metaphors which underline the subtlety in his novels and thus show the difference between them and the novels of Conrad. Warren Beck, for example, describes Faulkner's narratives as 'one of those brightly coloured Chinese eggs... which when opened, disclosed egg after egg, each smaller and subtler than the first.' Beck elaborates:

> There is no absolute, no eternal pure white radiance in such presentation but rather the strain of many colours, refracted and shifting in kaleidoscopic suspension, about the centre of man's enigmatic behaviour and fate, within the drastic orbit of mortality.[29]

Faulkner's modernism allows a variety of consciousness to reflect on the central concerns of his novels and each novel reveals a subtler variation of the technique: each novel gives the reader the task of fitting pieces together. The sum total of the fragments make the story, in much the same way, Faulkner once suggested, that a carpenter fits bits and pieces together to build a cabinet. *As I Lay Dying* (1935) is a good example of the technique at work. The story of the novel emerges through the interplay of fifteen narrators; each of these narrative fragments contributes to the central story which is the gruesome journey undertaken by the Bundren family.

Faulkner's analogy, however, though appropriate for *As I Lay Dying* could be misleading in the context of *Absalom, Absalom!* (1938). Here Faulkner's technique offers, perhaps not so much a finished cabinet, but the bits and pieces with which to build one. The narrators in *Absalom, Absalom!* are apprentice carpenters: curious but incompetent. Even though Faulkner tried to minimise the problem by likening the novel's technique to 'thirteen ways of looking at a blackbird,' it is more useful, as Richard Poirer suggests, to look at the novel as the work of historical recreation.[30] The narrators tell their story more in the manner of the historian, who, to paraphrase Albert Guerard, clarifies and verifies the past from often sparse, distorted and conflicting evidence, sometimes refusing to decide between alternatives and even describing his process of inconclusive reasoning.[31] The narration of Sutpen's saga thrives on the historian's sense of conjecture. Conjecture thus becomes the novels point of view, a vehicle for plausible creation of character and events. A double focus, akin to Conrad's in *Lord Jim* emerges, in which the observer-narrators themselves are centres of dramatic interest as well as the story they relate to the reader: *Absalom, Absalom!* is as much a story of Quentin, Compson, Shreve and their collaborating narrators as it is of Thomas Sutpen.

Ayi Kwei Armah employs similar techniques to those used by William Faulkner sketched above. *Why Are We So Blest?* (1974) bears great resemblance to *Absalom, Absalom!* Solo Nkonam, one of the novel's major narrators treats the stories of the other narrators Modin Dofu and Aimee Reitsch in the same way that Quentin and Shreve, with help from Rosa Coldfield and Mr. Compson, handle the story of Thomas Sutpen. In place of the skeletal story of Sutpen, Solo as it were, has Modin's notebooks:

> I searched them, filling in holes, answering questions I have asked myself and found no answers to, speculating, arranging and rearranging these notes to catch all possible meaning.[32]

Solo's need to catch all possible meaning coincides with the desperate need of the two Harvard roommates in *Absalom, Absalom!* to make meaning out of Sutpen's story. Solo arranges and rearranges Modin's notes to catch a meaning in the same way that Quentin and Shreve, and their collaborating narrators arrange and rearrange Sutpen's story. Seen in this way repetition becomes an inevitable element of their narrative technique. Repetition serves as an accumulative device which enables the narrators to tease out meaning from the numerous ambiguous situations in which they find themselves. In a recent study *Faulkner and Modernism* (1990), Richard Moreland describes this tendency on the part of Faulkner as 'revisionary repetition:' According to Moreland, 'this modernist strategy opens up a critical space for what the subject might learn about (that) structure in the different context of a changing present or a more distant or different past.' Quoting Sartre, Moreland talks about life for Faulkner developing in spirals; it passes again and again by the same points but at different levels of integration and complexity.[33] It is a modernist tendency well understood by Armah and used skilfully in *Why Are We So Blest*?

There is thus a kinship and affinity between the novels of Conrad and Ngugi as there is between the novels of Faulkner and Armah. A close examination of their narrative devices, their use of metaphor and of repetition and the way in which each novelist handles time reveals this. Here again, similarities in technique are matched by affinities in thematic concerns. Solo, who even before (his) death has become a ghost wandering about the face of the earth, bears a resemblance to Quentin who is also 'too young to deserve yet to be a ghost, but nevertheless having to be one for all that, since he was born and bred in the deep South.'[34] Both characters, typical modernist creations, are doomed through some cause antecedent to their own existence; both are victims of some large fatality marked for their respective societies, the American South for one and colonial and neo-colonial Africa for the other. Indeed Armah's Africa is portrayed in the same melancholy tone for which Faulkner's Yoknapatawpha county has become famous. Michael Echeruo is right to assert that 'Armah is for (us) what Faulkner was to the American South: A Jeremiah without Jehovah?'[35]

In the final chapter of this book I examine four novels which deploy what I describe as the communal perspective. These novels are written on behalf of communities and all the novelists probably agree with Achebe that 'their aims and the deepest aspirations of their society meet.'[36] In these novels the characters are not potential modernist authors impatient to rebel and leave their hostile, environment for the literary profession. Rather they see themselves as integral members of their community. We may agree with Mark Schorer that the devices of point of view enable the novelist to disentangle his own prejudices and predispositions from those of his characters but such a view needs modification with regard to these novels which deploy the communal perspective.[37] The novels emerge as the record of participant observers whose identification with the world they relate is almost total but they also reveal other voices looking over the shoulder of such observers and as in *Two Thousand Seasons* highlighting and endorsing the dichotomy created between 'them' and 'us.'

Several innovatory features emerge from such a concept of point of view some of which were hinted upon earlier in this introduction. It will be recalled that pronominal usage, for instance, can no longer be relied upon as a yardstick for determining point of view in the novels. Moreover, the reader who comes to the novels with the conviction that character is 'a paradigm of traits' or who joins character and psychological representation as 'the Siamese twins of novel theory' will face problems of interpretation.[38] The traits of the community may not be hard to describe as they are well itemised in *Two Thousand Seasons*, for example, and indeed the psychology may also be easy to understand but the reader will need to revise his views about what constitutes traits and whose psychology is being recorded in order to accommodate a human referent which is larger and more complex than the figures to which he has become accustomed.

Such an open theory of characterisation will enable the reader to see a figure with varying degrees of richness of detail not commonly associated with a single character in a novel. In *Two Thousand Seasons* the community of Anoa emerges as such a figure, so that the twenty narrators through whose eyes the story comes to the reader become mere manifestations or traits of this protagonist. They provide diversity to what is a unified whole or what we may now call a character. Armah's novel, like the early novels of Chinua Achebe, *Things Fall Apart* and *Arrow of God*, demand a review of the classical attribute of character that the reader has come to expect in a novel; such attributes as proper name, 'physical and moral nature' need to be transferred from the individual to the community. Similarly, questions which help characterisation such as who is he? and what does he stand for? are still relevant but in the novels under study they should read as 'who are they?' and 'what do they stand for?'

Innovative use of language in the novels provides the novelists with an effective tool to manipulate point of view and thus lead the reader to answers which such questions about character demand. It is true as Rimmon-Kenan observes that there are novels in which the language of the characters is individuated and distinguished from that of the narrator, but in *Two Thousand Seasons*, for example, Armah attempts to submerge the voice of the narrator in the collective narrative voice, making the plurality of the narrative an integral part of the novel's meaning.[39]

With Achebe in *Things Fall Apart* and *Arrow of God* such a voice finds expression in terse proverbial sayings and in the songs and tales, but Armah attempts, not too successfully, to create a completely new language through a reversal of symbols and metaphors and a combination of imitation and 'translation.' All the novels in this category are marked by a sense of performance in the manner of folktales. The narrators regard their task more as an exercise in 'verbal art' aimed at an audience of 'hearers' or 'listeners' than the narration of a story to passive readers. The awareness of an audience thus becomes an integral part of the novel's narrative structure and also helps in establishing point of view in it. The reader is required, like the audience at a folk session, to participate in the 'eloquent' story-telling in which he has become a part. This is true of *Things Fall Apart* and *Arrow of God*, of Gabriel Okara's only novel *The Voice* and of Ayi Kwei Armah.

The modernist's use of point of view is thus the binding theme of this book. It plays a crucial role in the concept of the novel held by all the novelists discussed. Each of the novels has various levels of emphasis through which point of view may be analysed. Thus only characterisation is common in the discussion of each chapter. It is held that the redistribution of the elements of character does not totally destroy it and that the method by which character and motivation are brought to the reader is paramount to the reader's understanding of the novel's point of view. Other features, however, differ. For instance, a novel whose primary perspective is to dramatise the events and actions as in the novels of James and Soyinka will be better understood if other dramatic elements such as the use of scene and action, or dialogue are taken into account.

The inward perspective as used by Joyce, Woolf and Awoonor requires greater attention to symbolism and to the uses of memory while the novel deploying the multiple perspective as in Conrad, Faulkner, Ngugi and Armah requires greater regard to its use of metaphor and the ways through which repetition emphasises the novel's central concerns. Language is a common denominator of all novels but attention to it becomes more crucial when the reader needs to distinguish between numerous voices in the novel as in the novels of Achebe, Okara and Armah's *Two Thousand Seasons*. It is also assumed that spatial and temporal setting may be common to most novels without becoming central to them as will be found in the novels of Chinua Achebe and Ayi Kwei Armah. Point of view thus provides a flexibility of method that allows a critic looking at these complex modernist novels to make adjustments according to a novel's main areas of emphasis.

To conclude this introduction, I should like to say one more word on the method I have used. I have clustered thirteen novels by British, American and African writers together, holding them up against each other and against the tenets of modernism to throw each into relief. In doing so, I may be charged with being formalist, even technicist but I have not been blind to the historical and social circumstances outside the texts that I have examined. The modernist novelist, a Joyce, Woolf or Awoonor may appear desperate, even obsessed by the search for style but is equally concerned with the troubled history of his society which in fact triggers his desperation and anguish in the first place. My close readings of these novels do not therefore altogether remove the study from an awareness of the historical and cultural background from which each writer emanates even if such a background is not foregrounded as some critics may want it to be.[40]

If the book succeeds it shows that there is a common ground between the African novelist and his British and American counterpart. It also shows that there are differences worth noting. In pointing out these similarities and differences I hope to demonstrate the originality of the African novelists. There is a lot to be achieved in this comparative strategy especially for the African writer who is only recently being accorded a place within the larger fictional universe. I agree with the authors of *The Empire Writes Back* (1989) who say that 'the strength of post-colonial theory may well lie in its inherently comparative methodology and the hybridized and syncretic view of the modern world.'[41] All the African novels that I have examined are 'complex and hybridized formations' which should be read neither as reconstructions of pure traditional values as quite a number of the literary nationalists tend to do, nor as simply foreign and intrusive as the Eurocentric critics suggest.[42] A process which consists in pointing out analogies, similarities and differences in novels which show artistic affinity is a more revelatory process than the parochialism which sometimes is presented with nationalist/racial sentiments. Chinua Achebe provides an analogy which should endear us to the method I have used here. Says Achebe:

> Let every people bring their gifts to the great festival of the worlds' cultural harvest and mankind will all be richer for the variety and distinctiveness of the offerings.[43]

In saying so Achebe is aware of the relations of power and the dispositions of critics he labels as colonialist critics but the international literary statesman makes this optimistic call which might bring the 'warring' factions together. The reader will find that in this book I try to make a contribution in the direction suggested by Achebe, one of the major writers in this study.

CHAPTER TWO

THE DRAMATISED PERSPECTIVE: HENRY JAMES, *THE TRAGIC MUSE*; WOLE SOYINKA, *THE INTERPRETERS*

Both James and Soyinka push their novels as far toward the spoken and the dramatic as they can. Both create scenes which are composed of the conflicting attitudes of the protagonists. These scenes and their underlying conflicts give the novels form and meaning; they determine their point of view. Mark Kinkead-Weekes observes similar tendencies in a study of Richardson who, it appears, clearly anticipated both novelists. Of Richardson's novels Kinkead-Weekes remarks:

> We have to measure the points of view against one another to understand how things happen and what will happen next; as scenes are repeated with variations, Richardson keeps giving his characters the freedom of another chance, which they use increasingly to determine themselves. Scenes become linked in chains, where apparent repetition points up significant differences and reveals development.[1]

It is thus not surprising that interpretation is at the heart of Richardson's modernist successors. James's and Soyinka's protagonists interpret others, are themselves interpreted by other characters and by readers who may assume the role of an audience at a play. The process is enhanced by a skilful use of scene and action and by the use of dialogue. Each character is made to play a significant role in the action. 'The action,' observes Edwin Muir, in a related context, 'begins never with a single character, but with two or more, it starts from several points on its circumference which is a complex, not a nucleus, of personal relationships.'[2]

If Soyinka or James was to begin his novel inserting a page announcing the 'dramatis personae' it could all be in order, for the first thing that strikes the reader of the novels is a sense of characters impelled by the need to engage in dramatic relationships with others. Characters in their novels have an inherent dramatic element in them which makes the relationships they subsequently engage in mere antagonistic attractions warring for their soul. Each of the major characters is portrayed as two men with scarcely a point in common. There are, thus, two concomitant dramatic situations posed in characterisation which consist of the drama within the character and the equally dramatic encounter he confronts in relationships.

In James's *The Tragic Muse*, there is Nick Dormer, bred up in a richly political atmosphere and with traditionally political antecedents, introduced to influences which push him in two opposed directions-into the House of Commons or the Artist's Studio. As if the situation were not complicated enough the reader soon discovers that Nick's nature defies any obligations. Choice is a form of tyranny for this modernist, highly imaginative, independent-minded and dreamy character. Nick Dormer, however, is not alone. Together with Miriam Roth, Peter Sherringham and other characters in the novel such as Julia Dallow and Charles Cateret represent the corrupt, political world against whose influence Nick battles. The 'web of relationship' into which all these characters are enmeshed is a source of drama. James offers the reader an exercise in contrast and comparison which he facilitates by arranging them as in a director's diagram. We are never allowed to lose sight of them on stage as they are presented to us as a lively and gregarious lot.

They shuttle from house to house, in and out of hansoms; we meet them at rehearsals, at restaurants and at playhouses or on several occasions simply walking, but they are very seldom alone. Indeed there is a close relationship between these characters: Nick Dormer and Gabriel Nash were schoolmates and Nick is a cousin of both Peter Sherringham and Julia Dallow. Gabriel Nash introduces Miriam Roth and her mother to his friends and again an intricate relationship develops. Often these characters act as one 'family:'

> ..... weren't they all caught in a common centrifuge through the hurt
> of gilded abstractions, full of flies reaching for a long time whisk to
> brush away thought smarts embedded in each sting. (p.221)

Soyinka's metaphor with regard to the characters in *The Interpreters* sums up much of what goes on in *The Tragic Muse*.

The key-word in all these close but intricate relationships is conflict, which is crucial to drama. In whatever way we see them, the relationships of the characters in the novel are built on conflict. Moreover, the drama that faces them is not usually a question of choice as they seem to imply, rather they are confronted with a dilemma in which any decision means some major sacrifice, capitulation or surrender. This is the situation facing Nick Dormer who through Julia Dallow and Charles Cateret, is confronted with the consequences of apostasy. In fact, he finds that he hardly gets a chance to make a choice. On his election, Nick confesses that 'he had done something even worse than not choose. He had let others choose for him (p.178). Conflict, for him, is poised in so many directions that he becomes 'a broken reed' destined as it were, to float with the tide. Yet the alternative is often beautiful, 'the beauty of having taken the world in a brave personal way' (p.125).

This modernist tendency to take the world in a brave personal way is recognised by Gabriel Nash who poses as a father, not only to Nick Dormer, but also to the other artist, Miriam, both of whom find in him an 'ambiguous but an excellent touchstone!' Nash both clarifies and confuses the two artists. He tries to outline the 'choices' more clearly but because he favours 'the artistic life' he tends to ignore the attraction which the political world offers his friends. To intensify the conflict and perhaps to confuse them further, he disappears without a trace, 'melts back into the elements, part of the ambient air,' as dramatic as the situations that he helped to invent, introduce and reveal.

Conflict within and among the characters in the novel takes further dramatic dimensions when these characters relate with the 'outside' world. Their lives are a reaction to all that happens around them, indeed, as critics have repeatedly pointed out, the interest in James's novels is not so much in the events but in the reactions of the characters to those events. Thus the corrupt reality is intensified to bring out the potential creativity of the imaginative consciousness. This is why James appears to have chosen his characters carefully; they are usually people of very high intellect, but in order to evaluate them properly James gives them rich and complex backgrounds against which their talents can be tested to their fullest realization. There is a sharp contrast, for instance, between the world of politics and the world of the artist when the action takes place in Charles Cateret's house. Everything inside the house down to the shoes is 'king-size,' grotesque, but attractive in its own way. When the reader learns that Cateret would have bequeathed $60,000 to Nick, he begins to see the nature of the sacrifice that Nick has had to make. The pull of the grandeur of the nation, of politics is so strong, it is not surprising that Nick becomes restless, walking in and out of the house. As if Charles Cateret, with his constant reminders of Nick's late father, was not enough, Nick is faced with an even bigger dilemma in Julia Dallow who is not only rich but is beautiful and is perhaps even in love with him. Faced with such 'monsters' and with only Gabriel Nash as the guiding philosopher, life, for Nick, presents conflict at its worst. It is no wonder that he comes out only in partial triumph.

In Soyinka's *The Interpreters*, Egbo and his friends face similar situations. Egbo, for instance finds that he is forced to make a choice, between taking over the inheritance of his father's kingdom or becoming a bureaucrat in Lagos; to set the war lord of the creeks against dull grey file cabinet faces of the foreign office (p.13). As in *The Tragic Muse*, Egbo in *The Interpreters* is not alone. Together with Sagoe, Bandele, Kola and Sekoni, he forms a community of interests as we find in James's novel. Background characters such as the Oguazors and Ayo Faseyi represent the world which Egbo and his friends seek to interpret. In addition to the corrupt politicians, Sagoe's employers at the Board of the 'Independent View Point,' the Oguazors and Ayo Faseyi' represent the 'plastic values' with which the interpreters strive to come to terms. They must, however, first come to terms with themselves. But because they are, like the major characters in *The Tragic Muse*, highly imaginative, independent minded and dreamy, they soon find that attempts to clarify their positions are fraught with complications. For them too choice is a form of tyranny and like the characters in James's novel they all have to face the consequences of apostasy.

Like James, Soyinka also 'enmeshes' his characters in a web or relationships which invites the reader to compare and contrast their actions with those with whom they come into contact. As in James's novel, Egbo and his friends are a lively and gregarious lot. *The Interpreters* presents an ubiquitous cast of characters who move from one town to another, from one night club to yet another night club, drinking with epicurean relish. They were all school mates and seem to find it easy to keep in touch. Their group instinct is noticeable when they are faced with a common dilemma, the outside world inspires unity within the group which eventually leads to severance. The unity is only a preparation, it seems, for intense dramatic moments. The close ties do not make the drama less complex, infact, the contrary is the case, for Soyinka, like James, is a master of the dramatic paradox. At moments when the cast is assembled, such as the night they all go to watch Joe Golder's play, they acknowledge that it is a night of severance, every man is going his way (p.245). Even when one of them, Sekoni, dies, their common grief only triggers separation and it requires the calm of Bandele to bring back some sense of community.

Yet even Bandele fails because conflict seems to be indispensable to their lives. The relationships of the characters in *The Interpreters* like those in *The Tragic Muse*, are built on conflict. Here too the drama that faces the characters is not merely one about questions of choice, they too are confronted with dilemmas in which any decision means some major sacrifice or capitulation. Like Nick Dormer, Egbo likens himself to a 'broken reed.' Perhaps, even worse than Nick, he seems at times incapable of floating with the tide. 'All his friends are doing something,' he admits, 'but (he) merely goes from one event to the other as if life was nothing but experience' (p.133). Yet, like Nick, he has so much talent and promise, indeed all his friends, especially the artist Kola, envy him. Egbo's varied experience is presented through comparison and contrast with his fellow interpreters and through the juxtaposition of his positive and negative features.

Contrast may be recognised for instance between Egbo and Sekoni who dares to be fulfilled. In the short period that he lives in the novel he acts as a foil to Egbo's recklessness and apostasy. As an electrical engineer he builds a plant but when he cannot get a chance to test it he redirects his energies to his latent talent and sculpts 'The Wrestler' which all the interpreters acknowledge is a great work. But perhaps Egbo's greatest foil is Bandele, the taciturn teacher, the mask of infinite patience who at times is like a timeless image brooding over lesser beings. Bandele, resembles Gabriel Nash in *The Tragic Muse* a great deal. Both characters are good-natured and they both go out of their way to help and comfort others. We have only one life, says Nash, 'that we know about: fancy taking it up with disagreeable impression' (p.26). Bandele exhibits a similar world view which irritates and exasperates the other characters, notably Egbo, Sagoe and Kola who cannot find reasons to explain his concern for the beach prophet Lazarus, for instance. Soyinka's method, like James's works through these contrasting relationships between the highly imaginative and active characters. Soyinka exploits the differences between these characters to very good use and makes it impossible to understand any character until the reader places such a character's point of view against those of the others.

This is why as in James's *The Tragic Muse*, the reader notices further dramatic relationships when the interpreters enter into contact with other characters outside their group. As in James's novel the interest in *The Interpreters* is not so much in the events but in the reactions of the characters to those events. Critics who read the novel as socio-political satire mediated on Soyinka's behalf by the interpreters do not do the novel much justice. It is true that the world of *The Interpreters* is a corrupt one but corruption is not Soyinka's subject. On the contrary, Soyinka, like James, is concerned with the way the characters react to corruption. Corruption is the excuse they use to review their lives, and the lives of other characters around them. It should not be forgotten that though they are interpreters of society the technique of the novel equally enables the reader to interpret them.

None of them, for instance, would want to be like Sir Derinola, the discredited Judge sleeping at the back of a limousine while his accomplice tries unsuccessfully to get a bribe from Sagoe, but beyond that, and beyond their abhorrence of 'plastic values' they are themselves just as confused. Kola speaks for them:

> Fitfully, far too fitfully for definite realisation of the meaning, he had felt this sense of power, the knowledge of power within his hands, of the will to transform; and he understood then that medium was of little importance, that the act on canvas or on human material was the process of living and brought him the intense fear of fulfilment. And this was another paradox, that he dared not truly be fulfilled. At his elbow was the invisible brake which drew him back from final transportation in the act. (p.218)

It is difficult to sympathise with the apostasy of the interpreters and Soyinka invites the reader to interpret their 'betrayal' as it compares with that of the Oguazors, the Faseyis and Joe Golder. Even the apparently ridiculous beach prophet Lazarus, as Bandele observes, seems to have done something more useful than most of the other interpreters. As Bandele says:

> ...One thing was obvious, this man did go through some critical experience. If he has chosen to interpret it in a way that would bring some kind of meaning into people's lives, who are you to scoff at, to rip it up in your dirty pages with cheap cynicism. (p.179)

The inability of the others to follow Bandele's trend of argument is a mark of their delusion and a reflection of the ironic view of the implied author. If they do clash constantly in their numerous gatherings and if they have more intense conflicts within them, their contact with their world merely aggravates these problems. In Soyinka, as in James, we move from crisis within the individual to that among individuals and eventually to the bigger clash with the outside world. In each case the movement generates dramatic tension best illustrated through the use of scene and action in the novels.

In *Some Observations on the Art of Narrative* Phyllis Bentley contends that:

> (The) scene gives the reader a feeling of participating in the action very intensely, for he is hearing about it contemporaneously, exactly as it occurs and the moment it has occurred; the only interval between its occurring and the reader hearing about it is that occupied by the novelist's voice telling it. The scene is therefore used for intense moments. The crisis, the climax of a sequence of actions is always narrated in scene.[4]

With regard to James and Soyinka, this observation, concise though it is, requires some modification. Phyllis Bentley is right in linking scene with action: Scene functions as an arena where the action takes place. But her relation of scene to the crisis, the climax of a sequence of actions does not apply to the James and Soyinka novels under discussion. Nor is it the case that there is an 'interval between its occurring and the reader hearing about it' for, here, the scene is the corner-stone of narration, characters speak for themselves, so do the actions and scenes. As F.O. Mathiessen remarks, James had 'the ability to endow some of his characters with such vitality that they seem to take the plot into their own hands, or rather, to continue to live beyond its exigencies.'[5] There is no story outside these chain of scenes; they carry the action forward. Because both novelists write 'to the moment they seem to write from moment to moment.[6] James's technical requirements consisted more in where to 'alternate' distribute and bring relief,'[7] than in the efficacy of the scenic method. Here is how he eulogised it:

> How through all hesitations and conflicts and worries...the desire to get back only to the big (scenic constructions, 'architectural effects') seizes me and carries me off my feet making me feel that its a far deeper economy of time to sink at any moment, into the evocation

and ciphering out of that, than into any other small beguilement at all. Ah, once more to let myself go.[8]

This was not misguided enthusiasm; most of the novels reveal a performed drama. They create life before our eyes; the characters behave as actors in a play, movement and behaviours being well documented in the series of scenes they enact. Each scene, as in drama, is 'copious, comprehensive, and accordingly never short... it treats all the submitted material' and possesses its logical start, logical turn and logical finish.[9] It is no wonder that James confesses in the preface to *The Tragic Muse* that he always had the happy thought of some dramatic picture of the artistic life.

Each member of the large 'cast' in *The Tragic Muse* is given a good chance to make his appearance felt. The novel's technique is described by Gabriel Nash:

> Ah, repetition recurrence: We haven't yet, in the study of how to live, abolished that clumsiness have we?...Its a poverty in the supernumeraries that we don't pass once for all, but come round and across again, like a procession at the theatre. Its a shabby economy that ought to have been managed better. The right thing would be just one appearance, and the procession, regardless of expense forever and forever different. (p.39)

The characters 'come around and across again' and the movement is determined by their actions as well as the actions of those with whom they enter into relationships. The technique of alternation enables James to provide 'relief' and to introduce a freshness into the narration.

The first nine chapters (scenes of the novel), for instance, are devoted to Nick's 'case.' They are scenes devoted to much activity, to the preparation for Nick's conflict the seeds of which are cultivated from the very first chapter or scene. Nick we find, is a dreamer it sounds for the moment like a bad word so when he tells his sister that 'all artists are in the same boat' there is an ominous fear, though the cause is not yet apparent, of someone rocking the boat and not long after this a potential rocker of Nick's boat, his mother, begins to make her presence felt; when art is mentioned she gets up to terminate the scene (p.51). But these are all 'rehearsals.' There are two rehearsals in this first segment of the story and they introduce Miriam Roth but, because her case is pending they remain rehearsals in a literal sense. The final scene that ends this first segment (act?) of the story is very significant and it deserves special mention. It begins very slowly; Nick and Gabriel are walking:

> They kept on and on, moving slowly, smoking, talking, pausing, stopping to look, to emphasise, to compare. They fell into discussion, into confidence, into inquiry, sympathetic or satiric and into explanation which needed in turn to be explained. (p.115)

This scene, however, takes a dramatic turn when the crucial issues are mentioned, the tension that Nick is undergoing begins to show and it is placed side by side with his friend's diligent, cool and "objective" way of looking at the process of living. Gabriel Nash describes life in dramatic terms:

> ...A passenger jumps over from time to time, not so much from fear of sinking as from a want of interest in the course of the company. He swims, he plunges, he dives, he dips down and visits the fishes and the mermaids and the submarine caves; he goes from craft to craft and splashes about, on his own account, in the blue, cool water. The regenerate, as I call them, are the passengers who jump over in search of better fun. I turned my summersault long ago. (p.117)

Nick's metaphoric boat springs to life in his friend's dramatic presentation and towards the end of the scene, towards its logical finish, the dramatic conflict is well poised. Nick has to first fight against himself, and as he confesses to his friends:

> Everyone that belongs to me that touches me, near or far: my family, my blood, my heredity, my traditions, my promises, my circumstances, my prejudices, my little past such as it is, my great future such as it has been supposed at it may be. (p.125)

The scandal of his apostasy will conjure horror, in his mother, his late father and Julia Dallow; for Nick, past, present and future are areas of confusion and conflict and with this conflict dramatically poised James alternates, turning the reader's attention to the other 'case,' that of Miriam Roth.

There are parallels and contrasts in James's presentation of the scenes and actions in this second segment of the story. Miriam's existence is 'a series of pasts assumed for the moment,' (p.130) and, like Nick Dormer, she has Peter Sherringham, who has committed himself to help her, to look after her affairs. She rehearses her part since it seems the nature of her art requires this of her and James presents the contrast in their approach to art through these series of rehearsals; this is her first major entrance. Three chapters are devoted to her 'case;' three scenes whose 'middle' also consists of a walk culminating in the startling revelation that Peter is in love with Miriam. This is material for yet more drama, hence James returns the reader once again to the alternative case.

By the third segment Nick has now won his seat in parliament and the seed of conflict is beginning to bear fruit. James's technique of delay and partial knowledge, which enhances the dramatic quality of the story, is becoming more polished.[10] In this segment skirmishes are made and dropped, as in the potentially explosive case of Charles Cateret's tantalising offer of a fine estate to Nick which is juxtaposed with Miriam's major performance in London as well as with Nick's now conspicuous flirtation with portrait painting. And when matters get worse the ubiquitous Nash arrives just in time to keep his word, as it were, to his old friends Nick and Miriam. By chapter twenty six the two cases are brought together, action quickens and the dilemmas become more and more complicated. There are two parallel scenes in this chapter, one at the theatre and the other at Nick's studio where tension is 'heightened' by the sudden arrival of Julia. The first scene shows how Nick's decision to take up painting is related to his first choice of a model for a portrait. She happens to be Miriam of whom Julia Dallow, Nick's cousin and benefactress, would not approve. Both Miriam and Nick Dormer are therefore surprised and tense when Julia suddenly opens the door and enters 'without making a sound.' Julia's eyes, the reader is told, rested on 'this embodied unexpectedness and grew pale' and all three characters become restless, (p.285). The parallel scene at the theatre is tense because the play in which Miriam is acting is 'ridiculous' and is a poor start to what is hoped would be a glorious career. This restlessness, hence increased activity assumes prominence and there is a breakdown in communication among the distracted 'actors.' All of them are disenchanted. These are moments of severance; everyone goes his or her separate ways: Julia to Paris, Peter after going in and out of hansoms disappears to Latin America until James reassembles all the cast again in that final 'play' to end the 'play.'

Soyinka employs similar techniques as those described above in *The Interpreters*, indeed with greater dexterity. Movement in Soyinka's novel is breath-taking, sometimes even confusing, but Gabriel Nash's law about recurrence works here as it does in *The Tragic Muse*. What creates the confusion in Soyinka's novel is the technique of creating mini-scenes through association. In *The Tragic Muse*, one action triggers another and a sense of sequence and order permeates the whole novel, whereas in *The Interpreters*, the association may be a mere word, an image, such as Egbo's 'talkative puddle' which leads to a dip into a completely different scene (p.5). Soyinka's ability to maintain a sense of unity in spite of this multiplicity of scenes is one of the good features of the novel. As in *The Tragic Muse* all the characters are performers and each character gets a good chance to act his part. Partly because of their inherent dramatic qualities each of them seems determined to out-perform the other.

In the first chapter of Part One the urgency and chaos which is consistent with their role is presented in the cacophony of the night-club. This night-club scene alone presents five separate actions which are depicted in the manner of stage drama. The scene introduces and develops the potential areas of conflict. The reader follows the interpreters in the first instance as they battle with a leaking night-club roof on a rainy night but we are suddenly taken to Egbo's Village to witness the burial place of his father where a hint is given of his 'apostasy.' A third scene outlines aspects of Egbo's dilemma by tracing some elements in his character such as the test of wills between him and his aunt's trading partner. The scene shows some of his independence and intransigence. In the fourth scene the reader is returned to the night-club where through a reviewing device we learn of Sekoni, whose significance in the story cannot be ignored.

The review even forecasts Sekoni's future and the final scene highlights the nature of the conflict between the interpreters, especially Sekoni, and the rest of society. In *The Interpreters* as in the *The Tragic Muse*, the actors are in 'the same boat,' the chaos and the incessant arguments are an index of their harsh predicament. Lasunwon is perhaps right when he likens their plight to that of the fish 'trapped' in an aquarium; 'closed in by avenue on which escape is so clearly written.' The fish is outraged, pauses in mid-motion and assaults through the mouth (p.19). It won't get out, of course, nor will the interpreters. Like Nick Dormer in *The Tragic Muse* the characters in *The Interpreters* are individually and collectively fighting their inner selves, their families, their traditions, their past and for that matter, their future. By the close of the chapter, Sekoni has already gone full circle; he lands in a mental hospital, an ominous sign, especially when it turns out that he is the only one among them who makes an effort, who dares to be fulfilled.

From this stage the action alternates between Sagoe and Egbo, the most dramatic of the characters. They carry us through dreams and real-life incidents such as Sagoe's raising of his former boss from the dead, or Egbo's affair with the undergraduate girl. These incidents are full of daring but are largely vulgar and obscene. They tell more about both men than the events they seek to represent. The first part of the novel ends with a gathering of all the cast for what is clearly a rehearsal for the second part. Mark Kinkead-Weekes has observed that, as in his plays, Soyinka has:

> A habit of using a two-part structure to transform our view of what we have been watching: a first predominantly satiric, comic and done in human terms; a second part tragic, mythic, and aware of the forces and perspectives beyond the human.[11]

In so far as this implies that the second part of the book is an exact repetition of the story of part one, Kinkead-Weekers is right. Where he errs is in implying that the second part is tragic; the whole purpose of resorting to Yoruba mythology is to highlight the comic possibility that the five interpreters will somehow tame chaos if they try hard enough, if they follow the example of the gods in whose image they are created. Ultimately the dichotomy in this novel serves a structural as well as a thematic function: by 'contrastive juxtaposition' the scenes display the glaring differences in the interpreters as well as the differences between their ideals and reality.

Part two of the novel, for instance, opens on the tragic death of Sekoni and immediately exposes the inadequacies of his friends. Only Bandele is able to cope with Sekoni's absence with a sense of calm and composure. All the others display the triviality that has hitherto dominated their lives. Sagoe needs his book of enlightenment to help him cope with the event but is as void as its sub-title suggests. Kola has clearly lost inspiration. Their friends' death is a major test which, excepting Bendele, exposes their shortcomings. They fail because they are not yet ready to follow the inspiration which their divine sources offer. The dichotomy also allows Soyinka to reassemble all the fragments of the first part of the story; fragmentation and reassembly are the major theme of the Yoruba myth of creation:

> ...these floods of the beginning...of the first apostle rolling the boulder down the back of the unsuspecting deity...and shattering him in fragments, which were picked up and pieced together with devotion. (p.225)

The devotion of the gods in picking up and piecing together is matched by a meticulous devotion on the part of the artist who also tries to piece together an otherwise chaotic first part.

In this second part of the novel, the first scene is again in the night-club but by now Sekoni, who was left demented at the end of the first part, is dead. However, it is not the death on which attention is focused since it is reported in a matter-of-fact-way; rather, it is the vibrations which it triggers among the surviving interpreters that is crucial. The scenes from now on depict the increasing knowledge or ignorance, as illustrated above, of the interpreters. The reader must notice a clear change in outlook on the part of Bandele, similar in character to Gabriel Nash in *The Tragic Muse*, who seeks to give a more concrete analysis of what they have witnessed and what their own actions amount to: 'he has gained knowledge of the new generation of interpreters.' The scene at Lazarus's church, for example, represents moments of honest stock-taking on the part of Bandele.

Soyinka uses Lazarus's church to turn the satiric lens on the other interpreters. By showing them as no better, perhaps even worse, than the charlatan prophet, Soyinka exposes them to the reader for ridicule. After several scenes of carelessly interpreting the conduct of others, they now ironically refuse to be interpreted minus Bandele that is. So as in *The Tragic Muse* they begin to go their several ways. At the theatre they all find 'it is a night of severance, every man is going his way (p.224). The final assembly at the Oguazor's is like the tortoise shell around divine breath. Soyinka puts back some semblance of order on this story but only just. What seems to have been represented here is 'an endless chain for the summons of the gods' which, as it happens, most of the interpreters refuse to answer to their peril. This last scene though more inconclusive than the equivalent one in *The Tragic Muse*, represents a possibility, it is an interval. Man and God will sooner or later seek to reassume the portion of recreative transient awareness which the first deity possessed (p.224).

Neither the scenes, nor the dramatic characters who interact in them would come to life without dialogue. The sheer impulsiveness and activity of the characters in the novels of James and Soyinka make dialogue indispensable, since it is only by expressing themselves in their own words that their drama comes to life. Also their gregarious nature, their fondness of interpretation and their powerful intellect makes discussion inevitable. Dialogue, in these novels, enhances a direct presentation. Through dialogue, the characters 'take over the plot of the story and their individual characteristics are better delineated; dialogue illuminates both the characters and the subjects and invites a greater sense of immediacy; in James's words' this is:

> .....really constructive dialogue, dialogue organic, and dramatic, speaking for itself, representing and embodying substance and form.[12]

Dialogue makes the scenes both James and Soyinka create nearer the experience of theatre. Sometimes whole chapters are composed exclusively of dialogue, at other times dialogue brings the scene to its climax or dialogue might point to potential areas of the dramatic conflict. Words dropped unobtrusively turn to be of immense significance; because these are very imaginative characters, the symbols they conjure in their discussion with other characters go a long way to illuminate the substance and the form of the story.

The Tragic Muse demonstrates a fairly consistent pattern. James introduces the characters, gives them a setting and then allows them to act out their parts through dialogue which in turn produces misunderstanding and clarification, often simultaneously. The forthright nature of the characters makes their dialogue more dramatic and for some, such as Grace Dormer, the implications of what they say go beyond their instinctive outbursts. James's introductions, by way of a brief narrative comment, are rendered in the manner of stage directions, as shown in the first chapter of *The Tragic Muse*:

> Three ladies and a young man, they were obviously a family a mother, two daughters and a son... After sometimes.... the young man rousing himself from his reverie addressed one of the girls. (p.9)

There then follows uninterrupted dialogue throughout the rest of the chapter.

More useful details emerge from the dialogue than in the summary; their own words reveal more about the potential rift within the family and the emerging polarity between 'the artists,' Biddy and Nick, and 'the public' Lady Agnes and Grace. The latter considers art as 'horrid and messy' and Grace is more concerned with the impending lunch than with discussions about the nature and function of art. The former are in the same boat as they say; thus by the end of the chapter it becomes evident that the lines of battle are drawn, and this, without a single comment by the narrator. This is James's way of letting the story speak for itself through its characters who already begin to show individual characteristics: Grace is clearly graceless, the mother is a 'British Matron' and Biddy is biddable since she appears prepared at the moment to be bargained for by the two worlds.

The pattern recurs throughout the novel. 'By their words' it appears, 'we shall know them.' Each scene begins with an introduction of the cast followed by extended dialogue between them; dialogue which, when handled by erudite characters such as Gabriel Nash, or by such theatrical characters as Miriam Roth, gives the feeling at worst of a good rehearsal and at best of good drama about it. The setting is often appropriate: dining tables at restaurants, at rehearsals in living rooms, a walk or a ride involving at least two of the major characters. Sometimes dialogue consists of an assessment of a character. This is one way of providing an objective assessment. In chapter eleven, for example, Peter Sherringham and Miriam Roth walk together, an exercise in which they reveal a lot about themselves, but much more significant, a lot is said about Gabriel Nash who would have remained an enigma but for such a moment of revelation through dialogue. Because he is such an incisive and accurate interpreter, yet one unwilling to give away his true nature, it is only when he is discussed by others that useful information about him filters through to the reader.

There are occasions when dialogue in *The Tragic Muse* serves useful comic purposes as when Peter makes a last desperate effort to carry off Miriam to a more 'exciting life.' As Miriam knows, all his argument is 'determined sophistry,' but he pushes it forward with such passion that it compels the attention, not only of the reader, but of an otherwise busy Miriam who already has an engagement and who besides, is not going to marry Peter anyway (p.464). Peter's comic illusions find their best expression in this chapter and towards the end it becomes clear that he has lost Miriam, that he never really had a 'case.' The whole scene is 'dialogue organic and dramatic,' complete with prompter, Mrs. Roth. The actors, though, know their lines so well that the prompter merely watches and listens; towards the end she offers some help but it is superfluous, the actors have had their evening. *The Tragic Muse* is full of these 'plays-within-the-play' and each gets its impetus through dialogue. Similarly, in the scenes between Nick and Charles Cateret and the subsequent one between Nick and his mother, when Nick is faced with the consequence of the apostasy he has just committed, dialogue plays a significant part. In both cases the dialogue reveals more clearly the irreconcilable positions between the 'parties' in contention:

> 'The pencil, the brush? They're not the weapons of a gentleman, said Cateret.' 'I was sure that would be your view. I repeat that I mention them only because you once said you intended to do something for me, as the phrase is, and I thought you oughtn't to do it in ignorance.'
>
> 'My ignorance was better. Such knowledge isn't good for me.'
>
> 'Forgive me, my dear old friend. When you're better you'll see it differently.'
>
> 'I shall never be better now?' (p.359)

Indeed Cateret never recovers from this shock and dies, leaving Nick, as expected, with nothing. Nick's callousness, as his mother sees it, and as Charles and Grace would agree, is incomprehensible.

In *The Interpreters* dialogue is so pervasive that inanimate objects such as Dehinwa's ward-robe and Egbo's 'talkative puddle' contribute to it; indeed ghosts join in useful dialogue with the living; for the interpreters life itself is one long dialogue. This includes even the stammering Sekoni who joins as a choral voice, but who usually provides a very useful bridge in an otherwise wide gap in opinion and outlook among the interpreters. It appears sometimes as if the other interpreters could do without the bridge but some of Sekoni's outbursts are indispensable to the novel's themes:

> 'T-t-to be afraid of gog-go-goodness. In an intelligent man, a fffear of b-b-beauty or g-g-good is c....cowardice.' (p.22)

It is significant that when he dies it is this bridge-like quality in him that the others miss most; the rainbow figure of Lazarus, the prophet, 'Sheikh's face de-metaphorphosed from the albino's (p.160) is not compensation enough. The failure of the interpreters to fulfil themselves is a result of a collapse of dialogue between them and their gods, between then and their fellow-men and the most crucial of all the collapse of dialogue within themselves. In all three stages, Soyinka presents this breakdown in communication via the actors themselves with very little intervention, far less authorial intervention than James's in *The*

Tragic Muse. As in James, most of the time the interpreters talk at cross-purposes but what they say throws light on their characters and this is further enhanced by the evaluation each brings to bear on the other.

Since each of them is an interpreter, and since each in turn is being interpreted, a complete picture emerges from the accumulated assessment that comes from the things they say and what others say about them. Sekoni's comments and conduct illuminate Egbo who in turn illuminates Kola, all of whom are assessed by Bandele, the timeless image brooding over lesser beings. Sagoe speaks and acts for himself. His 'voidante' philosophy reveals his frivolous life, as his alcoholism and his superficiality do. His talk is always that of a journalist, concerned endlessly with the surface and not bothering to probe deep into meaning. What each of the characters say when they leave Lazarus's Church is most illuminating:

> 'Why don't you go ahead and paint him, Kola? Then I would use the painting in my feature, give it some kind of dimension...I don't know how exactly, the idea is just winging its way into my brain.'

> Kola shook his head, 'No. I might paint him but not on the cross or any such waste of time, I was thinking of him as Esumare. Intermediary. As the Covenant, in fact, the Apostate Covenant. When Lazarus called him Noah, I thought about it then. He does possess that technicolour brand of purity.'

> 'Yes, yes, Egbo murmured.' 'And it is just as vaporous.' Bandele was mocking, lightly, 'Sagoe has his story, Kola has filled another heavenly space on his canvas, what are you getting out of this, Egbo?'

> Egbo turned angrily on him. 'What are YOU getting out of it?'

> 'Knowledge of the new generation of interpreters.'

> Sagoe exploded. 'You sound so fuckin' superior it would make a saint mad.

> 'You see,'Bandele said, 'You haven't even tried to find out. He asked you here didn't he? Have you thought why? Or do you believe the bull of the church thing alone? 'What else does he want?' Publicity of course. All the local prophets want publicity. Its good business. (p.178)

It is left to Bandele to expose their recklessness and ignorance. When Sagoe accuses him of sounding 'fucking superior,' he is of course accusing himself and the others, for all through the story, they have continued to behave as if they are models, and what models! Ultimately the novel's irony suggests that the difference between them and the Oguazors is one of degree. Those who see the book as an attack on the Oguazors and a corrupt society miss the point expressed so vividly and dramatically especially in the chapter from which the above dialogue has been taken. The point about *The Interpreters* is a failure of dialogue which illuminates as well as criticises all the characters.

The novelist using the dramatised perspective uses time as if in rebellion against the restrictions of drama because the novel spreads out experience and elaborates relations as against the tendency of the 'well-made play' to coalesce them into a set time-span. It is true as E.M. Forster insists, that no novel could be written without the consciousness of the clock,[13] but it is equally true as Mendilow suggests, that:

> Time assumes different meanings in different systems and varies from one frame of reference to another. Every good novel has its own temporal pattern and values, and acquires its originality by the adequacy with which they are conveyed or expressed.[14]

Two major conceptions of time manifest themselves in *The Tragic Muse* and in *The Interpreters*. Whereas James subscribes to the Western linear sense of time, Wole Soyinka employs the Greek and Eastern philosophies of cyclic time which, as he demonstrates, are also Yoruba, perhaps, African, concepts of time: 'Traditional thought, Soyinka says, operates not a linear conception of time but a cyclic reality.'[15]

In *The Tragic Muse* James adheres almost strictly to linear time. The novel begins in the present and though it makes occasional dips into the past it is fairly regular in plotting causal sequence, one event leads to another. The past has a strong grip on the major characters, particularly Nick, but its significance is shown only as it affects the present and perhaps the future; indeed sometimes past, present and future are areas of confusion and conflict but James never really abandons his steady movement in time. Information about the 'old days at Oxford' comes unobtrusively. The only instance of a pervasive past which sometimes threatens the reordering of events and perspective is the domineering presence of the late Sir Nicholas, Nick's father, but even then, his 'representative,' Charles Cateret, performs the job he is expected to perform namely to act as a source of inspiration for Nick. Reference is made to his ghost only once but the narrator is quick to remark that this is part of the hallucinations of Lady Agnes and not so much the work of Nick.

James exploits the lateral quality of the novel in the way in which, at times, the clock stops for certain characters so that others can function. James makes it impossible, for instance, for Nick and Miriam to see each other for ten months even though Miriam has been in London and is already becoming famous as an actress. It is Gabriel Nash, who originally introduced Miriam, who reintroduces her after ten months, by which time James finds opportunities to develop them apart to give equal attention to the two plots. Gabriel Nash himself comes in and out without much regard to a time sequence, indeed he 'melts back into the elements'; 'is part' James says 'of the ambient air.' Similarly Julia Dallow disappears after chapter twenty seven, reappearing only in chapter forty-seven. The reader only knows that she left for Paris. The duration of her visit can only be implied, but she is no longer crucial to the action by the time she disappears and so is left in Paris until James needs her to sort out the complication, or perhaps, further to complicate Nick's life. Only the novel provides avenues for such a flexible use of time which a modernist writer can use to good effect.

To come to Soyinka, however, is to notice a marked difference in the two writers' use of time. This difference is not accounted for merely by the linear and cyclic concepts of time which they employ; it seems to derive mainly from what Kola Ogungbesan describes as 'structural manoeuvres... of a man committed to a genre whose limitations he finds frustrating.' Soyinka appears to have written his novels, especially *The Interpreters*, as a rebellion against some of the strictures of drama and nowhere is this better demonstrated than in his use of flashbacks. Like a calendar-maker, Soyinka seems determined to create his own time: in the beginning was the night-club. Many modernist novelists use flashbacks, and many more manipulate chronological time but few have shown such iconoclastic disregard for any accepted time-scheme as Soyinka does in *The Interpreters*.

This is part of the reason why several critics condemn his novel but, as Kinkead-Weekes observes, 'no character in a novel can have a history until he is given one.' In an attempt to give Egbo and Sekoni such time-histories, Soyinka commits himself to a very bold venture which, because it is strange and indeed still rare in the African novel, is the subject of much adverse criticism. However, if attention is paid more to the significance that history plays in the novel as a whole, it will be found that the dexterous time shifts are in themselves part of the theme of the novel; they are the essence of Sekoni's "domes of continuity." Chapter One of the book contains the novel's story and structure; all that happens afterwards is mere repetition; recurrence.

The night-club is Soyinka's marker and the lives of the joint-protagonist literally begin and end there. Sekoni, for instance, has 'a reviewing device' which enables him to recall events from his past with ease. It is this device, perhaps, which makes it possible for the reader to know so much about the other characters from one spot. Thus we know about Egbo's past and about the demands he now faces and the nature of his apostasy. With regard to Sekoni, past, present and future become areas of confusion and by the end of the chapter he has been through all the phases of his life. His death, much later in part two is a non-event. Indeed, at that point in the novel the reactions of his friends to the news of his death, as observed earlier, is more significant than the event itself. The chapter thus sets the sequence, the pattern which is repeated in all the remaining chapters. There appears to be partial movement within a crowded night-club into several other places including Egbo's ancestral home. In time, however, the movement is far more complex, so complex that it is difficult to know precisely what moment is being described.

Part of this difficulty may be deliberate and could well mean, as Egbo implies, that someone has 'broken the crust of time' (p.10). Much of the discussion in this chapter as in the rest of the novel, is about time, Egbo is haunted by 'the spectre of generations.' The final scene of the chapter reassembles all the ages in the case history of Sekoni and though chapter two opens with the group of interpreters leaving the night-club, it is obvious that we have been through the essence of their story. In any case Sekoni is already in a mental hospital, it is as if the first cycle at least has come and gone. True, new characters are introduced, such as Lazarus, but he merely replaces Sekoni and Joe Golder is only a slight variation on the original group; they are all motherless children, away from home, Golder's song is their common cry. All they need is the link:

> It requires only the bridge, or the ladder between heaven and earth.
> A rope or a chain. The link that is all. After fifteen months, all that is left is the link.... (225)

The Interpreters is about the difficulty of finding such a link to complete a cycle, broken by the first apostate and from time to time, broken by those like Egbo and Kola who because of their apostasy cannot forge the required spirit to overcome the problem of fulfilment. Each of the major characters tries to find the link in the cycle. Some of them, like Sagoe, stumble from one error to another but there are those like Kola and Bandele who are more conscious of their limitations and are thus more positive in their efforts. Kola's canvas in which each of his friends is painted in the image of a Yoruba god is the most serious and the most concrete attempt to make the necessary link in time. But because each of the characters seems determined to out-perform the other, this modernist novel reads as a confusing stampede of events with a chaotic sequence. It can, however, be argued that time, chronological time, is not material in the novel. If Egbo lives his past and his present in one and the same breath it is precisely because time is theme in the novel.

Henry James and Wole Soyinka deploy almost the same narrative devices in their novels. James, however, is a more disciplined craftsman, fighting a modernists battle to create a style different from that of his comperes in the nineteenth century. Soyinka on the other hand, may be associated with the greater experimentation of the modernists of the twentieth century which James helped to cultivate. In Soyinka, therefore, will be found more innovations some of which he uses to good effect. For instance, Soyinka shows greater manoeuverability in the way he handles time in his novel while James's experiments fought shy of these possibilities. With regard to character, action, scene, and dialogue, there are many similarities: Soyinka probably borrowed from James some aspects of characterisation. In presenting scene and action, however, Soyinka the successful dramatist, does extremely well. Both writers also put dialogue to great use, both rely heavily on the way characters express themselves as an important element in the story. All their characters seem to take over the story, leaving both novelists, like good dramatic novelists, with stage directions.

Their vision is essentially a modernist, ironic one. As Ronald Wallace shows with regards to James:

> Faced with a world in which the preposterous, the trivial and the monstrous seem to rule James... marshals comedy as a weapon against chaos and absurdity.[18]

Soyinka harnesses the resources of African mythology in addition to a toughened modernist irony to confront the chaos in his own society. This is, perhaps, best seen in the way he handles time in the novel. But more important is the way both novelists create characters whose problem is themselves and the complex of their relations. The novelists considered in the next chapter offer a more inward picture of the way individual characters tackle the problem of the modernists' intense pro-occupation with techniques.

CHAPTER THREE

THE INWARD PERSPECTIVE: JAMES JOYCE, *A PORTRAIT OF THE ARTIST AS A YOUNG MAN*; VIRGINIA WOOLF, *THE WAVES*; KOFI AWOONOR, *THIS EARTH, MY BROTHER*

In the novels of Joyce, Virginia Woolf and Awoonor the reader is exposed to the mind of the characters in such a way that he becomes committed to the character's point of view. The novels of James and Soyinka could be said to move from the outside to the inward while the reverse is the case with those of Joyce, Virginia Woolf and Awoonor. *A Portrait of the Artist as a Young Man, The Waves* and *This Earth My Brother* are novels about the self. They may be read as a series of soliloquies in which 'a cosmic communication' is discerned between the protagonist and his many selves, or as in *The Waves*, between the protagonist and several identical characters. In each case the reader is invited to share in the experience so that what begins as the internalization of another's unexpressed thoughts and experiences ends up as a dialogue of many selves. This is the tradition which Joyce and Virginia Woolf have established in the modern novel.

In a recent interview, Kofi Awoonor acknowledged a kinship with this modernist tradition when he admits that the African novelist has 'entered a new period of monologue in which the self-search is something that has to be made.'[1] To understand the nature of point of view in the novels is to analyse this self-search.

Virginia Woolf's joint protagonists in *The Waves* provide a useful bench-mark for a study of the way in which the self-search is portrayed in her novel and in *A Portrait* and *This Earth*:

> The flower... that stood in the vase on the table of the restaurant when we dined together with Percival, is become a six-sided flower; made of six lives. (154)

This puzzle of the major characters epitomises the nature of the characterisation in all three novels. We may be studying one character but that character is so many people that it becomes difficult to pin down his individual characteristics. Earlier in *The Waves* a way out is suggested:

> ... A single flower as we sat here waiting, but now a seven-sided flower, many petalled, red, puce, purple-shaded, stiff with silver tainted leaves. A whole flower to which every eye brings its own contribution. (85)

In these novels, though the reader's eye 'brings its own contribution,' the myriad worlds of the novels as well as the host of sensations in the mind of the character provide further contributions and difficulties. It is a recurrent process renewed by character and reader throughout the novel.

In *A Portrait* Stephen Dedalus provides a classic example of the type of character described above. His numerous impressions sound incredible but this is because Stephen has many selves. There are, however, two main features in his characterisation. On the one hand there is the outer Stephen whose tingling sensations react to father Dolan's Cane. These sensations continue in other forms throughout the novel while on the other hand the reader finds the inward and thoughtful Stephen who listens and thinks so that he may understand. The latter is the mind that opens on the playgrounds in the early stages of the novel, 'the wide playgrounds swarming with boys,' and which ends up seeing strange figures advancing from a cave, figures who peer at him and seem to ask him something. This latter, lonely Stephen seems to taste joy in loneliness. Between this inner and outer Stephen and the dilemma that confronts both 'characters' lies the essence of this modernist novel's method. This is how the crisis is portrayed shortly after Stephen has spent his prize money and is broke again:

> How foolish he had been! He had tried to build a breakwater of order and elegance against the sordid tide of life without him and to dam up by rules of conduct and active interests and new filial relations, the powerful recurrence of the tides within him. Useless. From without as from within the water had flowed over his barriers: their tides began once more to jostle fiercely above the crumbled mole. (90)

The outer reality combines with the inner confusion to intensify Stephen's dilemma. At this point he seems to be a victim of circumstances and he is helpless. The bleak picture is nevertheless not entirely consistent with the character. Pleasant moments abound for the two Stephens. Both 'characters' have reliable friends who help them define themselves. The outward Stephen enters into relationships with women and with classmates which reveal another part of his nature. There is Mercedes, for instance, with her alluring eyes which flatter, taunt, search and excite Stephen, as well as Eileen of the long, thin, cool, white hair, the tower of ivory, and many others. School friends, such as Cranly, provide a useful intellectual board upon which the budding artist-cum-philosopher practices his numerous theories, as do the teachers and supervisors who see talent in the young man, such as the English Dean who learns his own language from Stephen. Since Stephen also has kind and understanding uncles and an indulgent, though improvident father, he really cannot claim to be lonely.

Yet he is. The source of loneliness can be found in the other Stephen whose mind 'tends to wither up like a flower of the desert that feels the simoom coming from afar.' (p.100) Several events and people represent these 'simoom winds.' Perhaps the closest and most touching is the poverty of the Dedalus household which creates disorder that nurtures a brooding mind:

> His silent watchful manner had grown upon him and he took little part in the games. The children danced and romped noisily and, though he tried to share their merriment, he felt a gloomy figure amid the gay-cocked hats and sunbonnets. (63)

There are others: injustice in early school days, such as Father Dolan's wrongful punishment; sin with a woman; temptation to join the priesthood; hostile, perhaps jealous, school mates who all appear like wild beasts whose feet pass in 'pattering tumult' over Stephen's mind. It is against these 'enemies' that Stephen declares his rebellion:

> I will not serve that in which I no longer believe whether it call itself my home, my fatherland, or my church: and I will try to express myself in some mode of life or art as freely as I can and as wholly as I can using for my defence the only arms I allow myself to use silence, exile and cunning. (222)

This is, however, only half the story. The rebellion apparently has limits as his diary entry of 11 April reveals:

> Would she like it? I think so. Then I should have to like it also. (227)

She is no ordinary girl; we have met her before:

> She seemed like one whom magic had changed into the likeness of a strange and beautiful seabird... Lone, long, she suffered his gaze and then quietly withdrew her eyes from his and bent them towards the stream, gently stirring the water with her foot hither and thither... 'Heavenly God!' cried Stephen's soul, in an outburst of profane joy. (155)

The reader notices worship, not profanity, nor is Stephen contradicting himself. He is only being consistent with his many selves. His various selves confront the magical woman in several guises as Eileen, Emma, Mercedes and Mabel Hunter, but her essence, however, remains unchanged: in each case the reader is reminded of a holy encounter which provides moments of ecstasy for Stephen.

In order to understand Stephen, therefore, we need to look for several characters in one. The two Stephens described are only a tip of the iceberg: more characters lurk beneath. It is not by accident that the mind is described in metaphors that represent vast spaces: a brimming bowl, a house, a theatre, a playground, an ark, a stream, the desert, and the sea respectively. Besides, the mind also reincarnates in human form, seeing and hearing voices, making the word flesh in the virgin womb of its imagination, touching and feeling. Joyce's modernism presents a complex difficult both for Stephen and the reader to understand.

In *The Waves*, Virginia Woolf appears to have found ways of making complete knowledge of character possible. Some of the difficulty of understanding the multiple nature of Stephen's character could well be solved through the method deployed by Virginia Woolf in *The Waves*. Bernard, Louis, Neville, Susan, Rhoda and Jinny melt into each other with phrases, share soliloquies, yet are different. Critics have described their relationship as 'magical' and Bernard, 'the phrase maker,' puts their case less modestly.

> We are creators. We too have made something that will join the innumerable congregations of past time. We too, as we put on our hats and push open the door, stride not into chaos, but into a world that our own force can subjugate and make part of the illumined and everlasting road. (98)

Later he intones:

> In the beginning, there was the nursery, with windows opening on to a garden, and beyond that the sea. (162)

The reader is called upon to witness a story of the Creation. This new modernist God has six, no, seven persons, and is also omnipotent. It is to his reincarnation, however, that the reader must turn for a better understanding of character.

The distinctiveness of all six major characters is never in doubt. A catalogue of their unique ways from childhood emerges as the story unfolds and as they grow the distinctions between them become more glaring. These differences are created largely through a series of similes and metaphors. Susan is like the seasons; Jinny is a rolling stone; Rhoda is 'a mistress of her fleet of ships;' Neville is like a hound on the scent; Louis is like a worm that has eaten its way through the wood of a very old oak beam; and Bernard is not one and simple but many and complex. In Bernard's character lie some crucial clues to the nature of the characterisation in *The Waves*. Bernard tries to fuse the other six selves in himself but in spite of his brilliant analysis of character he is unable to answer several questions fundamental to their nature. Bernard, though, asks the right questions:

> Who am I? I have been talking of Bernard, Neville, Jinny, Susan, Rhoda and Louis. Am I all of them? Am I one and distinct? I do not know. We sat here together. But now Percival is dead, and Rhoda is dead; we are divided; we are not here. Yet I cannot find any obstacle separating us. There is no division between me and them... This difference we make so much of, this identity we so feverishly cherish, was overcome. (p.195)

Bernard's questions and answers seem to be circular but they provide clues to the complexity of the novel's method. Virginia Woolf's style tempts the reader to recall a scientific analogy. As in Democritus's atomic philosophy, the characters differ in form and in their relations with one another, as the similes and metaphors demonstrate, but are all indivisible particles of the same universe, as Bernard so ably shows. Science and mystery could be said to unite in what Bernard describes as the 'eternal renewal, the incessant rise and fall and fall and rise again' (p.200).

The complexity in method is perhaps best represented, not by Bernard, the all-knowing phrase-maker, but by Louis, the man for all seasons. Louis is portrayed as a cross between the excesses of Bernard and the inactivity of Rhoda. He has two distinct lives:

> Mr Prentice at four; Mr Eyres at four-thirty. I like to hear the soft rush of the lift and thud with which it stops on my landing and the heavy male tread of responsible feet down the corridors. The weight of the world is on our shoulders. This is life. If I press on I shall inherit a chair and a rug; a place in Surrey with glass houses, and some rare conifer, melon or flowering tree which other merchants will envy. (p.114)

This humdrum, impressionistic existence is, for Louis, only a very minor part of his person. He claims:

> I find relics of myself in the sand that women made thousands of years ago, when I heard songs by the Nile and the chained beast stamping. What you see beside you,... is only the cinders and the refuse of something once splendid. I was once an Arab prince; behold my free gestures. I was a great poet in the time of Elizabeth. I was a Duke at the Court of Louis the fourteenth. (p. 15)

Louis's first life represents that which may be described as 'accurately and as minutely as possible' but the second life stands for that which is seen in shadow and may be described only in 'a moment of vision and faith.'[2] Louis, like Bernard, believes that their friend Percival who died in India might be the missing bit in their puzzle but Percival, 'Without whom there is no solidity,' only complicates their lives. He is, as Bernard admits, 'the complete human being' whom they have failed to be but at the same time cannot be. *The Waves* is a fuller representation of character than *A Portrait* but both are modernist novels whose sense of ambiguity is similar. Consequently *The Waves*, like *A Portrait*, ends on an indeterminate note:

> We have no ceremonies, only private dirges and no conclusions, only violent sensations, each separate. (p.105)

It is ironical, but perhaps true, that the greater the attempt to understand character the greater the mystery. These novels present character from the inside yet, though more sympathetic to the character's perspective than the novels of James or Soyinka, they are full of complexities. At the end of both *A Portrait* and *The Waves* the reader may wonder if these complexities, and not the understanding of the character, are the prime concern of both novels. Both novels separate and delineate characters only to complicate them further.

To come to Awoonor's *This Earth, My Brother* is to experience the same complexity as described in the novels of Joyce and Woolf above. The novel highlights the story of Amamu which turns out to be two stories of the same character running concurrently. Here is how Amamu's doctor puts it:

> ... I knew him personally, he was a brilliant lawyer, but some of these things do happen. Most of the time we cannot understand. (183)

The story which Amamu's doctor understands is simple and straight- forward, prosaic. The one he cannot understand is symbolic and complex, poetic. The brilliant lawyer Amamu, is a familiar figure with readers of African fiction which deals with colonial contact.[3] After a good education in his home country under colonial rule Amamu travels abroad where he qualifies as a lawyer. He sets up a very successful practice and is doing well by the standards of his country. He lives in a 'reservation' area away from the poverty represented by Nima and he is well-known, and outwardly he may be said to be a happy and successful man. The inward Amamu, however, is a complex similar to Louis in *The Waves*. His success in the outside world also bears resemblance to Louis's success. Both are men who, by following the path of convention, reach the top of their career, are success stories. Yet they are unhappy. The inward Amamu is restless and depressed:

> His sleep was sold forever for a love that was within and outside his grasp. For a dream that was unclear. It was at times like this that his headaches would come on. His head would become large, wanting to explode, bells would be ringing in it and he would want to scream. (p.81)

Home is described as a place of 'desolation and anguish' (p.29). Unlike Louis, however, and more like Stephen in *A Portrait*, Amamu has prepared his mind for escape. Like Stephen too there is so much to escape from: a frustrated marriage, a corrupt nation, uninspiring friends, and above all a wretched childhood in which the violent death of a mother has left the soul empty. *This Earth* invites the reader to share the soliloquies of this modernist muse and understand the man's inner impulses which the doctor and his numerous friends fail to grasp. All his soliloquies are addressed to 'a brother' who is expected to share in his predominantly sad and angered moods:

> This frame, smashed against such deadly countenances chained to the final idea of the death and decay of this body.
>
> It is the only avenue of salvation, in this angered mood, self-denial, self-effacement become twin weapons to be worn into an equal and equally inconsequential battle. Hear their battle cry, my brother... for you and me and all, a gathering must be proclaimed at our sacred grove, our worship must be renewed. (143)

To understand Amamu, however, is to feel him; the inner man seems accessible only via intuition: in the novel only two characters achieve this. One of them is Yaro, his houseboy:

> He knew with that desperate instinct that transcends blood that something terrible had happened. (176)

Much closer, though, is the mistress Adisa, who, like Stephen's woman, transforms into many shapes until she is indistinguishable from the divine woman of the sea. These two share Amamu's soliloquies. When he dies, the communion, as it were, is broken. Adisa reviews their relationship and highlights the complexity of the lonely Amamu:

> Their love was almost divine; its power was quiet and wordless. His loneliness and restlessness became part of her sacred responsibilities, for which she devised ritual acts of celebration and worship and sacrifice. This love was beyond the corporate confusion that hammered at his gates daily. (p.176)

A distinction is made between the humdrum nature of legal practice and a spiritual, mystical relationship with Adisa. These distinctions have been observed in *A Portrait* and *The Waves*. *This Earth* shares a kinship with the two novels in its presentation of character. Here is how Awoonor describes it:

> Somewhere in the true poem, the two dimensions of public and private attributes are unified. There occurs a deep relationship between the publicly owned linguistic landscape and the private esoteric magic land of the intimate poetic self.[4]

Awoonor's observation is similar to Virginia Woolf's concept of 'two faces to every situation.' In *This Earth* he resorts to a dual perspective in structure and theme in order to forge a link between 'the publicly owned linguistic landscape' and 'the private esoteric magic land of the poetic self.' One half of the novel is composed of 'poetic' chapters as in *The Waves* while the other half is a bald straight forward narrative of facts. This dichotomy reflects on the characterisation of the protagonist, Amamu, who, like Louis, is half real, half mystery.

Awoonor's method resembles Virginia Woolf's in *The Waves* but Joyce's manner of presenting Stephen Dedalus in *A Portrait* draws more obvious similarities. Both characters are iconoclasts. Amamu, like Stephen, has successfully dealt the blow to all the Gods that be. The nation is shown as rotten; his family is a sham; the ancestral gods are ineffectual, in his own words:

> A virtue shall elude mankind in spite of a million paschal lambs slaughtered and offered to greedy gods who will continue to doze in this millennium. (p.135)

Thus, like Stephen, he emigrates to the sea in search of salvation in the hands of an apparently spotless goddess:

> I will get away into the shadow of my tree to await the epiphany of my woman of the sea with hard nipples rippling on the waves parted by moon splash. (p.179)

When she appears, the ecstacy is similar to Stephen's epiphany in *A Portrait*.

> Here at last, he realised with a certain boyish joy, was the home of his salvation. (p.80)

The differences between Amamu and Stephen are differences of temperament and intent. The former, choosing the path of death, goes on a journey that should lead him, through the woman of the sea, to meet his ancestors already gone beyond. The latter, in acquiring weapons, is ready for another attempt, another form of adventure. One is middle-aged, negative, resigned; the other is young, positive, ambitious. Both journeys, however, represent a knowledge of self, especially of the waves that move within. Like their modernist counterparts in *The Waves*, knowledge for Stephen and Amamu, comes through search and pilgrimage and this process begins, and sometimes ends, in the mind.

Virginia Woolf's metaphor of a six or seven-sided flower is again an appropriate way of describing the process that unfolds the nature of the symbolism in the novels. From the parent flower there emerge several petals of different shapes and colours each of which contributes to the growth of the plant. The dominant symbol that emerges in these novels is that of life as a journey. We may thus see the journey as the parent flower from which all the others spring. Considering that all journeys have destinations, we may further distinguish three major categories of symbols in the novels: those symbols that represent the point of departure and those that stand for the homecoming while in between are the symbols that help to facilitate the journey. It is possible to envisage the journeys in symbolic terms because all three novelists only make a half-hearted effort to create the illusion of an actual journey taking place.

What goes on has been aptly described by Virginia Woolf in a comment on Sterne's novel:

> He was travelling in France indeed, but the road was often through his own mind, and his chief adventures were not with brigands and precipices but with the emotions of his own heart.

It is useful to recall George Moore's observation that 'every man has a lake in his heart and must ungird his lions for the crossing' because the journey which is meticulously undertaken in the three novels is a journey that does not 'observe certain laws of proportion and perspective.' The perspective is an inward one which piles up so many images that the reader may be justified if he feels that the symbols have become an end in themselves.

In *A Portrait* Stephen's journey is presented as a race and awareness of speed and competition dominates the story. Consciousness of this race, however, is displayed more by the inner than the outer Stephen though this distinction between levels of perception becomes apparent only as the story progresses and the reader becomes aware of it at significant stages throughout the novel. This early passage which describes Stephen's first days at school illustrates the salient features of the technique:

> The wide playgrounds were swarming with boys. All were shouting and the prefects urged them on with strong cries. The evening air was pale and chilly and after every charge and thud of the footballers the greasy leather orb flew like a heavy bird through the grey light. He kept on the fringe of his line, out of sight of his prefect; out of the rude feet, feigning to turn now and then. He felt his body small and weak amid the throng of players, and his eyes were weak and watery... He crept about from point to point on the fringe of his line making little runs now and then... But his hands in the side pocket of his belted grey suit. That was a belt around his pocket. And belt was also to give a fellow a belt. (pp.8-9)

The boy's awareness of his body invites comparison with other boys who are stronger and he realises that the odds are against him. He thus withdraws, keeps 'on the fringe of his line out of the sight of the prefect' and the 'rude feet' where he continues with a different exercise in which he thinks about words and begins to attempt making sense of them. The reader thus sees him from the outside when he is able to describe the playground and is conscious of himself before we move into his mind and see that he 'feigns to run now and then.' It is thus possible to delineate two playgrounds in the passage. One playground swarms with boys while the other is full of sensations and in it a different exercise with words takes place in contrast to the physical confrontation and competition in the first playground. *A Portrait* may be seen as a continuation of these exercises in the two playgrounds.

The prefects whose presence Stephen dodges are represented by the Jesuits, their religion, Stephen's family and his country and the rude feet stand for all those moments when he is jolted by incidents that seem to inhibit his exercise such as the retreat, the confession, the invitation to join the priesthood or the poverty of the Dedalus household. What strength the little frail, outside frame lacks as it confronts these obstacles is compensated for by an internal agility and sense of proportion which sometimes seems rather much for one of Stephen's age. Perhaps the consistency of tactics and purpose account for the eventual arrival at the point of destination. Here is how he describes another early stage in the journey:

> In the beginning he contented himself with circling timidly round the neighbouring square or, at most, going half way down one of the side streets: but when he had made a skeleton map of the city in his mind he followed boldly one of its central lines until he reached the Customs house. (p.61)

The pace quickens after this stage and the images that describe it now conjure speed.

> A side door of the theatre opened suddenly and a shaft of light flew across the grassplots. A sudden burst of music issued from the ark... His unrest issued from him like a wave of sound: and on the tide of flowing music the ark was journeying, trailing her cables of lanterns in her wake. (p.69)

'Sudden' appears in quick succession, and 'shafts' of light fly across and before long the movement is one of waves and tides.

Speed has so much become part of Stephen that when he attempts to 'construct a dam' to stem the momentum, the effort proves inadequate, 'useless,' 'the tides jostle fiercely above the crumbled mole.' Not even the sombre retreat of the Catholic priests can slow the momentum. The fiery words of the priest who conducts the retreat could well be Stephen's:

> The blood seethes and boils in the veins, the brains are boiling in the skull, the heart in the breast glowing and bursting, the bowels a red hot mass of burning pulp, the tender eyes flaming like molten balls. (112)

The following response to the sermon illustrates the level of speed which Stephen's race may be said to have gathered:

> A wave of fire swept through his body: the first. Again a wave. His brain began to glow. Another. His brain was simmering and bubbling within the cracking tenement of the skull. Flames burst forth from his skull like a corolla, shrieking like voices... (115)

The language is sharp and urgent, a word becomes a sentence and the flames which 'burst forth' from his skull are aided by 'waves.' There may be a retreat going on but the movement within Stephen is a mockery of the word. From the moment he picks up speed and the flames begin to roar the reader becomes aware of the inevitability of his subsequent exile. Stephen's mind is described as 'a cloister' through which gusts of wind blow. His mind has also been likened to other structures such as 'the theatre,' 'an ark,' 'a stream.' In the end it is as if this curious combination of structures has all been washed towards the sea which clearly is the destination:

> He looked northward towards Howth. The sea had fallen below the line of seawrack on the shallow side of the breakwater and already the tide was running out fast along the foreshore. (p.155)

We have come a long way from the stagnant pool at Clongowes. 'Where was his boyhood now?' he asks. The speed which Stephen gains surprises him as it does his peers and inevitably the reader. Not surprisingly the images now are of birds and of flight: 'When the soul of a man is born in this country, there are nets flung at it to hold it back from flight' (p.184). Stephen is presented as a bird that soars high above the nets cast to catch it. The bird, as it were survives the journey to the sea and not unexpectedly claims a prize in the woman of the sea 'whose bosom was as a bird's soft and slight, slight and soft as the breast of some dark-plumaged dove' (p.155).

So the journey or the race that begins rather playfully ends on a serious note. Stephen is presented as one able to combine the playful and the serious in order to cope with what turns out to be a difficult and complicated journey. The symbolism reveals the various stages of this modernist journey. There are false starts, as in the playground, unhelpful coaches such as Mike Flyn, as well as dubious techniques such as the retreat, but the assistance he receives is also tremendous and it leads him to a destination which turns out to be only a significant stop-over: 'I go to encounter for the millionth time the reality of experience' (p.228).

In *The Waves* as in *A Portrait*, life as a journey dominates the story. There is, however, a difference in the nature of the movement. Each character in the novel represents a symbol of speed. Percival, for instance, is often described in images that reflect great speed. This is partly because he dies young and because Bernard together with Percival's other friends see death as 'the enemy' which terminates Percival's 'gallop' in India. Percival's death is depicted as a consequence of too much speed:

> His horse stumbled; he was thrown. The flashing trees and white rails went up in a shower. There was a singe; a drumming in his ears. Then the blow; the world crashed; he breathed heavily, he died where he fell. (p.101)

In the accompanying 'poetic' rendering of the incident the images are of waves and sprays reflecting tremendous momentum:

> The waves broke and spread their waters swiftly over the shore. One after the other they massed themselves and fell; the spray tossed itself back with the energy of their fall... The waves fell; withdrew and fell again, like the thud of a great beast stamping. (pp.101–102)

Waves are seen as an aid or a hindrance to life's journey. The modernist novelist thrives on such ambiguous images and in this novel, the ambiguous image is also the novel's title. Half of the novel is an account of the movement of the waves and they are often, as is the case with Percival, used as a complement to the action in the other half of the novel. There are moments when the waves 'pause and draw out again, sighing like a sleeper whose breath comes and goes unconsciously' (5). They may thus gather their own momentum or initiate and reflect the speed of the human characters.

Bernard, for instance, could be said to walk, in contrast to Percival's speed, but even he admits:

> And in me too the waves rise. It swells; it arches its back. (198)

Bernard is aware of the 'eternal renewal' or what he also calls 'the incessant rise and fall and fall and rise again.' But he is in many ways a routine person: Tuesday follows Monday, then comes Wednesday. He is never content, however, with being a mere walker. He talks about 'a rushing stream of broken dreams, nursery rhymes and street cries.' Bernard lives long. He is the oldest of the major characters and this is put down to his 'precision.' He takes his time, he is preserved, as he claims, from the 'excesses' of his friends. His old age is thus seen as a mark of his control of the speeds (the waves) which control life.

Susan also symbolises the walking pace which Bernard so ably demonstrates. Like Bernard, she is married with children and since she has a farm and her 'stitching' to look after she can assume the leisure and easy pace which may not be harassed by waves:

> The brisk waves that slap my ribs rock more gently, and my heart rides at anchor, like a sailing-boat whose sails slide slowly down on the white deck. (p.31)

Louis symbolises a middle ground. He is used as if to bridge the gap between the routine, controlled pace of Bernard or Susan and the dizzy speed of Percival. He has developed an elaborate way of coping with the problems caused by 'waves' and conceives his role in complicated symbolic terms:

> My destiny has been that I remember and must weave together, must plait into one cable the many threads, the thin, the thick, the

broken, the enduring of one long history, of our tumultuous and varied day. (p.112)

Though Louis also hears 'the sullen thud of waves' he shows, as the passage indicates, that he is in control. Part of Louis's measured pace is derived from his idea that he has lived many thousand years but it is also a result of an almost identical harmonious relationship with nature as is the case with Susan. In him therefore may be found a bit of Bernard as well as a bit of Susan.

Jinny, however, 'rides like a gull on the waves,' (p.71) and Rhoda is like 'a ribbon of weed flung far' (p.72). Both women are 'rolled over' towards what seems to be an inevitable destination. They are not capable of running, not even of walking, and are quite satisfied to be part of a team and if possible enjoy the fruits of a communal victory, if any.

All the major characters thus become symbols which further throw light on the dominant symbol of life as a journey. Their journey as Bernard shows is fraught with dangers and death symbolises the end for each traveller:

What enemy do we now perceive advancing against us, you whom I ride now as we stand pawing this stretch of pavement? It is death. Death. Death is the enemy. It is death against whom I ride with my spear crouched and my hair flying back like a young man's, like Percival's when he galloped in India. (p.200)

There is a significant difference here between Joyce and Virginia Woolf in their symbolic interpretation of the journey. For Virginia Woolf all the journeys, as Bernard describes them in the above passage, end in death. Percival's 'sprint,' Louis's 'middle-distance,' and Bernard's 'walk' all lead to an inevitable death. The picture is bleak in contrast to Joyce's more positive homecoming in *A Portrait*.

In Awoonor's *This Earth*, as in the other two novels, the journey dominates the plot and is again the major symbol:

The long road begins here, begins from the foetal tunnel and winds serpentine through the grass, the river and the sun, for a covenant is drawn never to be broken, an oath is taken.

As in *The Waves* and *A Portrait*, levels of speed are crucial to an understanding of the nature of the novel's symbolism. Thus when Amamu is at 'the point of departure' elaborate preparations are made even though the ritual is complete when the oath is taken it is clear from the following passage that there is no cause to hurry:

> Crawling, crawling picking up and eating tasteless chicken droppings, is there no one here and this child is eating chicken droppings...

> Standing and falling scream scream into mother's bossom, little little goat Mother is not at home. Father is not at home...

> Picking up sounds. Ghosts are real. Real. But they walk faster, erect, they run, they jump. The darkness deepens into light...

> Bright bright days in the fields outside picking flowers, catching rainbow-coloured butterflies in a wild garden. (14–15)

Awoonor's language here not only mimes the thoughts of the child in its relationship with the adult world but it also reflects the pace at which these stages in the journey through life move. The pace is slow. The present participles give this effect but as the child begins to grow these participles are replaced by more urgent figures of speech, ghosts 'walk faster,' 'they run,' 'they jump.' But the language symbolises a world view and a process. The chicken droppings, the goat and the butterflies in a wild garden reflect a very rustic life just opening up for a beginner, and, for the child, ghosts are real. But the language also shows the rudimentary, unsure stages in the journey so far. It is a stage of crawling, standing and falling.

But this slow pace is soon accelerated:

> Chasing after tangible ghosts in the fields I caught one. That was my first catch... Then it flew away. It would not stay. For days I searched the field looking for it. (p.15)

Amamu's journey now gathers momentum and the reader is reminded of the symbol of the butterfly whose elusive quality invites comparison with some of the other people which he encounters on his journey. It is possible to interpret his successful law practice as one butterfly he has caught. His wife and his mistress Adisa could also be seen in this light. Amamu perhaps equates life's journey as a chase in the wild fields of butterflies.

Amamu also drives:

> Traffic was heavy... He was patient. After a few minutes he saw the hill he was waiting for. But he had misjudged the speed of the taxi from the centre of the town. As he turned into the road, swinging left, tyres screeched, the taxi driver jammed on his brakes, eased opposite him, and said with venom or bitterness, 'Your Mother's arse, don't you know how to drive?' (p.17)

He is only clumsy. The man on the wheels who meticulously describes the scenery for the reader is not quite the same as the man with the habit of withdrawal. The driver defines the nature and quality of his journey. The road presents problems for the unwary driver. But, like Louis in *The Waves*, Amamu knows enough to avoid the collision for a while. He is quite capable, as Louis is, of applying the brakes.

This Earth, however, abounds in characters who are unable to drive, who collide headlong. There is Paul Dumenyo, the demented priest, almost Amamu's double who as it were, falls by the wayside. Paul Dumenyo is always on the road and even when he becomes completely mad he is known more by his walk around the town than by his awful predicament. His favourite song is of a Christian Pilgrim:

> I am coming, Lord, Coming unto Thee. Wash me, cleanse me in Thy blood That flowed on Calvary. (p.103)

Dumenyo's song reinforces and complements Amamu's evangelical journey:

> There's no discouragement will make him once relent His first avowed intent To be a Pilgrim. (p.183)

Ibrahim, the cousin of Amamu's faithful house boy, also travels on this road and falls by the wayside. His movements from the north through the curious routes in Nima and his eventual death at the hands of his burglars are real but they can also be seen as symbols of a journey which proves too difficult for the traveller. The 'poetic' chapter preceding the description of Ibrahim's life recalls the symbol of the journey and makes reference to 'touchstones, billboards, boardings carrying illuminated messages' (p.48). It can be assumed that Ibrahim misreads the billboards. A character like Amamu's wife does not even seem to know where she is or whether she should travel at all. She simply vanishes into thin air, incapable of comprehending the quality of life's journey. Others take short cuts, like the two brothers who died fighting over a rat. When one is questioned he often replies that his brother had gone on 'a journey to Dahomey.' The soldiers who die in the Second World War also take a short-cut as does Amamu's mother who is cut down prematurely. Amamu's mother is one of those who hope, like Rhoda and Jinny in *The Waves*, that somehow the tide will carry them across. It does, and it is fair to say that *This Earth* is full of failed pilgrims.

As in *The Waves*, the Atlantic sea coast is perpetually battered by the tides from the ocean, washing away those who cannot drive. Amamu's tenacity, like Bernard's however, pays. But though his destination is similar to Bernard's he is more fortunate in a companion, not unlike Stephen's immaculate woman of the sea. Both Stephen and Amamu are presented as optimistic characters who use the sea as a special symbol of inspiration and courage. The characters in *The Waves* are equally tenacious but not as hopeful. There are striking similarities in the dominant symbol used by all three novelists. It is useful to read Awoonor's novel with *The Waves* and *A Portrait* in mind. Amamu's journey, like Stephen's, reaches its climax with the appearance of the watermaid, but, unlike Stephen, Amamu's pilgrimage ends with the enemy, death, so well known to Bernard and his friends in *The Waves*. Even the 'touchstones' and the billboards are strikingly similar. Thus the reader encounters butterflies and moths in all three novels as he does birds, streams and waves. Each of these symbols aid the journey undertaken by the highly introspective characters whose use of memory is also presented as a guide to our understanding the novels' dominant theme.

Memory constitutes the essence of the novels deploying the inward perspective as much of the activity takes place within the mind.[6] Memory is the link in the chain or, to continue our metaphor, memory serves as sign posts for the journey of the mind. The process may be described as one of fragmentation and assembly where a pattern eventually emerges from the numerous pieces. The writer wedges the pieces to complete the jigsaw puzzle. Much of this process consists of a series of images which are linked with events. The minds of the characters in these three novels are warehouses stocked with images of the past, the collection of which gives meaning to the events of the present and the future. But the novelist selects, and it is this selection that ensures a pattern. This may sound contradictory, since in the novels which deploy the inward perspective the images seem to 'roll in a laval flow.' But the modernist novelist who deploys the technique is as capable of manipulating language as his naturalist counterpart. He even does better than the naturalists whose fidelity to the difference between the 'Cathedral and the small girl' inhibits his perspective and selection.

In *A Portrait* Stephen's introspective nature is the perfect terrain for the mind's favourite activity, remembering. Always practising within his 'playground' he creates a pattern as the story unfolds. The mention of a word such as suck, for instance, leads first to a practice of its meaning, then to its association and inevitably to a memory of the night he had spent with his father at the hotel in Cork. This is the way Stephen's mind operates throughout the novel. It is through this process whereby all the senses of his mind and body are engaged in a recording process that a full picture of the nature and destination of his journey emerges. Stephen's mind, as the narrator tells us, is a 'fantastic fabric' woven of all kinds of shapes and colours. His outer frame may be weak but the same cannot be said of his mind. Two contrasting images keep coming up within the storehouse of memories. On the one hand, the reader notices what Stephen calls 'monstrous images' best represented in the vivid recording of the sermon at the retreat. These images torture the lonely traveller, indeed, towards the end of the retreat, Stephen's soul could be said to be literally on fire. Only a mind capable of 'winding in and out' like a tape could reproduce so vividly those sad moments when Stephen's sin 'oozes like a sore, a squalid stream of vice.' As he confesses, 'the last sins oozed forth, sluggish, filthy' (132). This image of filth persists. The poverty of Stephen's parents, for instance, is demonstrated in the lice he squashes, poverty serves as a symbol of the hell to which Stephen's soul has been condemned. It is significant that this slimy life which he first experienced in the hands of the school bully, Wells, never leaves him. It continues to appear in many forms. A pool of water is enough to remind Stephen of that faraway time when he shared a forced bath with a rat. Then there is the recurrence of the picture of the world as dunghill, plunged perpetually into darkness from which there seems no escape. Here, monstrous reveries come thronging into his mind or, more correctly, into the den. Darkness rules in this part and its meticulous recurrence in the mind of the protagonist serves as a reminder that here is a situation which calls for redemption. Stephen needs to reach for the light; he needs a lamp which will show him the way out of his cave and thus direct his steps properly to what must surely be the correct destiny: escape from those situations and people who seem bent on casting him back into damnation, into the sordid pool.

Just as Stephen's memory piles up sordid images by means of constant recurrence, so does the same memory serve him to fashion a path that will eventually lead him to light. The treachery of the other life is matched by the fidelity of the images of hope. The most significant images and the most persistent are those that relate to women. Eileen virtually dominates the first chapter in spite of politics and religion. She reminds Stephen of lovely and precious objects, a tower of ivory, a house of gold; her hair streams out like gold in the sun. Where in the other cluster there is darkness, here images of shining objects, represented by the sun, provide a strong antidote. Eileen's role is taken over by Mercedes in the second chapter. Her alluring eyes radiate and the constant repetition of her image reassures Stephen: the holy encounter continues in spite of the filth without. Both women are hand-maidens of the woman of the sea who is waiting patiently, as it were, for the success of Stephen's journey to her kingdom.

They are complemented by several other women who hold the lamp for Stephen to see his way out. The two main sides of Stephen's character are thus represented by two obvious contrasting images: darkness and light. One inhibits the journey, the other propels the traveller and a tortured but yet alert memory keeps Stephen on course. Memory is similarly used to highlight the contrast between dark and bright sides of Stephen's life.

Bernard's soliloquy early in the novel describes the way memory is used in *The Waves*:

> The bubbles are rising like the silver bubbles of image. I cannot sit down to my book, like Louis, with ferocious tenacity. I must open the little trap-door and let out these linked phrases which I run together whatever happens, so that instead of incoherence here is perceived a wandering thread lightly joining one thing to another. (p.26)

They are, in fact six trap doors all of which seem to open simultaneously and which give the coherence required for a composed story. Images are imprisoned within these doors and each time they are released they 'charge out' enjoying a certain freedom but aware also of the limitations of the freedom: there must be a wandering thread lightly joining one thing to another. What is most remarkable about *The Waves* is this ability described by Susan Gorky as 'Cosmic Communication' which enables the characters in the story accurately to define what the memory of the other five consists in. Perhaps as people who grow up together it is not unusual after all that they should think alike, or for that matter, have similar memories. Virginia Woolf's innovation shows that birds of identical feather do indeed flock together. However, these modernist muses show that, though the memories are the same, the images which are used to express them are different. This device of varied images also ensures the differences in characterisation. Images in the first chapter, for instance, of a ring, a slab of pale yellow, bird song, a globe, a crimson tasse, a great beast's foot, and a spider's web accurately separate the major characters. Memory here more than in *A Portrait* serves as crucial reference point. The six characters keep returning to the bench-mark from where they can properly

survey the road which it seems they have to construct for
themselves. Where Stephen had hand maidens, here the
protagonists must be desperately looking for their own markers.
Rhoda and Jinny could do with Stephen's luck but the nature of
their journey requires that they must create their own signposts.

Such a signpost stands conspicuously in the figure of
Percival. All roads lead to Percival. It is here that the traveller
must return for his map. This is why Bernard continues to regret
the day he refused to accompany Percival to Hampton Court. For
once, the guide was prepared to take the traveller to the sites
himself, but the poor traveller turned down an opportunity he
lives to regret throughout his journey. Whenever Bernard is
tormented by the 'horrible activity of the mind's eye' he
experiences this 'pounce of memory, no to be foretold, not to be
warded off' that he did not go to Hampton Court (p.179). As
with Bernard, so with the other five. Memories of Percival
constitute for them the only meaningful way of interpreting their
lives. Neville speaks for them:

> Into the wave that dashes upon the shore, into the wave that flings
> its white foam to the utmost corners of the earth, I throw my violets,
> my offering to Percival. (111)

They 'yelp like jackals biting at each other's heels but
assume the sober and confident air of soldiers in the presence of
their captain' (83). Memories of Percival unite their lives and give
the story its unity. Without him and his inspiration the rest are
incomplete, unprepared. The two moments in the story where
we meet Percival are the most moving and revealing moments. It
is also significant that Bernard's summary, which is a sketch of
memories to end all memories, places Percival's invitation in a
central position. It provides the 'pounce of memory' that he
cannot forget. The italicised 'poetic' chapters show images of
nature which also provide the signposts for all the characters.
They determine the progress that each of the characters make.
The first chapter sets the pattern:

> The sun had not yet risen. The sea was indistinguishable from the
> sky, except that the sea was slightly creased as if a cloth had
> wrinkles in it. Gradually as the sky whitened a dark line lay on the

horizon dividing the sea from the sky and the grey cloth became barred with thick strokes moving, one after another, beneath the surface, following each other, pursuing each other, perpetually. (p.5)

The evolutionary process which is described here is similarly reflected in the way the human characters are revealed to the reader. We begin with sunrise and end with darkness and are, through repetition, reminded of the importance of nature in the lives of these characters. Nature stands for the all-conquering 'hero' which Percival and his followers have failed to become. The change in the sun's movement is revealed gradually by a skilful use of memory.

In Amamu we find yet another withdrawn character for whom memory constitutes the essence of being. Since the beginning of the story is also its end, memory becomes indispensable to the narration. All the 'A' (poetic) chapters are exercises in memory and reflection. One, (chapter 6a) actually begins with the word remember. Amamu's memory also consists of a pattern of two opposing images. On the one hand there is the dunghill and on the other there is the butterfly. All the other images in the story may be grouped under these opposing categories. The dunghill is associated with darkness which in turn conjures the image of a cave. In this dark cave will be found all the filth of corruption in the country during and after colonial rule: 'fart-filled respectable people toiling in moth-eaten files to continue where the colonialists and imperialists left' (p.28). There is the unmistakable filth of Nima which lurks in the background. Nima provides Amamu with an opportunity to show that he is also quite capable of keeping the outer eye open. In what is clearly the best descriptive chapter in the novel, Amamu meticulously reminds the reader of the dunghill his country has become:

Nima skirts the west central part of the city like a vulture. No river runs through Nima. Only a huge open gutter that stinks to heaven. The City itself grew with a vengeance. Nima grew alongside it like an ever growing and eternal dunghill. (151)

In all his travels a lot of what he comes across reminds him of this dunghill. Yet:

In this dunghill we will search among the rubble for our talisman of hope. (p.92)

And here a path similar to Stephen's is followed meticulously. The elusive butterfly continues to prove more difficult to find, and as in Joyce, a host of hand-maidens, also with a lamp, help the traveller to move on course. Here also the image of the dunghill is contrasted with shiny objects, sunflowers, shining flames, gold, and as the traveller moves nearer his destination, the sun begins to break through the clouds. The moment is bright and it sparkles:

> She rose slowly, head first, adorned with sapphires, corals and all the ancient beads her mother left for her pubertal rites. She rose slowly from a dream sea. The sea was real: the sun was beating down hard and cruel.

Adisa, the dominant hand-maiden, smells of fresh earth upturned for the millet season in her native home. This is a sharp contrast to Amamu's wife whose presence brings 'dark clouds straddling the sky's span' (123).

Amamu's landscape is vast, stretching from Keta through London via Sweden to Moscow, yet memory serves him so well that his avowed intent is never shaken. In spite of the variety of people and circumstances that he encounters he has become such a master at puzzles that towards the end he joins all the pieces into a recognisable pattern. A chain of women leads him to the Watermaid and he displays an uncanny remembrance of friends and of the events that initiated the contact in the first place. Memory in Amamu has the power of uniting the impossible. Everything flows in a certain pattern for the searcher and traveller who has developed skills to be able to sift butterflies out of dunghills. Memory may be said to be the strong point of Awoonor' novel. Where Joyce and Woolf have a more restricted setting, Dublin and London, only marginally including other areas, Awoonor's extends to cover the world. All three novelists, though, display 'a perpetual lengthening shadow of memories' over their present experience. In the process they blur the boundaries between the past, present, and future.

The mind which creates its spaces is equally capable of creating its time which may, as with space, not be the same as that provided by the guide-book. In the modernist novels which use the inward perspective, time, chrolological time, is bent and broken to serve the psychological dispositions of the characters in the story. The multiple nature of the characterisation and the nature of the symbolism reflect the way time is also portrayed. Time is seen in different perspectives in its relation to nature, and in its relation to space. It may even be said that perspective on time conditions the flow of the narration. 'Glasses,' Sterne had said, 'can make an inch seem a mile. I leave it to future ages to invent a method for making a minute seem a year.'[8] Sterne went on to do in *Tristram Shandy* what he was going to leave to future ages but the novelists under discussion may be considered as his truest apostles. They all manipulate time as freely as possible in order to give the characters in the novels greater psychological perspective.

Thus chronological and mechanical time are often far from Stephen's mind in *A Portrait*. He changes the calendar days in anticipation of the Christmas vacation. He also carefully notes the lecture hours on his time-table and even compiles a diary toward the end of the story but all these exercises are subservient to the psychological time his mind creates. Because his mind creates vast paces it is able to see chronological time as a minor element in its world. When he tears dates off his Calendar, for instance, he is aware that the Christmas vacation is still a long way but he adds confidently that 'one time it would come because the earth moved round always' (p.14). The reader is then treated to a lesson in geography emphasising the superiority of space over time. When Stephen notices the lecture hours on his time-table he also remarks the unreliability of clock time: one clock tells him it is five minutes to five but there is another one near him beating eleven strokes. So he returns his mind to its introspective shell and considers his future role in the United States of Europe. These entries in his diary speak for themselves:

6 April: Certainly she remembers the past. Lynch says all women do.
Then she remembers the time of her childhood and mine if I was

> ever a child. The past is consumed in the present and the present is
> living only because it brings forth the future. (p.226)

The reader has already become used to this modernist's
sense of time and how in this process the spatial dimension takes
precedence over the temporal and a close connection is made
with nature which, after all, provides the vast expanse upon
which the mind works. Time is described mainly in relation to
space and nature:

> Consciousness of place came ebbing back to him slowly over a vast
> tract of time unlit, unfelt, unlived.

Elsewhere his soul traversed:

> A period of desolation in which the sacraments themselves seemed
> to have turned into dried up sources. (p.153)

Indeed nature, not time, is Stephen's main guide in life

> So timeless seemed the grey warm air, so fluid and impersonal his
> own mood, that all ages were as one to him (p.153)

Nature cools the loathing and bitterness in Stephen. The
moment may be depressing but the superior rhythm of nature
assures the troubled soul that somehow all will be well. It is in
the sea that Stephen recognises the presence of 'a new wild life
singing in his veins' (p.155). The sea and its waves continue
beating while mechanical time operates its monotonous beat. The
waves do soar and rage, have more flexibility, something
deficient in the other time. The mermaid who resides in the sea is
the custodian of this eternal ebb and flow of the waves and
enough has been said about her significance on Stephen's
consciousness. She represents the eternal renewal for Stephen.
This view of time affects the plot of the novel.

In the first chapter, for instance, where the attention of the
reader is focused on the 'playground,' past, present and future
mingle with such fluidity that it is difficult to distinguish which
is 'the moment.' In the first few pages of the chapter the reader is
introduced to the thoughts of the child but not long after that
Stephen is already established in school at Clongowes and is
shown to be settling down to some rhythm when he finds
himself in the infirmary. A long period is then taken to dramatize

a Christmas dinner party which in the narration is as present as the events we witness in the school. Yet it might well be the story Stephen tells his fellow invalid at the infirmary. As soon as the dinner party is over we are returned to the 'story' once more. This ability to dramatize events in such a way that each becomes part of the present consciousness is the advantage the modernist writer gets from taking chronology into his own hands and thus challenging the reader's conventional ways of looking at time.

Stephen's race has been recorded in such a way that he may rewind and edit the tape if and when he chooses. The choice is usually conditioned by 'the moment' which, in several instances, may just be a mere word or gesture. Each time squalor or dirt comes up a whole array of past incidents swarm back. The movement from Clongowes through Belvedere, to University is a recurrent one. It is no wonder that even at University the first things he remembers are those tormenting moments at Clongowes. Rather than measure time chronologically, Stephen has devised his own time measurement: Clongowes, Mercedes, and the small whitewashed house in the garden where he measured 'distance on the homeward and outward journey' (p.58). We have come to know that, for Stephen, distance is another way of talking about time.

The joint-protagonists in *The Waves* manipulate time in a similar manner as Susan's gesture here suggests:

> I have torn off the whole of May and June, and twenty days of July. I have torn them off and screwed them up so that they no longer exist, save as a weight in my side. They have been crippled days, like moths with shrivelled wings unable to fly. (p.36)

Susan's desperate gesture is an indication of the outlook the characters in *The Waves* adopt towards time. If we add her soliloquy to Louis's which consistently emphasises an ageless life, we notice a group of people desperate to take control of a situation which seems beyond them. None of them wants to go to the top to live in the light of 'this great clock, yellow-faced, which ticks and ticks.' Like Susan, and very much like Stephen, all the characters in *The Waves* do not trust mechanical time and they all plot, like Rhoda, to destroy it:

The two hands are convoys marching through a desert. The black
bars on the clock face are green cases. The long hand has marched
ahead to find water. The other, painfully stumbles among hot stones
in the desert. It will die in the desert. (p.14)

And it does. Here as in *A Portrait*, nature is the ally of the
mind. Nature destroys time so that the mind can create its own
or simply just live on; that is why, apparently pleased at the
conquest of time, Bernard claims that they are all creators. That
time which they create is a replica of nature: it lets fall its drop on
the roof of Bernard's mind; time for Bernard has become 'a
sunny pasture covered with a dancing light, it is spread as a field
at midday.' Here, as in Stephen's case, there is no past, no future,
merely the moment in 'its ring of light.' Preoccupation with the
moment dominates the narrative in *The Waves*. The story consists
of the desperate efforts of all six major characters to arrest the
moment, if possible, make it stand still. A very clear distinction is
made in this novel between the time of the mind 'which stretches
from Shakespeare to ourselves' and that other clock which marks
the approach of a particular person (p.185).

Having destroyed that other clock, however, they need to
create their own landmarks and here, as in *A Portrait*, memory
and a dramatized perspective plays a crucial role. Each soliloquy
seems to be tailored for the moment and the link between the
soliloquies, which sometimes seems incredible, as in chapter one
where Bernard and Susan seem to cue each other, ensures that
the stream, the new mode of time is kept constantly in flow. The
ability of the characters to know what the others are thinking
enables them to maintain the link in their own time span; except
for Louis, that is. Louis's sense of time, though also of the mind,
covers all seasons in a way which makes even Susan's ambitions
seem meaningless. Louis is a man of all seasons. There will
always be Louis, his father a banker in Brisbane, not just a Louis.
For him there is no particular meeting place between past and
present in spite of the attempt to 'defraud human history of a
moment's vision' (p.45).

The others, though, have found a new benchmark for
measuring time Percival. Like Mercedes in *A Portrait*, Percival
serves as a point for measuring time and distance. Bernard, for

instance is confused when he discovers that Percival's death and the birth of his own son occurred on the same day. Yet he must hold Percival's 'youth and beauty' since such an opportunity may never come again. In their pilgrimage Percival sets the pace and the time.

Percival's standard is, however, not the sole criterion for recording time. A good part of the narrative consists of the description of the rhythmic measurement of nature. The sun, the sea, waves, trees and birds operate a similar, though superior, rhythm from that provided by the other characters. Nature displays the variety which the characters stand for but which seems to elude them:

> The waves massed themselves, curved their backs and crashed. Up spurted stones and shingle. They swept round the rocks, and the spray, leaping high, spattered the walls of a cave that had been dug before, and left pools inland, where some fish stranded lashed its tail as the wave drew back. (p.112)

Rhoda or Jinny may be that poor fish which missed the wave. When Bernard contemplates his enemy, death, the waves are indifferent. They have the last word: 'the waves broke on the shore' (p.200). In *The Waves* too, nature is the criterion of time.

This is, however, not to ignore the other time which begins at the nursery. The narrative also takes us through chronological time if only to smash it. We follow the six, later seven, characters from nursery to old age as in the case of Bernard. Though this time itself sometimes flows as a stream it is nevertheless followed diligently. Perhaps that is why, besides Louis, the other characters seem particularly threatened by it. Time, here, as Percival's fate demonstrates, is a real enemy; its death merely produces ghosts which haunt the minds of the protagonists of the story.

Kofi Awoonor's intended title for his novel was *The Leaves of Time*,[9] and this passage from his incomplete novel aptly describes what happens in *This Earth*:

> I have no proper sense of time; measuring time by any mechanical means destroys the depth and autonomy that time, real time, in all its mystery and magic, imposes on all things. Time is EVENTS, time is PLACE IMMEASURABLE, BEYOND RECALL. Time is the record

of the mythic dimension of our interaction with our surroundings beyond the direct acts, beyond the IMMEDIATE recorded now. Time is the truth which is shattered, ungathered, unrecorded forever.[10] (Emphasis mine)

Amamu, like Stephen and Bernard, refuses to measure time by mechanical means. Instead he records time in places and events and sees it as the mythic dimension of 'our interaction with our surroundings.' Amamu is sometimes, like Louis, ageless: 'Sometimes I rode on the back of one of the small ghosts... rode through centuries I cannot recall' (p.14). The relationship between time, space, and nature, is a constant refrain of Amamu. Here are a few examples:

Yaro suddenly looked old; he wore for the first time an interminable age, an oldness that was not time's, an agedness of hills and rivers. (p.175)

A thousand raindrops shall dance in the fertile womb of time. (p.133)

Joe said time was a hermaphrodite offering the therapy of God and we must bend down, lie down and receive our divine medication at his/her hands. (p.105)

And the waves beat their eternal notes upon the shore as they washed against his body. (p.179)

This last line recalls Virginia Woolf's waves breaking on the shore even as Amamu, like Bernard, embraces death. But the agelessness of the watermaid also recalls Stephen and his woman of all time. Like Stephen, this woman of the sea, and her eternal powers, reassures a wary Amamu and keeps his pilgrim dreams alive. To think about her is to forget about time:

It seemed suddenly that the centuries and the years of pain of which he was the inheritor and the woes for which he was singled out to be carrier and the sacrifice, were being rolled away, were being faded in that emergence. (p.179)

In *This Earth* the mermaid also reincarnates in Amamu's cousin who died years ago when he was a child. Her message is an old one, only delivered in a youthful voice. Here, as in the other two novels, nature through the sea, its waves, the butterfly, the mermaid cancels mechanical time.

As in the other two novels, a sense of drama and a vivid memory obliterates the distinction between past, present and future all ages are one. Memory provides the time scheme and makes disparate events fit into a pattern determined as it were by forces outside of time. Yet *This Earth* also displays a considerable record of mechanical time. In some cases actual dates are given, such as Amamu's early days at school and all the incidents that were associated with them. But, here too, the fidelity of recording the dates and times is just another way of refuting their claim to order and precision. Amamu is the type of character who it seems has seen everything. It is no wonder that as he moves closer to his death he takes us back to his primer class. His modernist journey takes him through paths familiar to the characters of *A Portrait* and *The Waves*:

> The road winds through tomorrow, for there are no yesterdays, and tomorrow, they are wiped away by tears in the eyes of orphans, in the eyes of widowed women in the eyes of husbands who lost their wives in childbirth in the convent where white sisters in long gowns administer ether and cut open wombs with a pair of sewing scissors. Touchstones, billboards, boardings carrying illuminated messages proclaiming the covenant. (p.48)

Here, too, the present, the moment, is lost in the ebb and flow, the tears of orphans and widows. The suffering becomes itself an aspect of time. It is a touchstone that proclaims the covenant between the dead and the living. Amamu uses his accumulated experience from books and from travel to emphasise the fluidity of time. For instance, he claims kinship with Jesus whose ordeal he seems to undergo concurrently (p.48). It is as if he went to Golgotha. He also has an uncanny way of linking every event and person within his stream of consciousness. In chapter four 'a,' for instance, he is able to draw a list of all the women he has met in his travels and in his youth and as the list unfolds it becomes obvious that each of these women is just another manifestation, an epiphany, of the primal woman of the sea who, as in *A Portrait*, represents the ultimate measurement of time and place. Her patience conditions the movement of the character and helps to sustain him in his ordeal.

There is in his experience and breadth of coverage of time something striking about Amamu which it appears the characters of *The Waves* could do with. There is nothing of that desperation which is obvious in the conduct of Susan and Rhoda. Amamu is calm, he has seen it all, he is like some older version of Percival only perhaps more dreamy. While Percival has no mermaid, Amamu, like Stephen, seeks solace in his woman of the sea. However, the similar features outweigh the differences. In each of the novels, chronological time is manipulated to suit the temperament of the character. In this fragmentation new ways of assembly emerge. First the difference between time and space becomes blurred and time and events are indistinguishable. Each seeks a new mark upon which they can hang the disparate threads. In each case this new mark is found in nature which becomes crucial in this modernist war to obliterate the precision of the other time. With a new time dimension, confidence is engendered, only, in some cases, to be shaken by the monotonous but sometimes ominous, ticking of mechanical time. By singling out the watermaid as a source of inspiration and courage and as a benchmark from which they can look at other aspects of time, Joyce and Awoonor have found a way out of the intimidating presence of what Rhoda calls 'the great clock.' The minds of these characters having created symbols and space have added another element, time, to their long list of discoveries on their common journey.

The technique of the inward perspective reveals the novelist as an explorer into the inner recesses of the mind. For this voyage of exploration the novelist relies on memory and manipulates memory and time to show the complexity of the mind. The three modernist writers under study utilise these devices and some striking similarities emerge in their use of technique and in their thematic concerns. All three put their protagonists on a symbolic journey. Awoonor's protagonist is a cross between Joyce's optimism and Virginia Woolf's despondency. Awoonor has acknowledged a debt to Joyce but he also seems to have incorporated some of the devices that Virginia Woolf deploys in *The Waves*. Indeed, in structure *This Earth* bears direct resemblance with *The Waves* with its separate poetic interludes and separate straightforward narrative. The last three chapters of *This Earth* serve a similar function to Bernard's summary in *The Waves*. However, while Bernard is analysing the lives of his other friends, Amamu looks back at his own journey and attempts to place himself somewhere in the recurrent stream of life, a job which the watermaid seems to simplify for him.

The images and symbols used by all three novelists are very revealing. They confirm the view that all are devices which work toward the dominant symbol of life as a journey. As a result of this common focus the differences in setting between the three writers become blurred. All the symbols are deployed in an identical manner. For instance, the symbol of the mermaid appears in all three novels though it is given greater attention by Joyce and Awoonor. In an interview he gave in Texas in 1972 Awoonor had said of this mermaid:

> Right now in Keta there are magicians who cure all kinds of diseases and it is believed that they have spent years in the waters with this woman. She is a REAL.[11] (My emphasis)

No one need doubt the authenticity of the statement. What Awoonor did not say, however, is the way the mermaid has, in *This Earth*, been adapted to fit the bigger canvas his novel paints. Amamu's watermaid is greater than a herbalist's tool and I have tried to demonstrate the universality of the image as it is used by all three introspective modernist writers.

Awoonor's eclecticism, which draws from Joyce and possibly from Virginia Woolf, enhances his narrative technique. His novel deserves attention because it is a good story that blends the resources of poetry with straightforward factual narrative. Awoonor supports this view himself. 'Cultural purity,' he says, 'is a dangerous myth that can arrest a people's growth and impose false ideas of superiority on them.'[12] He also admits that a large community of African artists do return to their roots in order to forge artistic patterns, through the 'newly acquired European instruments.'[13] Awoonor's 'African dirge' sounds similar to the 'private dirges' of the characters in *The Waves*. It is possible to argue, as Richard Priebe does, that *This Earth* is a truly

African novel but it is an African novel written with a modernist's consciousness.

CHAPTER FOUR

THE MULTIPLE PERSPECTIVE I:
JOSEPH CONRAD, *NOSTROMO*;
NGUGI WA THIONG'O, *PETALS OF BLOOD*

If the novels of Joyce, Virginia Woolf and Awoonor are about the self then those of Conrad and Ngugi may be said to be about ideas. This is not to imply that individual perceptions are insignificant in the novels. On the contrary, both novelists are very concerned with the individual but they both present him as certain ideas, such as truth and honour, for instance, affect him and how his own views about these concepts shape his relationship with his environment. A complex network of ideas and personalities determines point of view in their novels. The perspective is as multiple as the characters in the novels.

The novels examined in the previous chapter deal with introspective protagonists whose concern with themselves is such that the novels sometimes read as if the novelists had no reader in mind. The novels of Conrad and Ngugi, however, are novels for the reader. They are, to borrow Umberto Eco's terms, 'open texts,' which actively involve the reader in their 'production.'[1] It is necessary to emphasise this point especially with regard to Ngugi because recent criticism of his novels has tended to suggest that they evoke a limited and predetermined response, namely, a scientific socialist orientation of society.[2] Such a view undermines the complexity of Ngugi's novels. Both *A Grain of Wheat* and *Petals of Blood* ask the reader to adopt more than one perspective. It is worth repeating here that it is Conrad's questioning technique which Ngugi most admired. Ngugi's wish to write a thesis on Conrad when he was a postgraduate student at Leeds, at a time when he had already published a novel and was, in fact, writing *A Grain of Wheat*, is further testimony of their kinship in method.[3] Discussion of point of view in his novels must account for this affinity.

The individual histories of all the major characters in *Nostromo* and *Petals of Blood* offer perspectives from which other major characters may be viewed. The characters display a dramatic partnership which places them in intricate relationships with one another but one which still highlights their individual consciousness and their unique need to discover a purpose and a direction in life. Isolation and community thus define the nature of the characterisation and the management of point of view as in the novels of Faulkner and Armah but the major characters in the novels of Conrad and Ngugi are not the speculative, passive, and sympathetic observers who repeatedly probe into the lives and events around them; instead, they choose and act and face the full implications of their actions. The sympathetic observer, such as Captain Mitchell claims to be in *Nostromo*, is superfluous.[4] The actions of the characters speak for themselves; sympathy and judgement are left to the reader who soon discovers that 'truth' in these modernist novels is the sum of many perceptions.

The scene involving Decoud and the Capataz of the Cargadores toward the end of the second part of *Nostromo* illustrates how well Conrad makes this technique work. Decoud and the Capataz of the Cargadores have been assigned the difficult and dangerous task of saving several silver ingots from the greedy hands of the Monterists and predictably they get into very serious trouble. This is how the moment is depicted:

The lighter was leaking like a sieve... The Capataz put into Decoud's hands the handle of the pump which was fitted at the side aft, and at once, without question or remark, Decoud began to pump in utter forgetfulness of every desire but that of keeping the treasure afloat... Decoud pumped without intermission. Nostromo steered without relaxing for a second the intense, peering effort of his stare. Each of them was as if utterly alone with his task. It did not occur to them to speak. There was nothing in common between them but the knowledge that the damaged lighter must be slowly but surely sinking. In that knowledge, which was like the crucial test of their desires, they seem to have become completely estranged, as if they had discovered in the very shock of the collision that the loss of the lighter would not mean the same thing to them both. THIS COMMON DANGER BROUGHT THEIR DIFFERENCES IN AIM, IN VIEW, IN CHARACTER, AND IN POSITION, INTO ABSOLUTE PROMINENCE IN THE PRIVATE VISION OF EACH. There was no bond of conviction, of common idea; they were merely two adventurers pursuing EACH HIS OWN ADVENTURE, involved in the same imminence of deadly peril. Therefore they had nothing to say to each other. But this peril, this only incontrovertible truth in which they shared, seemed to act as an inspiration to their mental and bodily powers. (p.247) (My emphasis)

If we agree with Conrad that 'silver is the pivot of the moral and material events, affecting the lives of everybody in the tale,'[5] then this passage clearly describes the narrative strategy of the novel, for each character, not just Decoud and Nostromo, in Conrad's large canvas is his 'own adventurer,' but who is united nevertheless by the common perilous fact of the silver. The silver is 'the crucial test of their desires,' and inspires their involvements in events which can only be appropriately seen as 'deadly peril.'

Perhaps the greatest 'adventurer' in this sense is Charles Gould; the undisputed, but uncrowned, 'King of Sulaco' whose history, on one level, could be seen as the story of *Nostromo*. His manifesto is a straight forward one:

What is wanted here is law, good faith, order, security. Anyone can declaim about these things, but I pin my faith to material interests. Only let the material interests once get a firm footing and they are bound to impose the conditions on which alone they can continue to exist. (p.81)

In pursuit of these otherwise plausible public and political goals, Charles Gould is 'decoyed' by these same material interests which had in an earlier period destroyed his father. However, his problem is not, as Decoud and Dr. Monygham claim, 'romantic idealism.' On the contrary, he is a very practical man, perhaps consumed by his fixed idea of justice but certainly not a 'romantic idealism.' The reasons for his failure may be seen in the contrasting qualities displayed by his wife. She is 'highly gifted in the "Art" of human intercourse,' has a 'humanising influence' on people and in her, 'even the most legitimate touch of materialism was wanted (p.50).' She goes out of her way to look after the interest of the old Garibaldino and her hospitals and schools, for all that Decoud may declaim, are a measure of her spiritual commitment. Charles Gould, in contrast, is active in a different but more disastrous way. He has become so occupied with the mine that he forgets even his own wife and their small circle of friends. As the narrative progresses, he speaks less and less, often making his decisions with the nod of his head, or a slight alteration of his facial expression:

> His silences, backed by the power of speech, had as many shades of significance as uttered words in the way of assent, of doubt, of negation even of simple comment. Some seemed to say plainly, 'Think it over,' others meant clearly 'Go ahead,' a simple low 'I see,' with an affirmative nod, at the end of a patient listening half-hour was the equivalent of a verbal contract, which men had learned to trust implicity. (p.60)

Gould opts out of the joy and pain of life exemplified so well by his wife; he becomes, instead, nothing more than a statue. He fails to take a deep look at his own motives and his activities, which, before his father's death, seemed not only practicable but genuine and honest. Even when he makes obvious compromises, such as bribing Sulaco politicians, he does not see the larger human contact which such actions demand, and, because he is unable to understand his own nature, he naturally fails to understand other people. Through him Conrad demonstrates, as Eugene Boyle remarks, 'the tragedy of self-recognition not attained.'[6] His failure though should be seen in its broader context; the other major characters whose histories could also be said to be subject of the novel provide a useful framework upon which the problems of self-knowledge and eternal demands can be assessed.

Dr. Monygham's downright view of material interests, for instance, presents a sharp contrast to the faith which Charles Gould displays but Dr. Monygham's observations also reflect a superficial view of what has happened to the owner of the San Tome mine:

> There is no peace and no rest in the development of material interests. They have their law and their justice. But it is founded on expediency and is inhuman; it is without rectitude, without continuity and the force that can be found only in a moral principle. (p.419)

It may be difficult to refute Dr. Monygham's claim and because he seems to survive so many generations and the unpredictable governments of Costaguana he could easily be taken to be the novel's authoritative voice. The strategy of the novel, however, allows no one character to enjoy such a role. Dr. Monygham's distrust of material interests and of fellow human beings, honest though it may seem, hides some very fundamental things about him. His face, the narrator observes, 'had something vaguely unnatural, an exaggerated remorseful bitterness' (p.308), the result, perhaps of the torture he underwent under Guzman Bento's rule. His experiences under this tyrant inflict a 'pain which makes truth, honour, self-respect, and life itself matters of a little moment' (p.310). No wonder, then, that he has little regard for these ideals. His idolatrous relationship with Mrs. Gould appears to be a way of exorcising himself of the demon that seems to haunt him but not even Mrs Gould's humanizing spirit can help the man who never recovers his self-respect. Toward the end he is no more than a bird of prey with 'a broken wing.' The history of his life highlights the predicament of a cynic who, though not fooled, as Charles Gould is, by any rationalised emotion, nevertheless has become the victim of self-abuse, obsessed with the idea that to be worthwhile life must be flawless. He gets his due 'reward' when Mrs Gould, his new found goddess, refuses to confirm his inveterate pessimism with regard to the character of Nostromo.

Martin Decoud, like Dr. Monygham, also rejects Charles Gould's 'fairy tale;' he is skeptical about 'material interests' but he too is unable to achieve any proper realisation of self. Decoud serves a very useful purpose in the novel because his dramatic schemes, such as the establishment of the newspaper in Sulaco, his gun-running and his eventual proclamation of independence for Sulaco, shape and direct the course of action in the novel. In place of Charles Gould's fascination with the treasure of the mine and of Dr Monygham's new-found idol, Decoud has beautiful Antonia Avellanos under whose charm he undertakes all his adventures. He is convinced, in spite of the crucial role he plays in the affairs of the Republic, that he is 'not a patriot, but a lover;' his only illusion, he claims, 'is the supreme illusion of lover.' Unfortunately, however, he too fails to discover the joy of life. He commits suicide when faced with a deep sense of loneliness in the dark gulf. All three complement one another. Each of them seems to represent what the other might have been and what qualities they needed to reach the self-discovery they seek, but, somehow, their lonely and curious lives often contradict the 'plausible causes' which each of them seems determined to defend. 'Things seem to be worth nothing by what they are in themselves,' the railway engineer once told Dr Monygham, 'the only solid thing about them is the spiritual value which everyone discovers in his own form of activity' (p.266). The doctor would not hear such nonsense and it may be assumed that neither the 'dumb' Charles Gould, nor the 'dilettante' Decoud would appreciate such talk; all are fooled in one way or another.

The last word in this novel, if any, must belong simultaneously to Emilia Gould and 'the magnificent' Nostromo, the Capataz of the Cargadores who gives the story its title. It is not a coincidence that Nostromo specifically wishes to confess his crime to the woman who alone represents the spiritual values so absent in all the other major characters. He has scored several major triumphs. He is, as his 'ugly' nickname implies, 'the most indispensable member of the crew.'[7] He is indispensable to the

Europeans of Sulaco; indeed, as Decoud remarks, he is the 'active usher in of the material implements for (our) progress' (p.161). But Nostromo also falls prey to all the destructive passions that cause the failure of his European counterparts, such as Gould's dumb faith in material interests or Decoud's idealised sensual love or Dr Monygham's mistrust of self. The crucial difference between him and them, however, is the way he manages, in spite of all the set-backs and his naivete, to salvage something from his failures. The reader must wonder what would happen had Decoud possessed the selflessness and courage which Nostromo displays. 'I have said the word,' he says, 'the spell is broken' (p.456), in defiance of Dr Monygham's inveterate pessimism, in spite of Gould's ignorant piety, and of Decoud's skepticism and disillusion. Toward the end of the novel, Dr. Monygham, who still seeks proof for his theory of the flawless man, hears a testimony of faith from Linda who, though betrayed, still loves her Gian Battista. 'It was another of Nostromo's triumphs,' the narrator says:

> The greatest, the most enviable, the most sinister of all. In that true cry of undying passions that seemed to ring aloud from Punta Mala to Azuera and away to the bright line of the horizon, overhung by a big white cloud shining like a mass of solid silver, the genius of the magnificent Capataz de Cargadores dominated the dark gulf containing his conquests of treasure and love. (p.463)

Nostromo's triumph can also be seen in the way he serves, together with the silver, as the unifying force in a story whose numerous fragments are sometimes frustrating. It may be overstating the case to call him a hero. Conrad's detailed histories of the other characters make such a distinction impossible, but Nostromo brings the efforts and the failures of the others into sharper focus. To understand him the reader must, however, also understand Charles and Emilia Gould, Decoud, Dr. Monygham and even Captain Mitchell for whom all these people, and the drama they enact, are 'historic.' *Nostromo* is not a novel about one major character but many; its meaning must be seen in their collective struggle.

A similar approach is needed to read *Petals of Blood* where the events and changes caused by material interests are also seen as chaos inside and outside each of the major characters. Ilmorog is for them what the silver represents for the characters in *Nostromo*: it unites and divides them in the way silver does the characters in *Nostromo*; the village which, like Sulaco, starts as 'a kind of neglected outpost of the Republic' becomes suddenly 'a centre of numerous activities,' which as in the other novel work 'in obedience to an invisible law.' This description of the early entry into the village by three of the major characters explains how the device works:

> They used Munira's bicycle. Sometimes all three would walk, one person pushing the bicycle. Sometimes all three would ride the bicycle with Munira on the saddle. Karega on the frame and Wanja on the carrier. But mostly THEY RODE IN A KIND OF RELAY. Karega would walk. Munira would take Wanja for a mile or so and leave her to walk on. He would come back for Karega and take him a mile or so past Wanja. Then Munira would walk. Karega would take the bicycle and go back for Wanja. Soon they looked like the earth on which they trod, enveloped by an enormous sky of white and blue. (p.106) (My emphasis).

The full complement of the team, in fact, includes Abdulla, an ex-Mau Mau fighter who has lost a leg in the struggle and whose shop in Ilmorog is the first rallying point of the events that unfold. The oddly contrived race takes them toward 'the kingdom of (self) knowledge' in which the reader is expected, like them, to find answers to the question also posed in *Nostromo*, namely: 'triumph and defeat; success and miserable failure... which (was) which?'[8] All start, however, with their own private motives which they each idealise into public ones so that the novel becomes the elaborate drama of conflicting witnesses bringing forward evidence that remains in doubt until all of it is assembled. In their bicycle ride the major characters show the alternating and interdependent relationship between the individual and the group, which, as in *Nostromo*, is a way of introducing the reader to the way point of view alternates from the individual to the community. Here, too, each character behaves as if utterly alone with his task yet is entangled in a complex of relationships.

The story of Wanja, for instance, is told in such a way that the reader could easily take the novel to be mainly about her. She is the driving force of Ilmorog:

> Under her firm guidance, Ilmorog suddenly seemed to expand: new roads, influx of workers, banks, experts, dances and numerous small trades and crafts. (p.310)

Like Nostromo, she is also described as one in a thousand, and, like Nostromo, is more vibrantly alive than any other character in the novel. Her unique experiences dramatically link all the major characters in the story. She runs the village shop in partnership with Abdulla and is expecting his child at the end. She has affairs with Munira and Karega, and is the mistress of all three businessmen whose murder is ostensibly the subject of investigation around which the story is built. All the chaos in the novel is, therefore, mirrored in her life which sometimes assumes mythic dimensions: 'Wanja has the beauty of a lioness,' and, true to her Sphinx-like nature, she destroys anyone who can not answer her 'riddle.' The real Wanja, however, is caught in 'the tension between the desire for active creation and a passive acceptance of her fate,' her major dilemma being that she does not seem to know exactly what she could create: 'She wandered from place to place in search of IT or for a man who would show her IT' (p.57). IT, is sometimes a child which eventually she is expecting, sometimes IT is money, which she seems to know how to make, but she is so muddled that in the end all these things become a burden:

> The wealth she had (so) accumulated weighed on her heavily, as if the jewelled, rubied cord around her neck was now pulling her and her very shadow to the ground. (p.295)

There are 'such changing colours of blue and red and green' that 'she cannot see anything clearly' (p.57), but the reader who analyses her point of view in context with that of the other characters can discover the success or failure of her adventure and why.

Her major problem, if we excuse her ignorance and helplessness, is, like Abdulla's, her past from which she cannot escape. Abdulla's past however, presents another dimension to the Ilmorog dilemma. His one leg should be a source of pride since it represents the freedom for which he fought but like his donkey, the leg is a mixed blessing. In one sense he gets the respect he expects, and deserves, but is lonely and unhappy. The reasons for his unhappy condition also make the story of *Petals of Blood*. He is regarded as 'the best self of the community, symbol of Kenya's truest courage' (p.228).Abdulla is central to the story because he exemplifies its public political betrayal and the way in which such betrayal has maimed people like him. His life from the time he enlists to fight in the Mau Mau war to the wretched existence after the struggle is a comment on the nature of the betrayal. But, like Wanja, he too is confused and at times his motives are suspect. Experience, however, seems to have clarified his ideas, indeed, if we must find a hero for this novel we must locate him in Abdulla's endurance, in his courage and his tragic daring. Of all the characters in *Petals of Blood* he alone triumphs against the odds; the child he is expecting from Wanja is his reward for a relentless struggle against material interests.

The same cannot be said of the two teachers, Karega and Munira, yet Ngugi, like Conrad, has so masterfully handled their characterisation that critics wrongly regard one or the other as the hero of the novel. Both Gerald Moore,[9] and Eustace Palmer,[10] declare Munira the hero of the novel while for Douglas Killam it is Karega who emerges in this role.[11] Yet the novel belongs to Munira, for instance, only in the sense that he is privileged to act the role of 'the narrator as participant observer.'[12] If he was not too keyed up with his new found evangelism he would, like Captain Mitchell, be no more than a tourist guide. Indeed as he strolls through the ruins of Ilmorog with Karega the third-person narrator describes him as a tourist guide and comments on the way he seems to enjoy the role. But, like Captain Mitchell, his testimony is doubtful, copious though it may be. The story is more dramatically enacted by the characters concerned. However, like Captain Mitchell, his important decision to settle in Ilmorog for twelve years where others have come and fled, ushers in all the other characters and sets 'the inexorable law of the metal power' in motion. There is a crucial difference though between him and Captain Mitchell. Both have vague ideas about what their 'missions' are, but, while Captain Mitchell is pleased to watch the 'historic' events that take place and point to a doubtful contribution to such events, Munira, on the other hand, is tired of constantly being an outsider, 'fated to watch adrift.' He struggles to liberate himself and as he watches the whorehouse he sets on fire burn, he kneels down to pray because, as he concludes, 'he was no longer an outsider, for he had finally affirmed his oneness with the Law' (p.333). We do not know the law to which he refers because he dodged such a question when it was put to him by one of his innocent pupils. To call him a hero will be over-stating the case, since it is clear that when he acts he does so out of an undefined sense of purpose. Because he fails as a hero in this moral sense and is thus unable to play a fuller part in the action as he would have liked he also fails to be the hero of the novel.

Karega is more difficult to handle. Since he is cast in the role of a socialist and since Ngugi has been identified with socialist ideas, critics such as Douglas Killam have interpreted his role to come closest to Ngugi's aspirations and therefore have seen Karega as Ngugi's and the novel's hero.[13] Karega may be Ngugi's hero but he is not the hero of *Petals of Blood*. It is true that he is the most politically active of the major characters but the novel's logic persistently shows that his activity is a mere repetition of a predictable pattern. Like Munira, Chui, and the lawyer, he has been to Siriana secondary school and been expelled. He arrives in Ilmorog not for any public cause but to look for Munira whose sister he has driven to suicide at least as far as Munira is concerned. The trip he organises to the city is eventually too much for him to handle and he inevitably falls on Abdulla's skill and experience to see them through. He may be a victim of material interests but so are the others, even though, unlike the others, youth and education are on his side. The reader can only wonder what such advantages would have done for Abdulla. The news he gets from detention about the impending workers' strike cannot be compared to the highly symbolic import of Abdulla's child by Wanja; especially if it is remembered that even Abdulla's adopted child, Joseph, is already beginning to make an impact on his elders. This is not to ignore the intricate web of relationships that surround Karega, for indeed he seems to have the habit of dropping in at the most crucial moments in the history of Ilmorog but his stature in the novel must be measured against the contribution made by the other major characters. Such is the skill Conrad deploys in *Nostromo*. Ngugi's rendering of narrative perspective is similar to Conrad's in this regard.

The questioning spirit that characterises the novels of Conrad and Ngugi gives them a densely metaphoric texture which reveals characters who, like Inspector Godfrey in *Petals of Blood*, are constantly 'sifting words, storing phrases and looks and gestures, also looking for a line, a key, a thread, a connection, an image that would tie up everything together' (p.299). As image presses upon image, the characters seem like Karega, 'to wrestle with each, fix it, make it yield the secret' (p.214) that appears to elude them. Indeed, metaphor is such a pervasive feature of the style of these two novelists that it sometimes seems that a metaphorical reading is the only way of making sense of the novels: they constitute the conceptual constants of the novels and are consequently the reader's major vehicle for determining the point of view. However, as the examples of some of the characters will show, metaphor sometimes leads them into a 'linguistic mistake' which prevents them from seeing things in their substantial uniqueness, rather, they interpret events as signs. Only the reader is privileged to see through their mistakes and arrive at an interpretation that escapes all but a few of them.

In *Nostromo* Conrad presents a single dominant metaphor in the silver of the mine from which all the characters may be interpreted because the novel is about their insights into the nature of material interests. The novel's figurative language extends the uses of this metaphor by multiplying motifs which reinforce the centrality of silver in the course of events. Silver, as Emilia Gould observes, is 'not a mere fact, but something far-reaching and impalpable, like the true expression of an emotion or the emergence of a principle' (p.99). But Silver is real in the novel as the property of the Gould Concession. It has provided jobs for thousands of people, and is 'the biggest thing in Sulaco and even in the whole of the Republic' (p.98). Its 'palpable' form may also be seen, even before he is corrupted, in Nostromo's buttons, his whistle and his ring, even the colour of his horse is silver-grey; indeed, as Decoud observes, the man seems 'to disdain the use of any metal less precious than silver.' However, in spite of its dominant substantiality, the silver has a powerful 'shadow' which is responsible for the enormous metaphorical undercurrent of the novel. The gulf that separates the substance from the shadow also has substance in the Placido where Decoud and Nostromo hide the silver entrusted to their care but there is also the moral gulf which separates the characters in the novel. All the characters seem to operate within a 'moral darkness' as do Decoud and Nostromo when they take the silver away. Only two characters see the 'light.'

Of these, the most conspicuous is Emilia Gould. Conrad has made light and Mrs Gould indistinguishable. Light as metaphor expresses the clarity of her vision and the remarkable difference between her perception and that of even her husband who, though close to her, is unable unfortunately to benefit from her radiance. When the chaos in Costaguana reaches Sulaco, all the streets are dark except the light from Mrs. Gould's carriage, and as she 'passed in, all the lights went out in the street, which remained dark and empty from end to end.' It often appears that the more light she radiates, the greater the darkness around her. She radiates a light of her own:

> The half-light under the thick mass of leaves brought out the youthfulness of her face; made the clear, light fabrics and white lace of her dress luminous. Small and dainty, as if radiating a light of her own in the deep shade of the interlaced boughs, she resembled a good fairy, weary with a long career of well-doing, touched by the withering suspicion of the uselessness of her labours, the powerlessness of her magic. (p.428)

Nostromo also radiates light. Through him it can be said that Emilia Gould's labours were not useless after all. The Captain of the Cargadores had hitherto been satisfied with his 'reputation' but after what appears to be a 'long bout of intoxication' he wakes up from a fourteen hour sleep into the full light of the day and like a 'man just born into the world' begins to feel his way about. As 'the darkness of the sky descends to the line of the horizons,' he begins to ask questions and draw some useful conclusions. Now he feels the pinch of poverty for the first time in his life. His poverty is twofold. On the one level he is spiritually poor, not having, until now, any purpose in life, simply dreaming, but on another level he also discovers that he does not even possess anything tangible, that he has been 'betrayed.' For all 'the Nostromo here and Nostromo there,' the poor man discovers he has not even been paid for his labours. The truth is bitter:

> Kings, ministers, aristocrats, the rich in general, kept the people in poverty and subjection; they kept them as they kept dogs, to fight and hunt for their service. (p.443)

Nostromo's bright moments also yield some useful insights into other characters: Captain Mitchell emerges almost accurately as a person 'fitted by education (perhaps) to sign papers in an office and to give orders, but otherwise of no use whatever, and some-thing of a fool' (p.545); and Dr. Monygham bears a resemblance to the vulture he encountered as soon as he woke up. But even before the encounter with Dr. Monygham in the large Customs building he is attracted by the 'unexpected sight of two lighted windows.'

The light enables him, as it were, to overcome the powerful cynicism (darkness?) of Dr. Monygham; he reminds the doctor, as he did the vulture, 'I am not dead yet.' Nostromo's long swim across the gulf is thus a metaphor which draws the reader's attention to the difference between the old Capataz of the Cargadores and the new Captain Fidanza. He has now washed himself, has come out of darkness and is no longer satisfied with a doubtful reputation. The confession he makes to Emilia Gould is the crowning point of his climb from darkness to light. Decoud on the other hand commits suicide because the darkness of the Gulf overwhelms him:

> When Nostromo put out the candle in their lighter, it was to Decoud
> as if his companion had destroyed by a single touch, the world of
> affairs, of loves, of revolution... No intelligence could penetrate the
> darkness of the Placid Gulf. (p.237)

Similarly, Dr. Monygham, for all his wisdom and
experience, has too many 'dark' sides to his character; his history
is clothed in secrecy and in rumours (Chapter Eight). His mind is
so dark that not even Mrs. Gould's light seems able to penetrate
it. Charles Gould suffers the same predicament, his life 'was like
being a prisoner in a cavern of bandits with the price of your
ransom in your pocket, and buying your life from day to day '
(p.263).

Closely associated with darkness is the metaphor of weight.
The 'blackness' whenever it is mentioned is shown as weighing
heavily on the characters in question 'like a stone.' Everyone
carries this weight, even Mrs. Gould has it around her neck like
an albatross. The test of character lies in the ability of the
individual to throw away the burden. Mrs. Gould and Nostromo
manage but the result for the other major characters is disastrous.
Silver is shown as a heavy 'lump of metal' but its weight is also a
metaphorical comment on what happens to those like Decoud,
who cannot handle it properly. There is an ironic twist with
regard to Decoud when he puts the four ingots of silver as a
weight to help him sink quicker after his suicide. He is aware of
the significance of the weight of the silver but alas only
negatively.

The 'shrieking ghosts' that haunt the Azuera, which also
seem to haunt most of the characters are a product of the real and
metaphorical darkness depicted in the novel. Like the darkness,
the ghosts serve as tests of character, they provide the ominous
background against which the bizarre histories of the characters
can be better understood. The ghosts take palpable shape in the
form of the two gringos described as 'spectral and alive, and
believed to be dwelling to this day among the rocks under the
spell of their success' (p.18). They are reminders of the crowd in
Sulaco who, like the ghosts, are now 'rich and hungry and thirsty
a strange theory of tenacious gringo ghosts suffering in their
starved and parched flesh of defiant heretics.' In his repentance

Nostromo can be likened to the 'mozo,' 'the poor four-footed beast,' permitted to die because it was 'without sin.' The metaphoric terms Conrad uses are integrated into the thematic, descriptive and narrative structures of the novel so that with the silver, the darkness and light, ghosts and weights it is usually difficult to distinguish between metaphor and fact. Sometimes, a densely metaphoric sentence is enough to tell the reader what to expect from a character, such as this description of Mrs. Gould:

> Coppery glints rippled to and fro on the wealth of her gold hair. Her smooth forehead had the soft, pure sheen of a priceless pearl in the splendour of the sunset, mingling the gloom of the starry spaces, the purple of the sea, and the crimson of the sky in a magnificent stillness. (p.437)

Apart from the light she radiates she also has colour in her life which she provides in contrast to the achromatic lives and views represented by the other characters in the story. Conrad's metaphors work in a chain-like fashion, one dominant metaphor linked to several other related metaphors all of which shape our interpretation.

In *Petals of Blood* Ngugi also operates a chain of related metaphors. There is, however, a significant departure, because though Ngugi, like Conrad, is concerned with material interests and the effect they exert on individuals, and though he also refers several times to 'the molten beast of silver' and the results of its 'crushing weight' and its 'empty metallic promise,' silver is not the dominant metaphor of the novel. Ngugi has kept Conrad's dense figurative language but has deployed the metaphors in the same fragmentary fashion as he has done for the characters. In the search for an image that would tie everything together he has used and dispensed with several images along the way.

The first of these pervasive metaphors is the metaphor of fire. Like the silver in Nostromo, the reality of fire is everywhere in the story. Arson and the death of the three business men trigger the investigation which is the novel's background plot. Fire has englufed Wanja's abode three separate times and Munira seems always to be the agent or the victim of fire. But the image of fire is used in the ambiguous manner of modernists and is thus amenable to several interpretations. For Munira, who is the novel's greatest carrier of metaphor, 'man's life is God's sacred fire that had to remain lit all the way from the ancestors to the child yet unborn' (p.88). Fire also purifies: when Munira burns the effigy of the girl who caused him to 'sin' in his youth he is convinced that he has purified himself, that he has exorcised the demon and can now live a different and better life. Even when he burns the whorehouse it is with a view to 'save Karega.'

The fire in *Petals of Blood* engulfs almost every chapter. Even though Munira causes the big fire it is significant that each of the major characters has contemplated the use of fire as way of solving their problem. All the characters, to use Munira's cliche, have been baptised by fire. Experience, especially if it is as bitter a one as all the characters seem to encounter, is usually seen as exemplification of the destructive fire of life. Wanja who is always at the centre of fire, is described as 'the bird periodically born out of the ashes and dust' (p.281). The language is itself fiery; Karega's head is often 'ablaze,' there are 'flames in Wanja's mind,' sometimes 'embers of curiosity' are 'stoked to a growing intensity,' 'the bright flames' of people's dreams usually die, 'leaving only ashes,' there is a 'burning pool' in Nyakinyua's stomach (pp. 53, 62, 65 and 98). There is thus a clear distinction between the destructive nature of fire, and the inherent fire in everyone which can also be put to very positive use. Karega's fire seems to be burning for the right purpose as Abdulla's before him, but Munira, unfortunately, is too obsessed with the fixed idea of purification to put it to any useful purpose. He has been an outsider and has not allowed the fire to burn. When he attempts to kindle it, the results are the opposite of what he expects. Wanja's fire usually is lit by other people, once by rivals, and once by accident, but when she chooses to make her kitchen 'the most important element in the drama' she unleashes forces she can no longer control. As 'the tongues of flame from the four corners of her whorehouse form petals of blood,' it is left to Abdulla who carries a different fire to save her and his child from destruction.

Blood and fire are closely related in the novel. As with fire, blood is seen as an indispensable part of man but it may also, like fire, acquire dangerous dimensions. It appears at its worst in the murder of the three businessmen. The heavy tankers, the reader is told, squelch tar on a long trail across the plains of Ilmorog to feed a 'thousand arteries' of thirsty machines and motors. What they carry is the blood of Ilmorog. The new tools divide homes and sever the blood bond as they complete their destructive journey. In contrast, there is a kind of 'blood-letting' which is seen as positive and creative. This is given poignancy in Abdulla's one leg which he has sacrificed so that his people may be free. All the Mau Mau fighters belong to this category of people whose activities are seen as a way of cleansing the land of 'bad' blood.

The image of the flower which has petals of blood becomes relevant in this latter context because flowers, like the fighters, are seen as the only beautiful aspect amidst the destruction. Munira's figurative mind establishes this curious link between flower, blood and murder:

> The security and the defences around my life-long twilight slumber were being cut at the roots and I felt the pain of blood-sap trickling through hearts, veins and arteries awaking from years of numbness.... The very movement of her skirt was a razor-sharp knife in my inside. And yet the knife seemed to cut deeper and sharper when I did not see the skirt. (p.244)

Munira is thinking about Wanja and his own relationship with her but it is all a mixture of her skirt, which seems to be beautiful, and razor-sharp knives, which are clearly dangerous. It is no wonder that he is unable to resolve this chaos within him and ends up a murderer himself.

The thengeta flower which also has petals of blood is yet another image used as a metaphor of harmony and chaos. It has healing powers and should, when turned into drink, 'be taken with faith and purity in one's heart.' When the quartet of Abdulla, Karega, Wanja and Munira take it, however, they start a series of confessions which leads to more conflict among them. Munira finally discovers, for instance, that Karega was responsible for the death of his sister and is determined to be avenged. But the severest consequences of the misuse of this beautiful flower are seen when the three businessmen buy the patent for brewing the alcohol from it and turn most of Ilmorog into a drunken and divided city. When they finally die in Munira's fire it is, to use a cliche, as if they have been playing with fire by toying with the thengeta plant. The thengeta is a central metaphor in the novel. Munira's early irritation and confusion when his pupils confront him about its petals anticipates the greater confusion which the flower engenders. It becomes a tool which shows the effects of the manipulation of the people by the businessmen who turn their favourite symbol into an 'opium' to enhance their exploitative designs.

Another pervasive metaphor which is used as a comment on the activities of the characters in the novel is that of life as a journey. Here too there are many 'real' journeys in the narrative. The people of Ilmorog, for instance, march to the city of Nairobi to present their problem to their Member of Parliament. Munira makes several trips to and from Ilmorog; on one of them Wanja and Karega use his bicycle in a sort of relay until they reach their destination, but the journeys are also toward the kingdom of knowledge, `toward Bethlehem'. After the journey, however, 'a devil (came) into their midst and things were never quite the same again,' because as Karega and as all of them discover in stages, 'there were those who waited in shadowy corners' to trap travellers on the way. The epigraphs which introduce each part of the novel highlight the significance of the journey. Read together they become 'Walking toward Bethlehem to be born again... La luta continua.' This invites comparison with Yeat's cycle and the cyclic nature of the story itself as it is revealed in the lives of the characters shows the importance Ngugi gives to the metaphor of the journey. Karega's situation, for instance, reveals its double metaphorical import. First he makes the journey through his mind, through memory and through the books sent to him by the lawyer, but he also considers his experiences in contact with other characters as manifestations of the journey and sees each of them as a stage in his own particular journey. This is why he pays so much attention to the Trans-

Africa Highway which will link Ilmorog with many other parts of Africa and force the otherwise quiet village into a journey which all the other transformed villages have undertaken. As with the characters, so with the town. The journey usually emerges as a cyclic phenomenon, they all keep going round and round and consequently most of them are confused. Like Conrad, Ngugi uses colour to define the nature of their confusion. Both Munira and Wanja, who are more confused, find it difficult to separate colours. The only one which they seem to see clearly is unfortunately red, itself an ambiguous colour.

Ngugi also uses silver as a metaphor of wealth and of corruption and like Conrad, deploys it as a way of differentiating characters. Morality is judged by the reaction of each character to the 'metal power.' As with Conrad it usually acts as a weight that brings down those who cannot use it properly. The fate of Chui, Mzigo and Kimeria is the result of the wrong use of material interests. Unlike Conrad, however, Ngugi though he also refers to 'an invisible law,' seems to imply that the law could be changed if, as is the case with Abdulla, some daring is combined with selflessness. Abdulla emerges from Ngugi's novel as a conquerer of material interests, who, unlike Nostromo, has not been corrupted. These metaphors, however, do not fall into any neat pattern. To list and describe them as has been done here is not to undermine the complexity with which they are introduced to the reader. They are as much a problem to the reader as they are to the novel's main characters.

The recurrence of these images or metaphors in simple or cumulative repetition is one of the hallmarks of Conrad's and Ngugi's narrative method. All the characters in the novels are tortured by 'the repetition of past patterns.' Some of it is the product of their own mistakes which make them impose interpretation on the things they encounter, implying in the process that their lives are a series of repetitions, in most cases 'a series of calamities.' The device, therefore, serves as a comment on the point of view of individual characters but it is also a tool for investing the metaphors in the novels with a greater variety of concepts than the local expressive image may grant. Through repetition, the image becomes an emblem of the particular notion that it carries but as the images multiply the notions also increase until it becomes impossible to make sense of the story without assembling its fragments. The questioning posture which the novels assume and the way they begin in mid-term or at the end also make repetition inevitable.

It is difficult, for instance, to make sense of *Nostromo* until the reader assembles the various ideas which are associated with Silver as well as the attitude each character brings to bear on the image. Conrad devotes the first large section of the novel to the 'Silver of the Mine' and, within this section much emerges about its history, but a lot is also known about the major characters as it seems their lives are 'tied to the mine.' It is a thing that could provoke a 'tumult of words and passions.' For Charles Gould 'the mine had been the cause of an absurd moral disaster, its working, he asserts, must be a serious and moral success' (p.61). For the wife the essence of its history is the essence of her married life (p.62). The horses in the story have silver trappings and everything about Nostromo is associated with Silver. It is the novel's centre of dramatic interest; the silver mine becomes an institution, 'a rallying-point for everything in the province that needed order and stability to live.' Sometimes Conrad shows its significance through constant repetition within a sentence or in a very short passage:

> When the carriage moved on he took off his hat again, a grey sombrero with a SILVER cord of tassels. The bright colours of a Mexican serape twisted on the cantle, the enormous SILVER buttons on the embroidered leather jacket, the row of tiny SILVER buttons down the seam of the trousers, the snowy linen, a silk sash with embroidered ends, the SILVER plates on headstall and saddle... (p.113) (My emphasis).

The novel literally 'jingles' with Silver, it is impossible to take count of the number of times the word and an accompanying idea are mentioned. The section ostensibly devoted to it ends with a very powerful and metaphoric gesture of Nostromo who cuts off all the silver buttons of his coat, reinforcing his poverty but also displaying how much he cherishes his reputation. The silver enslaves people, destroys some, or simply weighs others down; there are eighteen different times in which the motif of weight is used to add to one of the most oppressive attributes of the silver. On five different occasions, it is indicated that the silver is tied for safety around Nostromo's neck. The same image is also used for Mr. Gould who also carries the silver, like Martin Decoud, as a heavy load. The image of a load eventually works literally when Decoud sinks under the weight of the silver ingots.

Events also seem to repeat themselves in the novel, sometimes with uncanny coincidence. Dr. Monygham, for instance, dogs Nostromo so closely that Nostromo cannot help observing that he was the last person he met when he was heading for the Gulf and he is the first person he meets as soon as he comes out of his long swim across the Gulf. The doctor is on this, and on other occasions, something of a demon that seems to haunt people like Nostromo in the most unlikely places such as the large empty Customs House. He is twice depicted as a vulture, hunting for prey and is never far from scenes of disaster. Other images of ghosts also abound in the story: its background is fixed in the ominous Azuera 'gringos' whose plight the Costaguana people seem to be living all over again. Even the courageous Mrs. Gould can not help seeing the repetition of events:

> She saw clearly the San Tome mine possessing, consuming, burning up the life of the last of the Costaguana Goulds, mastering the energetic spirit of the son as it had mastered the lamentable weakness of the father. A terrible success for the last of the Goulds...
> (p.428)

The parrot in her house is a reminder of this unfortunate situation. It keeps chanting Viva Costaguana, as if to remind the so-called patriots of the numerous times they have shouted slogans without actually living up to their patriotic dreams.

Repetition is also used to pinpoint the ubiquitous nature of characters like Nostromo and Captain Mitchell, and Conrad usually accomplishes this by the use of stock phrases. Each time Nostromo is mentioned, he is referred to either as 'the incorruptible;' or 'the indispensable.' He is also severally 'invaluable,' 'one in a thousand,' 'usher-in,' 'trusty,' 'a man absolutely above reproach' (pp. 373, 435, 118 & 165). These phrases are repeated so often that it is no longer necessary to mention Nostromo by name. Captain Mitchell writes his own curriculum vitae and he is so consistent that it is also not difficult to identify him; when the word 'historic' is mentioned, and it creeps in often, we know that he cannot be far away. Patterns of such verbal repetitions thus enable the reader to identify certain characters and they also serve as a way of determining the interpretation other characters and the reader may bring to bear on such a character. If we sometimes find them overdone it is because Conrad uses them to reinforce our view on the characters.

The resonance that silver invokes in *Nostromo* has a near equivalent in the image of fire in Ngugi's *Petals of Blood*. Fire begins and ends the story. All the major characters are connected in one way or the other with fire, indeed, besides Ilmorog, it is the other crucial force in the novel. Wanja is constantly chased by fire, and she is a fiery woman herself. It is no coincidence that the big fire that constitutes the plot of the novel should emanate from her whorehouse. All the other characters are also fiery. Munira, for instance, has so made it a part of his life that he has managed to reduce fire to cliche. He only sees things when they are 'flaming' and it is not surprising that he is the one that sets Wanja's whorehouse on fire. Abdulla and Karega have all contemplated the possibility of cleansing the rot in their lives and in the world outside with fire; towards the end of the story Abdulla is in fact approaching Wanja's house with a box of matches. All the characters try to exorcise by fire but in vain.

However, Ngugi also gives considerable attention to the root causes of the fire. Through these causes he is also able to differentiate between characters because their attitudes to fire usually is a comment about their outlook on their problems. Munira sees it as a purifier and he repeats this image several times, once even burning an effigy to prove his point and eventually burning three businessmen to 'save' Karega from Wanja. He has always carried fire and has felt inhibited from using it until he takes the momentous decision to obey the 'law.' Abdulla's fire burns in more positive directions, although he too, like Karega, does not forget the destructive aspect of fire.

Similarly all the characters seem to agree that money is the root cause of their problem and the motif of money whether as the 'molten beast' or as 'silver coins' or as 'the glittering metal' is pervasive throughout the story. Like the silver in *Nostromo* it constitutes a great burden, all the characters are 'weighed down' by money, an expression which is used on eight different occasions.

Events also repeat themselves very often in the novel as in *Nostromo*. The story of the series of expulsions from Siriana Secondary School is the most conspicuous but the past of each of the characters seems also to repeat very familiar patterns. Wanja, for instance, does not really seem to move forward. Her observation about her predicament is accurate:

> May be nobody could really escape his fate. May be life was a series of false starts, which, once discovered, called for more renewed efforts at yet another beginning. (pp. 337–338)

She is right, as Abdulla also observes:

> You played your part, and then you left the arena, swept aside by the waves of a new step, a new movement in the dance... (p.340)

For all the characters in the novel, the dance is always the same, even the steps they take bear an uncanny resemblance. The coincidence of four people from the same village of Limuru caught in this new village of Ilmorog and all facing the same dilemma sometimes seems unconvincing but they are such different and lively people that Ngugi cannot be accused of forcing the pattern.

Ngugi, like Conrad, makes good use of patterns of verbal repetitions. They help, as in Conrad's novels, to differentiate between characters. Each time Munira is mentioned, for example, notice is drawn to the fact that he is an 'outsider' a 'strange-man,' 'fated to watch adrift,' he has an 'overwhelming sense of always being on the outside of things;' there are at least fifteen different times when the reader's attention is drawn to this aspect of his life (pp. 23–24 ff). It becomes his identify but it also prepares us for his culminating act which as he claims is done so that he too can become an insider. Patterns of 'blood,' 'arteries,' 'red petals' reinforce the image of blood and the murder that takes place on two levels in the story: the murder of the people of Ilmorog by exploitation and the counter-murder by the Mau Mau fighters. As in Conrad, these patterns help to determine the attitude of each character and are therefore the reader's indispensable tool for discovering their point of view. We know them better through these constant reminders.

Modernist novelists use repetition as a device to reinforce the potential of the metaphors they employ and to highlight further the psychological state of the characters but they also deploy it through the use of highly figurative verbal patterns to differentiate between characters and their points of view. Because they seem to be more concerned with universals, they tend to construct their narratives with very little attention to time.

The impression of time which the reader gets from a reading of the novels of Conrad and Ngugi is one of chaos. This is not only because in its modernist form the material of the novels is fragmented in time and distributed among many narrators, as is the case with Faulkner; it is because of an almost total absence of plot. Because the novels usually are the 'historical' accounts of individual characters they often seem to be engaged in 'rivalry' so that the baffled reader is faced with numerous competing claims of credibility. Each of them 'behaves as if utterly alone' with his job, hence the novels do not pay attention to any sense of sequence. Time is not the unifier in these novels. The reader must look for dominant metaphors and for dramatic relationships but cannot expect to make sense of what is present and what is past in the novels. Time is the enemy, not in the Faulknerian sense in which an oppressive mythical time runs a cycle of doom, nor is it the overwhelming phenomenon which the characters of Joyce or Woolf seek to arrest; here, the characters in question act as if they are completely unaware of time.

Nostromo, for example, is full of 'immortal' people. Though the titular hero and Decoud die, they seem to remind the reader of the two gringos 'living' somewhere in the Azuera. Nostromo's activities are so stupendous that it is sometimes difficult to imagine that they were all accomplished in one lifetime not even Captain Mitchell's rhetoric can find words complete to cover the activities of the magnificent Capataz. It is significant that Captain Mitchell is unable to put a time on the achievements of Nostromo: he simply says 'years ago' he engaged a runaway Italian sailor. The novel is full of these generalisations about time and this is deliberate. The 'present' of the story is hardly noticeable Captain Mitchell is 'explaining' the birth of the Republic of Sulaco to foreigners and this is in fact after the death of Nostromo. Yet Nostromo and several of the characters take the story, as it were, from his mouth and live it before the reader.

Nostromo is a novel that relies on atmosphere for its power, rather than on a sequence of events. This is why when the novel opens great attention is paid to creating a mysterious background. 'The eye of God himself,' the natives say, 'could not find out what work a man's hand is doing in there and you could be free to call the devil to your aid with impunity if even his malice were not defeated by such a blind darkness.' Soon after this the reader is introduced to the revolt which has resulted in the break-up of Sulaco from Costaguana after which the question is asked; 'Has anything ever happened here for a hundred years before today?' It is quite a while before the great impact that the silver has made on the area begins to show, then the reader is taken through 'brief' histories of all the major characters but must wait until the 'story' is one-third narrated before he encounters Martin Decoud who 'incidentially' is the founder of the Republic whose history is the subject of the novel.

All the present activities in the plot occur within three days but the number three has become something of a fetish in the Republic's history. Everything connected with it is given in threes: the three Isabels, the three villages, the third of May, everyone sees things in threes. Consequently, it is not possible to say that the number of days reflect a time sequence; they simply are part of the legend. In *Nostromo* the characters live forever, or outside of time, and this thematic ploy influences and shapes the narrative.

There is a greater semblance of order and sequence in *Petals of Blood* but even here the 'present' of the story is also very thin. Munira has, within a period of ten days, been able to narrate the history of Ilmorog. The story, however, runs away from him; the other characters take control of their lives and dramatise their own stories in a way which leaves him, like Captain Mitchell, a mere tourist guide. 'Time' he admits 'was a vast blankness without a beginning, middle and end' (p.191). *Petals of Blood* begins from the end. When the novel opens the principal actors in the drama have already been rounded up for questioning in connection with the murder Munira's fire has caused. The novel should thus narrate a sequence of the events that lead up to the incident but it develops instead into the record of the individual histories of all the characters. When Munira begins his own version of history, he dates it back to the twelve years when he first came to Ilmorog but the story that unfolds is no longer a twelve-year history; it goes back to the time when Ilmorog was 'a small nineteenth century village' and traces its history to its modern industrial status. As the history of the village is inseparable from the characters, each of them ends up telling us everything about their past. However, it is almost halfway through the novel that the alcohol from Thengeta releases their tongues and forces them to fill in the details that have been missing.

Ngugi also employs a time-scheme that may be likened to the relay which Karega, Wanja and Munira conduct on the latter's old bicycle. The characters seem to pass their narratives from one to the other in the form of a relay. But it is a curious relay which merely ensures a questionable 'solidarity.' The total impression is more of a cyclic movement. The repetition of past patterns helps to create this cyclic nature of time. Even when all the characters concentrate on the twelve-year history, they do not seem to move very much. It is more than halfway through the narrative that the first five years are 'completed.' Movement is generally 'slow' and confusing but here, as in Conrad, technique and theme unite to emphasise the chaos inside and outside the characters.

The devices which Ngugi deploys in *Petals of Blood* bear great resemblances to those used by Conrad in *Nostromo*. Ngugi's acknowledgement of a debt to Conrad does not, therefore, come as a surprise. Ngugi, however, has written novels which are more than mere derivations from those of his mentor. Both writers fragment their material and present it through the multiple perspectives of several major characters and both stretch the use of metaphor so that their novels demand interpretation through an understanding of the complex interfusion of metaphors. Their method is deployed with some variation by Faulkner and Armah.

CHAPTER FIVE

THE MULTIPLE PERSPECTIVE II: WILLIAM FAULKNER, *ABSALOM, ABSALOM!*; AYI KWEI ARMAH'S, *WHY ARE WE SO BLEST?*

Speaking generally of Faulkner's narrative technique, Karl Zink describes it as 'the material under the lens of a microscope which,' Zink observes, 'is examined at progressively increased powers of light or lens, so that the watcher enjoys a process of discovery as the material grows in complexity from simple outline and takes on breadth and depth.'[1] The reader of *Absalom, Absalom!* would do well to bear Zink's metaphor in mind. Faulkner encourages the reader to make discoveries by making the characters in his novels initiate the process. Each character appears to have a special 'light' or 'lens' without which the novels cannot be interpreted. James's centres of consciousness, for instance, determine the point of view which pervades his novels but in the novels of Faulkner the reader is expected, as in the works of Conrad and Ngugi, to participate actively in the story. There is in these novels an imaginative sharing of experience in which the reader is invited as 'a secret sharer.'

The method probably influenced Ayi Kwei Armah; the reader of *Why Are We So Blest?* notices a close affinity in method. Narrative perspective is distributed among several characters in the novels in a Faulknerian manner. Both writers display an acute sense of community and their awareness of a larger community affects the way they present character. *Two Thousand Seasons* is an experiment in creating this sense of community and it generates a communal perspective but *Why Are We So Blest*? is best seen in the light of Faulkner's novel.

William Faulkner's *Absalom, Absalom!* and Ayi Kwei Armah's *Why Are We So Blest*? are novels in which a variety of consciousness reflect on the central story of the novel but they are also novels where these consciousnesses that ponder over the story are as much the center of focus as the story which their narratives seek to present. Because they are lost in their private obsessions, they are only able to view the stories through their distortion of vision; they tend to miss the true meanings of the tragedy in which they take part, and, as in *Fragments* and *As I Lay Dying*, the reader gains greater knowledge from their biased interpretation of the characters and events. In both novels, the objective existence of the story is the collective product of the working of the minds of the speculative narrators whose stories are verified by the reader who must make allowances for the interests and biases of the narrators. Both novels gain in complexity from this multiplicity in perspective. Here, too, as in Conrad and Ngugi a fair balance of sympathy and judgement emerges from the rapport between participant narrators and the subject of their narration; between the reader and the subject; between the reader and the participant narrators and finally between the reader and the story as a whole.

In *Absalom, Absalom!* two major narrators Quentin and Shreve collaborate with two others Rosa Coldfield and Mr. Compson to tell the story of the rise and fall of Thomas Sutpen. Rosa Coldfield's account chapters one and five is strange, almost bizarre; the Sutpen that emerges from her account is 'an ogre, some beast out of tales to frighten children with' (130). Miss Coldfield has no good word for her subject whom she seems determined to see as diabolical and incomprehensible. Her frenzied account hardly seeks to explain the man's behaviour which, like Sutpen's refusal of the marriage between his daughter and Charles Bon, is, for her, 'without rhyme or reason.' The reader is to understand Sutpen as the man who came from 'nowhere,' with 'no background,' who 'tore violently' a plantation, married a wife and 'begot' two children. When Rosa is finished Sutpen remains a bewilderingly inexplicable phenomenon. It is not possible from her account to regard him as anything but a phenomenon, for Rosa Coldfield's Sutpen seems devoid of any human value. Rosa Coldfield, however, has a major contradiction to resolve because of her engagement to Sutpen. In her soliloquy in chapter five she tries very hard to resolve the contradiction. Here she mellows and begins to talk about the subject in human terms:

> If he was mad, it was only his compelling dream which was insane and not his methods: it was no madman who bargained and cajoled hard manual labour out of men like Jones. (p.137)

Sutpen is no longer the man who it seems 'was not articulated in this world' (p.112). Miss Coldfield's contradictory story tells more about her own life than about Sutpen's. By her own admission the reader knows she was born into 'some curious disjoint of her father's life and left on his (now twice) widowed hands' (p.120). With a background like that she remained a child 'living in a womb-like corridor where the world came not even as a living echo but as dead incomprehensible shadow' (p.133). Her inability to understand Sutpen, therefore, stems not so much from the fact that the latter is a demon, which in some respect he is, but rather from her inability to step out of her 'womb-like corridor.' There are human beings outside the corridor but to reach them Miss Rosa needs more effort than her 'devious intricate channels of decorous ordering' (p.115) can allow. The reader knows much about Miss Coldfield but must look elsewhere to find answers to fill the many holes she has left in the story of Thomas Sutpen.

Mr. Compson attempts to go beyond the 'ogre' image and seeks to represent his subject differently. His early account describes Sutpen thus:

> A man with a big frame but gaunt now almost to emaciation, with a short reddish head which resembled a disguise and above which his pale eyes had a quality at once visionary and alert. (p.26)

Mr Compson's Sutpen, though incomprehensible, is at least a human being: a man who, 'given the occasion and the need, could and would do anything' (p.38). Mr Compson's story is a great advance from Rosa Coldfield's hysterics. Details of Sutpen's arrival, his tortuous task of settling down, his marriage and his children all fall within that Sutpen himself later describes as his 'design.' But it is not long before the reader discovers that, for all his detached narration, Mr. Compson is not only biased but is himself unable to explain his 'subject' fully. In spite of his recognition of the intricacy of the story he is trying to tell, and of the complexity of the characters, he assumes a patronising tone and begins to separate Sutpen's generation from his and to pass it off as 'uncomplex':

> People too as we are, and victims too as we are, but victims of a different circumstance, simpler and therefore, integer for integer, larger, more heroic and the figures therefore more heroic too, not dwarfed and involved but distinct, UNCOMPLEX, who had the gift of living once and dying once instead of being diffused.. (p.73)

It turns out, in fact, that he has merely replaced Rosa Coldfield's religious interpretation with a more secular one; substituting her fiendish images with what he describes as 'a horrible and bloody mischancing of human affairs' (p.83). His vagueness is partly the result of his ignorance of vital information he does not know the full history of Charles Bon and partly the product of a cynical and detached mind which is determined to absolve itself of the 'follies' of its past. The son notes this cynicism when he equates his room-mate's uninvolved remarks with those of his father: 'He sounds just like father.' Mr. Compson's cynicism and superior airs make it difficult for him to probe for motive and rationale, and by the end of his narrative, the reader knows more about Sutpen but not enough. To accept Mr. Compson's doctrine of Fate as the real ruler of the story is as unhelpful as Rosa Coldfield's fiendish account; in both cases, sadly, Sutpen is still a riddle. That is why Mr. Compson resorts to metaphor when he is faced with contradiction:

> They are like a chemical formula exhumed along with the letters from that forgotten chest... you bring them together in the proportions called for, but nothing happens; you re-read, tedious and intent, posing, making sure that you have forgotten nothing, made no miscalculation, you bring them together again and again nothing happens: just the words, the symbols, the shapes themselves, shadowy inscrutable and serene. (p.83)

But this sophistry reveals more about Mr. Compson than the people whose lives he is trying to describe. The reader can sympathise with him but must look further for better clues to solve the Sutpen puzzle.

Thomas Sutpen, by means of a conversation with General Compson, tells his own story in chapter seven. Unlike the other narrators, Sutpen's story is free of distortion, he is trying to probe objectively into his own past. He emerges as a man of action who has embarked on a quest to accomplish what he describes as his 'design.' In its essence the design is simple: to found a dynasty in which his son and the rest of his descendants shall have all that he lacked as a child; wealth, power, and untainted respectability. However, like Mr. Compson, though with different motivation, Sutpen seems determined to disown his past. It is this desperate need to escape his past that complicates what he sees as a very simple design. The shame of his rejection at the door of a wealthy plantation owner by a 'monkey nigger' is compounded with that of his first marriage to a woman who has part negro blood. He tries to buy his way out of both dilemmas because, for him, 'the ingredients of morality were like the ingredients of pie or cake and once had measured them and balanced them and mixed them and put them into the oven it was all finished and nothing but pie or cake could come out' (p.212). Unfortunately, however, nothing ever turns out the way Sutpen expects; he merely moves from one 'mistake' to yet another mistake, committing the same 'crimes' which had triggered the design in the first place. His rejection of his Spanish wife and his subsequent refusal to acknowledge his son are as appalling as the action of the plantation owner who turned his father and the rest of his family into virtual slaves. The reader admires his courage and his sense of duty and sympathises with his inability to understand, and hence modify, the pattern of the design he sets out to accomplish, but his obduracy which in the end hinges around a desperate need for a boy leaves his life, and subsequently the lives of his sons, Charles and Henry, a puzzle.

All the versions of the story so far do not seem to 'pass' the 'inexplicable' death of Bon at the hands of his brother Henry. The enigma of this murder, which Rosa explains in terms of demonic powers and which Compson attributes to fatality, provides Quentin and Shreve with an excuse to embark upon a quest for identity. In order to accomplish this, they both present a largely cooperative version of the Sutpen story, 'both thinking as one, the voice which happened to be speaking the thought only the thinking become audible, vocal; the two of them creating between them out of the rag-tag and bob-ends of old tales and talking' (p.249). In tracing the history of Thomas Sutpen, Shreve sometimes sounds cynical insisting for instance on referring to the man as Faustus, sometimes even reverting to Rosa Coldfied's images of demon and Beelzebub, but even Shreve makes a more committed effort to understand the character and to seek motives for the otherwise bizarre account which Rosa Coldfield and Mr. Compson present. It is appropriate as Donald Kartiganer suggests, that they both concentrate on the two sons, Charles and Henry, as this suits the condition of their own youth: sons still seeking their maturity, potential lovers still dreaming of passions they cannot admit are usually confined to books.[2] Their story is thus initially a story of love and youthful heroism, of potential incest. However, because of their dynamism, they soon discover that to pursue the theory of incest as the possible motive for Charles Bon's murder would leave Bon a mere exploiter of Judith: Bon would thus be portrayed as one who would either have his heritage or his recognition. Quentin and Shreve reject this easy moral and instead 'invent' Bon's negro blood. In making this lead from the theme of incest to that of miscegenation, Quentin and Shreve separate themselves from Rosa Coldfield and Mr. Compson. Their story, in contrast to Rosa Coldfied's and Mr. Compson's, extends itself just at the moment of its apparent completion. Both Quentin and Shreve seek to understand the characters by immersion, by total identification; 'two, four, now two again, according to Quentin and Shreve, the two, the four, the two still talking' (p.285). This is not to say that they do not have their own private interests and biases. For all his superficial cycnicism, Shreve's growing interest in the story betrays his suspicion of the emptiness of his own life: 'I just want to understand it if I can and don't know how to say it better. Because it's something my people haven't got it. Or if we have got it, it all happened long ago across the water and so now there aint anything to look at every day to remind us of it' (p.269). For Quentin there is the haunting memory of the South out of which he seeks to find a meaning. What they have both achieved, through their own historical recreation, is a definition of the meaning of history for Shreve who has very little and for Quentin who has too much. In each case they have found strategies to relieve the pressures of their private anguish, something which Rosa Coldfield and Mr. Compson also try to achieve but with very little success. Theirs is a modernist triumph of the creative process in which creator and subject unite.

In *Why Are We So Blest?* Modin Dofu's story is both a search for the meaning of his African past and a speculation about the present. In recreating the story, however, Solo Nkonam is conditioned by his own psychological and social past which gains additional light from the background provided by his 'double,' so that, while Modin may be said to be the novel's center of dramatic interest, providing much of its action, Solo's more speculative mind is the authority through which the reader experiences the multiple import of the novel. The 'uncanny complementarity' of their lives gives the novel its complexity which is further enhanced by the voice of a third narrator, Aimee Reitsch. Here too, as in *Absalom, Absalom!*, the objective existence of the story is the collective product of the workings of the speculative narrator whose interest and biases the reader must take into account. Sympathy and judgement emerge from the rapport between the reader and Solo, between Solo and the pair of Modin and Aimee, and between the reader and the characters's search for meaning.

The structure of *Why Are We So Blest?* provides a further clue to the nature of its characterisation. Its thirty chapters are divided almost equally between Solo and Modin, eleven for Solo and thirteen for Modin, even though Modin's notebooks are meant to be the novel's major source of material. The parity in structure reflects the complementary nature of their relationship, a point which Solo takes care to emphasise:

> I see myself in the couple; I see them in me. The man in me: the African absolved into Europe, trying to escape death, eager to shed privilege. (232)

But as Solo's research into Modin's notebooks continues, it becomes obvious that there are, along with the similarities, differences of a very fundamental nature. By his own confession, Solo is a 'failed revolutionary' watching what he would like the reader to believe is a stubborn, incorrigible idealist. Toward this end, Solo tries to portray himself as a compassionate and troubled observer: 'I wept for him, in impotent acknowledgement of a destiny shutting both him and me within its destructive limits' (p.247). Pain and compassion drive him to 'help' the couple but it soon becomes obvious that he is not just impotent but is merely 'filling time, surviving emptiness.' Solo is like some younger Mr. Compson, though not quite as open-minded as Quentin, trying to justify his inactivity and failure. His reaction to the notebooks is not surprisingly a mixture of 'curiosity, fear, suspicion and despair' (p.267). His references to an impending doom, his acute sense of futility, of an 'ordained disease,' of life as a 'vicious medium' in which he could only move against strong `resisting forces' often remind one of Mr. Compson's 'horrible and blood mischancing of human affairs.' Solo identifies similarities between him and Modin merely to show how 'suicidal' the latter's actions are and to demonstrate how much better it would be to choose the path of inaction. For all his compassion and identification, Solo sees himself as the wiser, older man, who has seen it all and is thus able to look at the futility of the efforts being made by the younger man. Modin of Solo's monologues, like Mr. Compson's Sutpen, is one of those misguided people who do not seem to realise that the prize for action, no matter how plausible, is frustration because there is always the 'ordained destruction, the destiny held out to (us)' (p.83). Solo's pessimism says it all:

> I read him, watching me, a spectre from an unwanted destiny,wondering how little time he had to go before his fire also went out and he too was reduced to me. (p.257)

Modin's notebooks, however, do not reveal the kindred spirit which Solo seems at pains to discern. Like Solo, he is disgusted with some of his experiences in the United States and, even more than Solo, he is also conscious of the disadvantages, even dangers, of being a marginalised African in a white dominated world. Indeed, he has come close to death in one of his encounters with people Solo would describe as white slavers and it can be argued as Fraser does, that Modin is racist. But, for Modin, life is a 'revelatory process' and one setback is not enough reason to generalise as Solo is so often prone to do. His relationship with Aimee, for instance, shows his positive qualities, and is not, as Solo would imply, another trap into perdition. He tries to relate to Aimee as a fellow human being as her own notebooks confirm and their commitment to each other, even if their experiences seem to differ, is total. Things begin to worsen when Aimee, not Modin, falls back on cliche such as 'bourgeois hotels,' or 'revolutionary hotels,' when she begins to brand Modin 'racist,' 'coward' and 'bourgeois,' cliches which their previous experiences ought to have rendered meaningless. Modin's efforts should be seen as a genuine attempt to cancel generalisation, not, as Solo implies, simply another example that there is a destiny 'shutting them within destructive limits.' There is a crucial difference in the ambiguous relationship between Modin and Solo. Both are idealistic in temperament, and in their awareness of the preponderant realities of human behaviour are pessimistic, but, while Modin channels his pessimism and melancholy into positive protest, Solo, like Mr. Compson, recoils into the kind of didactic protest whose only aim is to justify itself. Modin makes retreats but not as repudiation of principle, simply as signs of natural human weakness and weariness; his pendulum usually swings back into positive action. Quentin's reaction to a similar ambiguous situation is instructive: 'It's when you realise that you don't need aid' (p.307). Modin's refusal to surrender principle even when he seems overmatched by circumstances such as his experiences in America and his bitter experience at the hands of the French 'army' intensifies his melancholy but it also enhances his human dignity. He emerges, in spite of his seemingly passive posture in most of his Congherian experience, much larger, more heroic than Solo and in the process also exposes the shortcomings of Aimee whose experiences should have taught her the futility of stereotypes but who, when faced with the odds, returns unfortunately to the same problems, the emptiness of her life at Radcliffe, and perhaps to her frigidity, which Modin had helped her to overcome. Both Solo and Aimee are aware that there must be other exits out of the dilemma in which they find themselves. His analysis of the African past, which he defines as slavery and of the contemporary educated African whom he also sees as another kind of slave, is brutal, but it never ends in the same kind of 'solution' which Solo proffers. His retreat into Laccryville, if it had occurred, would have been one of his many efforts at bringing back pieces of his life which he tells us he is in the habit of 'flinging dangerously wide indeed' (p.158).

The reader may thus sympathise with Solo's anguish which he graphically portrays and may indeed note several similarities between his experiences and those of Modin but Modin's notebooks present, in spite of their uncanny complementarity, a completely different point of view from that of Solo. Modin's point of view gains its complexity through its convictions based on experience and through the collaborative notes of Aimee who serves as a third narrator and whose voice stands both as an indictment upon her own behaviour and proof of Modin's reliability. But, as in *Absalom, Absalom!*, only the reader has this comprehensive view of the stage. To understand these two modernist novels is to penetrate the ambiguities through which the narrators try desperately to fight their way.

Ayi Kwei Armah's concept of character and the way he executes it in *Why Are We So Blest?* is similar to that of William Faulkner. There are affinities between *Why Are We So Blest?* and *Absalom, Absalom!* Both writers demonstrate the ways in which the technique of multiple perspective is deployed in a novel through skilful use of metaphor and repetition.

Since the aim of the novels is to demonstrate the protean nature of perception and since each character brings his individual perspective to bear on the central concerns of the novels, each trying to catch a meaning, metaphor becomes a useful, almost indispensable, instrument for enriched meaning as well as a tool for defining and advancing narrative. Each metaphor aims at solving the problem of the individual and consequently the problem of the novel but just as it may easily penetrate ambiguity it may sometimes complicate meaning: the character may invent a metaphor to enable him see but the same metaphor, because of its flexibility, may blur the intended meaning. Some metaphors are inadequate, while others are elaborate and sophisticated depending on the level of perception of each character. Metaphor, here, serves the primary function of helping the reader to distinguish between characters: the more complex the metaphor, the more complex the character. Metaphor also defines and emphasises structural and thematic motifs; it is a code, sometimes a baffling one, which hides the 'true' meaning of the novels from the isolated consciousness of the character and sometimes even from the reader. In *Absalom, Absalom!* and *Why Are We So Blest?* metaphor is the customary form of statement.

Indeed in *Absalom, Absalom!* there is a great problem of ambiguity as a result of the pervasive nature of metaphor. The problem is compounded by the nature of the novel's characterisation and its manipulation of point of view whereby Sutpen, who is the novel's subject, is himself a metaphor to be explained while at the same time his 'design' is also a metaphor which presents obstacles for him and for those who seek to explain it. Each of these narrators also experiences this doubling in metaphor, each has his or her 'design' and each in turn fashions metaphors which illuminate or complicate their own story or the story they try so desperately to tell. It is, as one critic has remarked, like 'a Hall of Mirrors, repeating tableaux in a progressive magnification where echoes multiply into the dissonance of infinite overtones to unfold complex, mysterious, obscure and incomplete meaning;'[3] or, to use Quentin's words:

> May be nothing ever happens once and is finished. May be happen is never once but like ripple maybe on water after the pebble sinks, the ripples moving on, spreading, the pool attached by a narrow umbilical water-cord to the next pool which the first pool feeds, has fed, did feed, but this second pool contains a different temperature of water, a different molecularity of having seen, felt, remembered, reflect in a different tone the infinite unchanging sky. (p.215)

Quentin's metaphor explains the way metaphor generally works in the novel. It is useful to single out an incident and identify it as 'the narrow umbilical water-cord' and see how metaphor works through doubling to render and complicate meaning. Such an incident is the murder of Charles Bon by Henry Sutpen. This incident 'ripples' throughout the novel; it is the culminating point of Sutpen's design and both Sutpen and those who seek to understand or explain him must 'pass' this incident. The response of each narrator to the incident shows their degree of perception and their imaginative skills. Rosa Coldfield's metaphors are inadequate to cope with this 'mystery.' For all her hysteria and her frightening calvinistic images of demons and ogres, she is unable to explain the incident which she is forced to admit is 'without rhyme or reason.'

Mr. Compson is a greater maker of metaphor than Rosa Coldfield, even inventing appropriate ones to match the temperament of the characters he creates, like this very pertinent one for Judith Sutpen:

> You are born at the same time with a lot of other people, all mixed up with them, like trying to, having to, move your arms and legs to all the other arms and legs and the others all trying and they don't know why either except that the strings are all in one another's way like five or six people all trying to make a rug on the same loom only EACH ONE WANTS TO WEAVE HIS OWN PATTERN into the rug. (p.105) (My emphasis).

The reader remembers Mr. Compson for such metaphors and they help, perhaps, to reveal the sophistication of his mind but as he correctly admits '(it) does not explain.' 'It' refers again to that murder of Charles Bon which, for all his detachment and expertise, he is unable to explain. But perhaps the metaphors he employs hinder his perception. Such metaphors as his 'Greek characters,' his 'Cassandras,' tell us more about him than about the subject he seems to handle with so much erudition. Metaphor may thus be its own enemy as well as the characters' as it proves for Sutpen, Rosa Coldfield and Mr. Compson.

However, Quentin and Shreve seem determined to make metaphor work. In doing so, they move more freely than the others from one metaphor to another. They move more freely between fact and metaphor and from one metaphor to another metaphor for it, a technique similar to the one they use in describing Sutpen's starts and false starts:

> He decided that maybe he was wrong in being free and so got into it again and then decided that he was wrong in being unfree and so got out of it again. (p.149)

The roommates are able to do this because they combine the best elements of the material at their disposal. Whenever Shreve, for instance, finds Rosa Coldfield's 'demons' useful, merely perhaps to prod Quentin, he applies them but he can also revert to the detached tone of Quentin's father such as this poignant description of Charles Bon's son:

> With a face not old but without age, as if he had had no childhood, NOT IN THE SENSE THAT MISS ROSA COLDFIELD SAYS, she had no childhood, but as if he had not been human born but instead created without agony of man or agony of woman and orphaned by no human being. (p.161)

Such metaphors are typical of Mr. Compson but the two Harvard undergraduates do usually go beyond such metaphors to create symbols in which they can believe more firmly, such as the lawyer they invent to 'calculate' 'assets' for Charles Bon's mother. Indeed in such cases they tend to believe more in their own metaphors as they do in the case of the lawyer than in the characters. This ingenious technique finally leads them to the theory of miscegenation as a more plausible reason for Charles Bon's murder than the incest which all other accounts seem to suggest. Both Quentin and Shreve are still not satisfied that this is in the nature of the complicated use of metaphor in this novel but they, more than the others, approach a meaning that makes sense.

Why Are We So Blest? though not so problematic, presents the same principle of doubling in its use of metaphor. Modin's life is the metaphor Solo is using to explain his own past. However Modin himself needs 'a key to break into the code' (p.26) that will give meaning to his own life. The image that comes most readily to mind is the Ananse design he notices in Dr. Lynch's house:

> The design was a mask: a pained, human face, a huge head, huge, bulbous, all-seeing eyes, pained, distorted ears open to all possible

sounds, super-imposed on a shrivelled mouth are nostrils cramped with hard control. The limbs emaciated, reduced to spindly lines were attached directly to the human spider head. (p.32)

In order to penetrate the mask, Solo seems to ask what to him is a very simple question: 'What is this love we suffer from, impelling us to embrace our own destroyers?' (p.181). As this question relates to the third narrator it is useful to examine what she stands for and why Solo considers her crucial to the explanation of his and Modin's demise. Is she actually the obstacle they must surmount to reach the true meaning of their lives? Solo seems to think so but in this he faces the same kind of problem as Mr. Compson; the problem of inventing inappropriate metaphors to explain 'phenomena.' In his anguish Solo sometimes even sounds like Rosa Coldfield with his 'destroyers,' 'predators' and 'deserts.' But all these are, like Coldfield's, figments of his troubled imagination. His justification stems from his unsuccessful 'affair' with a white woman, a Portuguese girl whom he manages to convince himself, in spite of all the dissimilarities, resembles Aimee the American girl who is Modin's friend. However, the diaries of Modin and Aimee reveal a relationship which is not congruent with Solo's destructive metaphors. This is how Modin reports it to Naita who, incidentally, he has turned into a metaphor of motherhood and source of inspiration:

We would lie for hours, me in her, talking about her notes, my thesis, the pointlessness of the academic life in general and its particular childishness here. I did not feel lonely any more. We can't help serious involvement, Naita. I did not want to. I tried your normalising outlets. They almost killed me. I don't feel dissipated anymore. I am NOT dissipated anymore. It is so difficult to explain real things across distances, Naita, but that is not my fault. (p.157)

From this it is clear that Solo's obstacle is himself; he is his own barrier to understanding. Here, too, metaphor is its and the character's enemy. In seeking to render meaning through it, the character complicates the issues and ends up revealing more about his own problem than the one he or she set out to solve in the first place. In seeking to read Modin as a metaphorical enactment of himself Solo ignores all the facts against such a reading and for all his 'painstaking' reading and re-reading of the notebooks continues to see people in the shadows that he has created and not as they really are.

Modin is different. He invents metaphors which he tests against experience and is willing to move from one to another. Thus he explains his relationship with Mrs. Jefferson as one with:

> The Western European damsel in distress, the valued prize after the conflict between dragon and knight. But the conflict now grows in complexity. There is no knowing who the knight may be, and who the dragon, for this is one of history's crossroads, and old values may or may not get changed. Standing at the crossroads, Sandra, the American youth, prize after the great cataclysm, from which she would be the only certain gainer. (p.157)

But all this changes when he is confronted, not with 'Sandra,' but with Aimee Reitsch, a real woman who has a problem and with whom he throws overboard all the metaphors of destruction with which Solo would agree so much. His melancholy and his withdrawal and his eventual death are not proof of the theory he has developed, they stem more from Solo's inflexible outlook and from Aimee's own sudden withdrawal from the real world which they had both known. By its nature metaphor ought to be flexible. It may thus be said to have failed if it does not possess its elementary quality of transference. Quentin and Shreve have shown how successfully this can work but Solo and Aimee, like Mr. Compson and Rosa Coldfield, have also shown how it may fail to serve that function for which it was invented, thus leading to further complexity. Though *Absalom, Absalom!* displays in greater detail the richness and complexity of metaphor, its technique of doubling is seen at work in *Why Are We So Blest?* where persistent images of sex and the eventual torture at the end of Modin by means of a ghastly sexual scene highlight Armah's skilful use of metaphor's doubling effect. The black man's 'skill' and 'pleasure' are also his bane, the novel seems to imply.

Repetition, as stated earlier in the discussion on Conrad and Ngugi, is implied in the very nature of novels that deploy multiple perspectives. Since the numerous consciousnesses reflect on one or more themes there are inevitably cases of recurrence. The novels are thus, more than other types of novels, complex tissues of repetitions, and of repetitions within repetitions, linked in chain fashion to other repetitions. Repetition is at the heart of Faulkner's conception of his task as a novelist:

> All the moving things are eternal in man's history and have been written before, and if a man writes hard enough, sincerely enough, humbly enough, and with the unalterable determination never, never, never, to be quite satisfied with it, he will repeat them, because art like poverty takes care of its own.[3]

The novels discussed here fulfil this task through their repeated probing into known details, examining and re-examining such details for valid interpretations and explanations. The process enriches the novels by creating a movement from simple outline to complexity and depth. Since the novels imply that life is metaphor that needs explanation, the process of arrangement and rearrangement provides the necessary device to create this meaning.

Absalom, Absalom! thrives on repetition. It is in the very nature of the story. The reader knows the whole story from page one and the rest of the book merely seeks valid explanation which will flesh the skeleton. Each new narrator goes over the ground covered by the previous one but the technique is such that repetition is not simply a twice-told tale, but reveals more to the reader. This is because of its double focus. Each narrator has a handicap which makes it impossible for him or her to know all the details of the story. Rosa's frenzy reveals a lot about Sutpen but because she never aims to see him as anything other than as demon the reader misses some of the details of his arrival in Jefferson which Mr. Compson eventually fills in. Mr. Compson delineates the technique very well, when he describes Charles Bon's letters: 'familiar in shape and sense... You bring them together in the proportions called for.. you bring them together and together again' (p.83).

Part of the reason and success of the technique is to be found in its subject which essentially is about the meaning of history. Each of the narrators repeatedly probes into the past which in this case is dominated by one person to find the meaning that suits their particular temperament.

Repetition is best seen at work in *Absalom, Absalom!* in the use of metaphors. In order 'to catch all possible meaning' metaphors are not easily disposed of in the novel; instead they contain the seed for further analysis. Even Miss Rosa's fiendish metaphors do have their value for Quentin and Shreve and Mr. Compson's elaborate metaphors for Ellen Sutpen attract the young men a great deal. Her figure as a butterfly caught in a gale and 'blown against a wall and clinging there beating feebly' attracts the attention of Quentin and Shreve who want to sympathise with her predicament as her marriage to Sutpen seems clearly to have just been another adjunct to the 'design.' She never really features as a human being. Even more attractive are the metaphors which express the thoughts of her daughter Judith. Both narrators are interested in Judith's story because they are concerned with a story that speak of love and heroism and Judith's desperate attempts to make her own 'pattern on the loom' of life fascinates the Harvard roommates and so they happily take over from where Mr. Compson left off.

Total identification also enhances the accretive nature of the story:

> Yes, we are both father, maybe it took father and me both to make Shreve or Shreve and me both to make father or maybe Thomas Sutpen to make all of. us (p.215)

Throughout the story, especially in the last four chapters where the young men take control of the narrative, this process of complete identification is repeated, thus adding complexity to the drama that unfolds.

Why Are We So Blest? employs a similar accumulative device. Solo is seeking valid explanations for his and Modin's predicament and the search leads him to scrutinise the latter's notebooks: he has 'read them, put them aside and returned to them' (p.149). Solo elaborates on the technique and defines its purpose which is illustrated in a passage which has been used in section three to show how metaphor works. It requires quotation in full again:

> I try to fit my pieces of that life together, hoping to understand? That hope too is dead in me. I arrange the pieces, rearrange them. My

impotence simulates impotence. Often, what seems a reasonable arrangement I know is false. It is not understanding I am reaching for. I have time to kill an infinity ahead of me, and these notes are reduced to something to help a defeated man survive empty time. I arrange them, rearrange them. (pp.231–232)

Solo's desperation is evident in the repetitive way he keeps returning to expressions such as 'I could not have helped him.' A constant need for justification haunts him every way so that he keeps coming back to the same theme over and over again.

Total identification enables him to continue talking about Modin as if he were a second self. His anguish is not as convincing as Quentin's or Shreve's but his pretensions are the same: he wishes to see 'an uncanny complementarity' between himself and Modin. Whenever he speaks about him, therefore, he speaks as if his voice were a representative one on behalf of what he calls 'life's failures.' Like Quentin, he is a ghost wandering about the face of the earth in search of a double.

The structure of *Why Are We So Blest?* is also repetitive. Of the thirty 'fragments' only six are seen through the consciousness of the third narrator. This is meant to emphasise Solo's anguish as the reader soon finds, that, in spite of his claims for the notebooks, the story is one of the troubled conscience of the speculative, 'guilty' Solo. Like Quentin, he makes the subject of the story subservient to his real desire to elucidate the meaning of history for himself. Modin, like Sutpen, is the excuse Solo uses to penetrate into himself by using his past. In doing so Solo repeats details by instalments. As he remarks:

It is not merely the quantity of the notes. I could go through them, turn and return. They would hold new meaning every time. But they take their vengeance on me. (p.149)

Repetition, here, as in *Absalom, Absalom!* points to a qualitative, rather than chronological, development. The first entry that Solo discloses from Modin's notebooks, for instance, reveals a desperate person on the verge of suicide, one who has given up everything: lectures, scholarships. This is the character that interests Solo. As he moves backwards and forwards in the notes he is only interested in arranging them in an order that will suit his temperament so that even though much of the positive

Modin appears in the notebooks, the sad, dispirited character is the one with whom we are supposed to be familiar. Some parts of the notes have dates but dates do not interest Solo because he is seeking a development in qualitative, not chronological terms. In all the novels, this disregard for chronology is central and will be examined in detail as it throws more light on the novel's multiple shifts in focus.

The novels of William Faulkner and Ayi Kwei Armah present obstacles to the reader seeking continuity because their material is fragmented in time and distributed among multiple narrators. The fact of broken chronology is, however, not new to the modern novelist. But, while time for Joyce and Virginia Woolf may be seen as something which the individual consciousness can 'arrest,' Faulkner and Armah generate, instead, a reversible or circular time scheme through which the past is identified in the present and the present in the past. Thus, myth plays a central role in their conception of time: in their novels there is constant interplay between historical time and mythical timelessness. This is reflected in the structure of the novels and in the numerous voices of the narrators whose consciousness are agonisingly aware of the inconquerable and overwhelming nature of time. There is some sense of chronology such as the nine days the Burden family take to bury their relative in *As I Lay Dying* but the mythical dimension dominates the narratives. In discussing time in the novels, therefore, it is useful to consider three main aspects; the chronology which through flashback or through 'present' action influences and shapes the novels and the historical and mythical time which are the dominant features of *Absalom, Absalom!* and *Why Are We So Blest?*

Absalom, Absalom! is all about time because its subject is the meaning of history. Yet the narrators themselves are continually frustrated by the paucity of historical details to which they must assign temporal intelligibility before they can link the past with the present. The novel is an exercise in this frustrating task which even the most knowledgeable narrators, Quentin and Shreve, find daunting. Quentin and Shreve are trapped by what, to them, is purely myth but they both realise that they must turn it into history. In their world the present hardly exists since their cold undergraduate study and a short letter from Quentin's father are all that constitutes the present. Yet in another sense the present is 'absent' because there has always been too much of the past; it has become impossible to distinguish between, say, 1833 and 1909 because Quentin feels he is still breathing the same air and can even hear the church bells that rang in 1833.

Part of their dilemma stems from the historical figure they are trying to recreate. The movement of Sutpen's family gives an indication of the nature of the problem:

> He didn't remember whether it was that winter and then spring and then summer that overtook and passed them on the road, or whether they overtook and passed in slow succession the seasons as they descended, or whether it was the descent itself that did it and they not progressing parallel in time but descending perpendicularly through temperature and climate... it didn't have either a DEFINITE BEGINNING OR A DEFINITE ENDING. (p.184) (My emphasis).

All the narrators build their story upon this timelessness. Rosa Coldfield is simply overwhelmed and can only fall back on her religious background to help her fit the pieces together. She fails because time and history are against her. She is an ageing woman who is aware she has little time left. Perhaps this explains the frenzy with which she narrates her story. And in her frenzy she leaves many events unexplained. History is distorted through her vision and it is left to the others to reconstruct it. Mr. Compson tries to manipulate history to suit his temperament by removing Sutpen as far away, psychologically at least, as he can. Even he, with all his detachment, curiously concludes that he is probably dealing with a phantom. According to him, Charles Bon is 'born of no woman' and is 'impervious to time.' So, even though he starts off recreating history, he ends with a myth which is as ambiguous as the events he had sought so much to make real. His great stumbling block, Charles Bon, does not explain.

Quentin, the most inventive of the narrators, is 'older at twenty than a lot of people who have died.' But the greatest feat the two roommates perform is to break the barrier, at least metaphorically, between past and present.

Four of them there, in that room in New Orleans in 1860, just as in a sense there where four of them here in this tomblike room in Massachusetts in 1910. (p.290)

This crucial link helps their recreative task and opens them to interpretations which the distorted accounts of the previous narrators were unable to arrive at. *Absalom, Absalom!* treats history as a riddle which time alone cannot solve. indeed time provides the obstacle to any solution. Its fragmentariness underlines the disorderly nature of historical fact but the attempts of Quentin and Shreve point to possible uses of time and history.

'For a moment I saw something elemental in that look, something so old. The face itself way young, but the expression on it could have come from the depths of ages of sadness.' (p.59)

In *Why Are We So Blest?* the same philosophy of timelessness features not only in the cyclic vision which Solo presents as in the above quotation but in Modin's own accounts of history. Modin links his past-communal, racial- with his present and declares both as forms of slavery. In his obsession with the past, the future, as in Faulkner's *Absalom, Absalom!* ceases to mean anything: 'I want to think of future things' he writes, 'but these memories are strong. They will not leave me' (153). Later he reflects:

For me now, things happening again in retrospect happen slowly. Not the single events themselves they do not take so long. But whatever I see again gets immediately connected to events in the past, so that what took a minute happening now spends fifteen passing through my mind (p.154)

Modin like Quentin, in *Absalom, Absalom!* also links past with present in such a way that they become indistinguishable. Slavery, for instance, is, for him, not a thing of the past.

This is the Modin that Solo wishes to study and with whom he identifies. When he refers to Modin's young face bathing in generations of sadness he is perhaps reading his own face through a mirror but he has tried so much to link their two fates that the reader must assume that, in time, they belong to the same 'timelessness' which is responsible for their mutual destruction. Solo is killing time, filling emptiness. Time may be 'a revelatory process,' for some but Solo is merely turning in circles again and again.

Chronological time undergoes a lot of manipulation in *Why Are We So Blest*? Some times in Modin's notebooks do bear dates but most do not. Consequently, Solo arranges them to fit his own requirements. Since, in fact, he is only interested in providing the resemblance between himself and Modin the events and the dates are not important. What matters is the significance Solo attaches to them. Thus, Aimee's transcript is first released chapter 3 - showing her 'impatience' and her 'exploitative' tendencies long before the reader knows who the woman actually is and what is her connection with the other narrators. Meanwhile Modin appears in the second chapter as a desperate lonely man even though the reader discovers that this has not always been his way of life. All this happens before it is revealed that he has come to study on a scholarship but has forfeited it, hence his desperation and frustration. The narration of *Why Are We So Blest*? is controlled by means of a qualitative rather than chronological development. This is the method of *Absalom, Absalom!* as well. Both novels seek to find a meaning for history but both end up as puzzles or perhaps as pointers that history is what the individual makes of it. This is the position of all the narrators in the two novels. Consequently, chronological time is immaterial to the demands of the style whose main purpose seems to point to a time which knows no limits and which may not be arrested in the manner, other modernist novelists suggest.

CHAPTER SIX

THE COMMUNAL PERSPECTIVE: CHINUA ACHEBE, *THINGS FALL APART* AND *ARROW OF GOD*; AYI KWEI ARMAH, *TWO THOUSAND SEASONS*; GABRIEL OKARA, *THE VOICE*

CHINUA ACHEBE'S *THINGS FALL APART* AND *ARROW OF GOD*

The protagonist of *Things Fall Apart* is not Okonkwo, but Umuofia. The same can also be said of *Arrow of God* whose main character is not Ezeulu, impressive as he is, but the community of Umuaro. Both communities, to use Achebe's terse proverb, are like the lizard; if it loses its tail it soon grows another. Okonkwo and Ezeulu are tails of the lizards, Umuofia and Umuaro. Achebe has redistributed the elements of character to reflect this shift in emphasis and though critics acknowledge 'the strength and stability' of the communities, few have paid attention to this significant feature of the African Novel.[1] Nelson Wattie's article, 'The Community as Protagonist in the Novels of Chinua Achebe and Witi Thimaera,' points the way to this innovation. Wattie observes that:

> The world which is being described and discussed in (this) novel the complex gossamer network of contacts and relationships which bind the community together is its true protagonist. As the discussion progresses, the tensions which strain and stretch this network toward breaking point are revealed to the reader, and this, MORE THAN

THE PROGRESS OF OKONKWO'S LIFE, IS THE CENTRAL ACTION OF THE NOVEL. Okonkwo, in fact, is an anomaly within this pattern, because he acts against the true values of the community by taking part in the ritual murder of his foster-son Ikemefuna.[2] (My emphasis).

Because critics have gone in search of individuals whose 'traits' they can identify, they have ignored the central characters of the novels and have placed emphasis on the progress of both Okonkwo and Ezeulu. Both *Things Fall Apart* and *Arrow of God*, however, oppose such a reading. It is true that Okonkwo and Ezeulu are major characters in the respective novels but it is equally true that they are presented in contrast to more fascinating protagonists. Achebe sets out to discover his own tradition and the reasons for its collapse; both Okonkwo and Ezeulu are to be seen as tools for the realisation of his goal. Both characters suffer from an ignorance of context and the reader sympathises with their inability to penetrate the minds of their communities and, through their characterisation is able, as both Okonkwo and Ezeulu are not, to understand the moral codes that govern their communities.

The communities of Umuofia and Umuaro tower above all other named characters in the novels. Achebe achieves his aim of giving his people dignity by capturing the flavour of the life and speech of communities whose ways were threatened by the forces of 'civilisation.' It is tempting to link his portrayal of these communities with a similar picture by William Faulkner of the folk of Yoknapatawpha County but Faulkner's community acts in his novels as a chorus, akin to the impression created by Hardy and other nineteenth and early twentieth century novelists. Of more interest, perhaps, are the novels of the Scottish writer Lewis Grassic Gibbon (Leslie Mitchell) whose portrayal of the setting and people of the Mearns by means of a 'sharply and poetically recreated impression of folk speech rhythms partly Scots partly English,' is similar to Achebe's method.[3] The communal perspective deployed by Achebe (*Things Fall Apart* and *Arrow of God*), Armah (*Two Thousand Seasons*) and Okara (*The Voice*) enables the novelists to get as close as possible to their people's ways and to try to see things from their point of view. The method demands a review of our ideas on character in the novel.

In *Things Fall Apart* Umuofia emerges with its own space and time, its own ideological system and its own standards of behaviour. The reader is invited to enter into the mind of this community and to become familiar with it through its voices and to perceive it as if from within and consequently to assume a point of view internal to it. If, as Roger Fowler has shown, characters may be put together from a stock of physical, behavioural, psychological and verbal attributes, then in Umuofia, more than in Okonkwo, may be found the true protagonist of *Things Fall Apart*.[4] The community is a 'round' character whose development the reader can follow in great detail. Its role in the structure of the plot is crucial, indeed, the point needs repetition that the community, and not Okonkwo, plays the most significant role in the plot. Things fall apart for Okonkwo but the complete breakdown of values in the community forms the core of the novel.

An 'assemblage of traits' could be put together for Umuofia. The community, as critics never tire of pointing out, is 'proud, dignified and stable.' It has been castigated for its 'brutality' and 'savagery' and competitive and materialistic tendencies. Umuofia has been praised for its resilience and for its shrewdness and humanity.[5] These positive and negative qualities give it character, but those who enumerate them are quick to withdraw such status and to invest it instead in Okonkwo and in other minor characters in the novel. Yet only when we understand Umuofia can we appreciate the role played by these other characters in the novel.

The personification of Umuofia enables us to interpret the community as we do characters in a novel. When Ezeudu goes to warn Okonkwo of the impending death of Ikemefuna he announces that 'Umuofia has decided to kill him' and when Ezeudu himself dies the narrator observes that:

> The first cock had not crowed, and Umuofia was still swallowed up in sleep and silence when the ekwe began to talk, and the cannon shattered the silence. (p.84)

Often the narrator breaks the character into manageable and more easily identifiable components and attributes. Here is a typical portrait of Umuofia at one of its moments of crisis:

> It was the time of the full moon. But that night the voice of children was not heard. The village ILO where they always gathered for a moon-play was empty. The women of Iguedo did not meet in their secret enclosure to learn a new dance to be displayed later in the village. Young men who were always abroad in the moonlight kept their huts that night. Their manly voices were not heard on the village paths as they went to visit their friends and lovers. Umuofia was like a startled animal with ears erect, sniffing the silent, ominous air and not knowing which way to turn. (p.139)

The portrait reveals children, women and young men but these soon merge into a single unit whose predicament is likened to that of an animal sniffing the silent, ominous air. In peace or in crisis the community emerges as a single force. The bond of kinship and the need to speak with one voice surpass all other needs. When they celebrate, the entire neighbourhood 'wears a festive air' and one man's behaviour is often interpreted in terms of the larger group. When Okonkwo beats his wife in the Week of Peace the priest reminds him that the evil he has done can 'ruin the whole clan.' 'If one finger brought oil,' the elders say, 'it soiled the others.'

Umuofia is a collective individual. Achebe creates the character out of a clear understanding of the meaning of community. The existence of this collective individual, as Schmitz has observed, in a related context 'rests upon ties of place, and upon ties of friendship, shared feeling and common belief.'[6] This feeling is never lost in the novel. Moreover the reader comes across a character who is at once violent and even evil but one who is equally humane, lively and unforgettable. As he follows this character from the festivals, through the bad moments or simply enjoys the day-to-day banter, he seems to keep the company of a friend, a shrewd and understanding friend who is capable of laughing at himself but who is confident enough to point out the follies of other friends and enemies.

The disaster which befalls Umuofia is terrifying and Achebe portrays it, not through the downfall of Okonkwo, whose career often goes against the grain of the community, but through the unmasking of an egwugwu, which is the essence of the group:

> That night the Mother of Spirits walked the length and breadth of the clan, weeping for her murdered son. It was a terrible night. Not even the oldest man in Umuofia had ever heard such a strange and fearful sound, and it was never to be heard again. It seemed as if the very soul of the tribe wept for a great evil that was coming or its own death. On the next day all the masked egwugwu of Umuofia assembled in the market-place. They came from all the quarters of the clan and even from the neighbouring villages. The dreaded Otakagu came from Imo, and Ekwensu, dangling a white cock, arrived from Uli. It was a terrible gathering. The eerie voices of countless spirits, the bells that clattered behind some of them, and the clash of matchets as they ran forwards and backwards and saluted one another, sent tremors of fear into every heart. For the first time in living memory the sacred bull-roarer was heard in broad day-light. (p.132)

The awesomeness of this episode cannot be compared to Okonkwo's pathetic death and it is simplistic to equate his suicide with the death of the clan.[7] Indeed the community watches Okonkwo sometimes with amused detachment: 'Looking at a king's mouth,' says one elder, 'one would think that he never sucked at his mother's breast' (p.19). The contempt with which elders such as Uchendu treat him shows his real standing, not only in the community, but in the novel as well. His poor imagination makes him see issues only in black and white. 'If a man comes into my hut and defaecates on the floor, what do I do? Do I shut my eyes? No! I take a stick and break his head. That is what a man does' (p.113). Achebe uses his kind of mentality to underline the complexity of Umuofia.

Okonkwo pursues his ambitions in defiance of a reproachful community. He ignores its codes and customs and displays a complete insensitivity to human feelings. That is why he kills his foster-son and treats his own son with such disdain. He reminds one of Thomas Sutpen in Faulkner's *Absalom, Absalom!* Both men may be said to have a bad 'chi' and Okonkwo, like Sutpen, suffers from that innocence which sees the ingredients of 'success' as those of a pie or cake: 'Once you measure them and balance them and put them into the oven it was all finished and nothing but pie or cake could come out.'[8]

Thus he imagines that all his community requires of a man is that he should acquire titles, wives and barns full of yams. These material things are indeed the controlling fibres of the community but he ignores the fundamental ingredient of discipline and consequently makes the worst of what someone like Uchendu or his own good friend Obierika would have assimilated into the accepted order of things. Here, for example, is part of Uchendu's and the community's philosophy:

> You think you are the greatest sufferer in the world? Do you know that men are sometimes banished for life? Do you know that men sometimes lose all their yams and even their children? I had six wives once. I have none now except that young girl who knows not her right from her left. Do you know how many children I have buried children I begot in my youth and strength? Twenty-two. I did not hang myself, and I am still alive. If you think you are the greatest sufferer in the world ask my daughter, Akueni, how many twins she has borne and thrown away. Have you not heard the song they sing when a woman dies? 'For whom is it well, for whom is it well? There is no one for whom it is well.' (p.95)

Uchendu may sound like an incurable optimist but he is prepared at least to place the events in his life into their context and to view them with less passion than Okonkwo, 'the roaring flame.' Most other people in the community share the point of view put forward by Uchendu:

> There were many men and women in Umuofia who did not feel as strongly as Okonkwo about the new dispensation. The white man had indeed brought a lunatic religion, but he had also built a trading store and for the first time palm-oil and kernel became things of great price. (p.126)

This sense of accommodation affects their relationship with outsiders.

In *Things Fall Apart* the outside world is represented by the Christian missionaries, who convert Okonkwo's son, and by George Allen who imprisons Okonkwo and others for burning down a church. Both the missionaries and the Colonial establishment display an arrogant superiority over the people of Umuofia but their assumed superiority is not any more dangerous than Okonkwo's ignorant and dangerously individualistic point of view. Okonkwo invalidates the habits and customs of the community and is as much a threat to it as are the missionaries and George Allen. Gerald Moore is right to assert that Okonkwo 'is not a typical Igboman.'[9] He merely abstracts, as Sutpen does in *Absalom, Absalom!*, those evil tendencies from the controlling fibre of the community and exploits them without caution for the purposes of his own ambition: 'to become one of the lords of the clan' (p.92).

Okonkwo has wrongly been interpreted as a true representative of his clan. He has thus been shown as a powerful person, which he undeniably is, whose ambitions are thwarted by a confused clan. But if we look closely at other characters in the novel it is easy to see that the issues are not as simple as Okonkwo often makes them seem. It can be argued that the community is not strong enough to control its Okonkwos and that its ways have become vulnerable but this argument becomes suspect when the views of a cross-section of the community are taken into account. Obierika, for instance, questions some of the strictures of the community but admits that there is 'complexity.' Other elders question the customs constantly and some of these customs are shown to be dynamic. Achebe's method makes each character in the novel appear as if to prove or invalidate a custom. Such is the role, for instance, of the couple that die on the same day, enacting in death their rapport in life. In reviewing their relationship Okonkwo cannot understand why any man would consult a woman before carrying out a project but this is only one of many things about Umuofia he cannot understand, to his cost. His failure to understand these things affects his son Nwoye who sees Umuofia through his father's eyes. Since his father has misread the community it is to be expected that Nwoye's reading is equally wrong. Achebe's method expects the reader to see individuals in the novel only in their relationship with the community whose standards, though faulty at times, provide a commanding perspective.

'The world,' says Ezeulu, 'is like a mask dancing. If you want to see it well you do not stand in one place' (p.46). The Chief

Priest's metaphor is useful in reading *Arrow of God,* for, though he exerts great authority in the novel, his character, like that of Okonkwo, cannot be understood fully until we unravel the protagonist of the novel, the clan of Umuaro. Like Umuofia, Umuaro is personified throughout the novel thus enabling the reader to interpret the community as a character. Metaphors that describe individual conduct are used to portray Umuaro:

> Umuaro had grown wise and strong in its own conceit and had become like the little bird, nza, who ate and drank and challenged his personal god to single combat. (14)

The same metaphor is used later to depict Ezeulu's behaviour and the strained relationship between him and the community is often presented as a confrontation between two difficult individuals. As the Chief Priest himself ruminates:

> His quarrel with the whiteman was insignificant beside the matter he must settle with his own people. For years he had been warning Umuaro not to allow a few jealous men to lead them into the bush. BUT THEY HAD STOPPED BOTH EARS WITH FINGERS. They had gone on taking one dangerous step after another and now they had gone too far. They had taken away too much for the owner not to notice. Now the fight must take place, for until a man wrestles with one of those who make a path across his homestead the others will not stop. Ezeulu's muscles tingled for the fight. Let the white man detain him not for one day but one year so that his deity not seeing him in his place would ask Umuaro questions. (p.160) (My emphasis).

Ezeulu views the community as an individual with 'ears and fingers' but also highlights its collective nature when he sometimes refers to 'them.' When the 'fight' approaches he imagines a multitude of voices and the stamping of countless feet but often returns to the once person who is neither Nwaka, his 'arch rival,' nor Captain Winterbottom, his friend and enemy. The 'person' in question is Umuaro. David Caroll is right to observe that the dilemma in the novel is 'a matter of personalities.'[10] Caroll, however, fails to point out that the personalities are Umuaro and its Chief Priest. All the other characters, to use Ezeulu's own word, are 'insignificant.' They may all be portrayed in great detail, indeed Nwaka is an unforgettable character, as are

Winterbottom and the missionaries, but the centre stage belongs to Umuaro. The 'major' characters in the novel are only means by which the reader may get to the complex nature of the community.

Arrow of God records Ezeulu's fruitless attempts to become a hero of his people. His failure denies him similar status in the novel. As he well knows:

> His power was no more than the power of a child over a goat that was said to be his. As long as the goat was alive it was his; he would find it food and take care of it. But the day it was slaughtered he would know who the real owner was. (p.3)

The Chief Priest seeks to augment his power but eventually concedes defeat to the community. It is common among critics to regard Ezeulu as the hero of the novel and thus to read it as a clash between his individualism and the claims of society.[11] Such a reading is justifiable but as has been shown in a similar case regarding Okolo in Gabriel Okara's *The Voice*,[12] Ezeulu's characterisation provides a perspective on Umuaro; it leads the reader to a fuller understanding of the community which is the novel's centre of dramatic interest and its major character. The reader is able to take over where Ezeulu's sanity ends and may sympathise with his predicament without failing to observe the vibrant community which has upstaged him.

Umuaro, through Nwaka, defies Ezeulu's bumptiousness. Nwaka is not just a surrogate for a jealous Idemili as Ezeulu would have us believe, he is a man of many titles who knows and speaks the mind of the community. No wonder that he often beats the Chief Priest at debates. Nwaka knows the nature and origin of Ulu, a god carved by the community to protect it from marauders, and will not be fooled by Ezeulu's arrogance. The elders of Umuaro agree with him. It is not that Umuaro is always right, indeed part of its story which Achebe reconstructs in the janus-faced manner of a modernist novelist is a record of confusion and a near absence of values. But what attracts the reader is not their incessant quarrels, it is their ability to live life to the full in spite of all the difficulties that confront them. Perhaps this explains why Achebe devotes much attention to festivals which cannot be explained away as 'sociological passages.'[13] They are an attempt by the author to present a comprehensive picture of traditional life. They give a full picture of the character of traditional life. They give a full picture of the character of Umuaro which is often ignored because critics look to Ezeulu, Nwaka, Akuebue and Ofoka as the main characters in the novel. It can be argued, however, that these other named characters are traits of Umuaro, aspects of a very complicated character.

There is plenty of evidence in the novel to support the argument. Even Ezeulu cannot release himself from the strong grip of the clan. Nwaka's resplendent wives often exhibit the brighter, ceremonial side of the community. 'Their walk,' the narrator comments, 'was perforce slow and deliberate, like the walk of an Ijele Mask lifting and lowering each foot with weighty ceremony' (p.68). Nwaka himself exhibits those qualities most admired by the clan, he has taken many titles and is 'owner of words.' A gathering of Umuaro elders calls itself Umuaro because they believe their wisdom is conferred by the community. Discreet voices such as those of Ezeulu's friend Akuebue and of the forth-right elder Ofoka merely reinforce the communal voice. Akuebue is the first to remind Ezeulu that no one wins judgement over his clan. The clan speaks in all these voices in the story.

The exceptions of course are Captain Winterbottom, his deputy, Clarke, and the missionaries who convert Umuaro to the Christian faith. Captain Winterbottom may appear to stand poles apart from Ezeulu but they have a lot in common. Like George Allen and Okonkwo in *Things Fall Apart*, both Winterbottom and Ezeulu are enemies of the clan. They are both dangerously individualistic and Achebe uses them to show the limitations of seeing things from one perspective. One of the great ironies of *Arrow of God* must be Ezeulu's inability to heed his own philosophy which conceives the world as a mask dancing. Ezeulu unfortunately stands in one place and is thus unable to see the mask well. Captain Winterbottom similarly suffers from this fixed perspective, indeed in other matters, as when he sends Oduche to school, Ezeulu does better than his 'ally,' Captain Winterbottom. The missionaries in their zeal to win over converts are even worse than either Ezeulu or Winterbottom. The narrator presents them in an ironic vein:

> Mr. Goodcountry not knowing the deviousness of the heathen mind behind the growth of his school and church put it down to his effective evangelization. He wrote a report on the amazing success of the Gospel in Umuaro for the West African Church magazine, although as was the custom in such reports he allowed the credit to go to the Holy Spirit. (p.215)

Mr. Goodcountry does not deserve the harvest; it is clear that his god reaps where it has not sown. Each of these characters is used by Achebe to build a case for his community, a case which in *Things Fall Apart* and *Arrow of God* the communities ably demonstrate through the skilful use of proverbs, songs and tales.

The language of *Things Fall Apart* more than any other aspect of its technique determines the novel's point of view. This is because Achebe allows the characters to speak in their own idiom. 'Among the Ibo' the narrator asserts, 'the art of conversation is regarded very highly, and proverbs are the palm-oil with which words are eaten' (p.5). The language of the novel is one of proverbs, songs and tales. Its essence lies in 'skirting round the subject before hitting it finally.' The playfulness is a mark of the confidence of a narrator sure of his subject as it is a reflection of the ease and assuredness with which the people of Umuofia conduct their business. In the novel, the line between this confident narrator and a self-assured community can be very thin as in this description:

> The night was very quiet. It was always quiet except on moonlight nights. Darkness held a vague terror for THESE PEOPLE, even the bravest among them. Children were warned not to whistle at night for fear of evil spirits. Dangerous animals became even more sinister and uncanny in the dark. A snake was never called by its name at night, because it would hear. It was called a string. And so on this particular night as the crier's voice was gradually swallowed up in the distance, silence returned to the world, a vibrant silence made more intense by the universal trill of a million million forest insects. (p.7) (My emphasis).

The swift movement from the detached narrator who records the fears of 'these people' to the participant narrator who reports the 'vibrant silence' of the night is typical of the novel's method.

Umuofia is simultaneously 'they' and 'we' and this subtle combination of detachment and participation helps Achebe to manipulate point of view. The reader would do well, however, to bear in mind that the main interest of the novel is communal and that 'the impression of village reminiscence, anecdote, gossip, and formal "tales of Okonkwo," mixed with folk tales, songs and sayings'[14] which Neil McEwan observes in it are aimed at giving a full picture of the character of Umuofia.

The devices which McEwan outlines are crucial in the story because the community speaks through them. Perhaps Achebe is right and the novel is a process of education because the tales and sayings are indispensable instruments toward an understanding of the novel's purpose. As 'teaching aids' they are couched in simple language, the mark, perhaps, of a good teacher. Part one of the novel, for instance, records several lessons on the bond of kinship most of which appear in the form of tales told by 'foolish' women and children. These tales skirt around the subject and it is left to the reader (hearer) to deduce their meaning. Their greatest asset is simplicity as the beginning of the famous Tortoise tale demonstres:

> 'Once upon a time,' she began, 'all the birds were invited to a feast in the sky. They were very happy and began to prepare themselves for the great day. They painted their bodies with red camwood and drew beautiful patterns on them with uli.'

> 'Tortoise saw all these preparations and soon discovered what it all meant. Nothing that happened in the world of animals ever escaped his notice; he was full of cunning. As soon as he heard of the great feast in the sky his throat began to itch at the very thought. There was famine in those days and Tortoise had not eaten a good meal for two moons. His body rattled like a piece of dry stick in his empty shell. So he began to plan how he would go to the sky.' (pp.67–68)

It is tempting to ask what a simple tale about Tortoise is doing in a novel which treats the downfall of a community. By the end of the story, however, the connection between Tortoise and Okonkwo becomes evident. Both characters stand out from the rest. As with Okonkwo's relationship with his community, Tortoise is of the birds and yet not of them and when the moment of truth comes both he and Okonkwo are shown the way out. In seeking to become 'all of you' they pervert the meaning of community and both are clipped of their borrowed wings.[15] Similarly simple tales, such as the one even Okonkwo himself can remember, about Mosquito and Ear, reflect a world view (p.53). These animal stories carry the virtues which Umuofia esteems, such as the magnanimity of the birds in giving Tortoise wings, but they also contain the vices which the community condemns, such as Tortoise's greed. Moreover the manner in which they are told captures the flavour of the life and speech of the community. The feast in the sky, for instance, is consistent with the festive atmosphere that marks much of the novel and the attendant preparations made by the animals who painted their bodies with camwood and made beautiful patterns on them with uli will all be familiar to both women and children in the community. The reader also recognises that Tortoise's starvation which went on 'for two moons' reflects a manner of speaking and a way of calculating time which is consistent with the cosmology of the people of Umuofia.

Besides the tales and the inevitable songs which accompany them Achebe also uses quoted speeches to capture the flavour of the people's thoughts:

> 'Tell the white man that we will not do him any harm,' he said to the interpreter. 'Tell him to go back to his house and leave us alone. We liked his brother who was with us before. He was foolish but we liked him, and for his sake we shall not harm his brother. But this shrine which he built must be destroyed. We shall no longer allow it in our midst. It has bred untold abominations and we have come to put an end to it.' He turned to his comrades, 'Fathers of Umuofia, I salute you,' and they replied with one guttural voice. He turned again to the missionary. 'You can stay with us if you like our ways. You can worship your own god. It is good that a man should worship the gods and the spirits of his fathers. Go back to your house so that you may not be hurt. Our anger is great but we have held it down so that we can talk to you.' (p.134)

The third-person omniscient narrator introduces the parties involved, interpreter, missionary, and elders, but allows the people to speak for themselves with no further comment. Thus the church becomes a shrine and when the spokesman pauses he seeks authority and support from 'Fathers of Umuofia' who would understand 'abominations.' The reader may wonder if the church or the abandonment of twins, or an outcast system qualify for the term but the self-assurance of the elder which makes him speak patronisingly to Rev. Smith whose 'brother was foolish' but whom they 'liked' nevertheless, encourages the reader to re-examine the abominations. 'The world has no end' says Uchendu, 'and what is good among one people is an abomination with others' (p.99). The Priestess of Agbala calls the converts the excrement of the clan and sees the new church as 'the dog that (had) come to eat it up' (p.105). Such confidence derives from the fact that these characters are linguistically at home. Achebe makes them feel at home. The tales, songs, proverbs and other wise sayings provide the community with a solid base from which to view their 'enemies;' the devices enable them to state their case. Bernth Lindfors is right to observe with regard to the proverbs that they provide them with 'a grammar of values.'[16]

Achebe does not insist that the community is always right, indeed it is sometimes woefully wrong. The impersonal narrator, who often gives way to a participant observer, emerges to laugh occasionally at Umuofia, as when he depicts the role of the rain maker:

> And now the rains had really come, so heavy and persistent that even the village rain-maker no longer claimed to be able to intervene. He could not stop the rain now, just as he would not attempt to start it in the heart of the dry season, without serious danger to his own health. The personal dynamism required to counter the forces of these extremes of weather would be far too great for the human frame. (p.24)

In this passage the religious fervour of the people gives way to the scientific consciousness of a sceptical narrator. This doubting narrator who unobtrusively surprises the reader is the same one who tries in the court scene in chapter ten to explain Okonkwo's absence in the crowd to his wives, but, as often happens, he is upstaged by the efficiency with which the Egwugwu despatch their case. The community's 'terrifying' masks are meant to frighten the sceptic. What the novel reveals is a rich and complicated community.

Arrow of God is studded in communal lore. The reader may be justified if he feels that the language is too rich and that the novel reads more like an anthology of wise sayings than as a serious story about the break-up of a community. It can be argued, however, that the novel depicts a serious battle of words in which the best speaker wins. Umuaro is blest with good speakers, indeed, it has bestowed the title of owner of words on Nwaka whose debates with Ezeulu represent the clash between the community and its Chief Priest. Their debates are often a rich source of communal tradition. Ezeulu is even able at times to include a short tale to enhance his argument:

> Once there was a great wrestler whose back had never known the ground. He wrestled from village to village until he had thrown every man in the world. The he decided that he must go and wrestle in the land of the spirits and become champion there as well. He went and beat every spirit that came forward. Some had seven heads, some ten; but he beat them all. His companion who sang his praise on the flute begged him to come away, but he would not, his blood was roused, his ear nailed up. Rather than heed the call to go home he gave a challenge to the spirits to bring out their best and strongest wrestler. So they sent him his personal god, a little wiry spirit who seized him with one hand and smashed him on the stony earth. (pp.26–27)

Umuaro's love of wrestling which features at some festivals provides the Chief Priest with a useful motif for his tale. The link between the world of men and the world of spirits which is sometimes manifested in his physique and which he so graphically relates is familiar to his audience and to the reader who is never allowed to forget the centrality of religious belief in the novel. Ezeulu ends his tale with two wise sayings: 'The fly that has no one to advise it follows the corpse into the grave;' 'let the slave who sees another cast into a shallow grave know that he will be buried in the same way when his day comes' (p.27). Such cryptic messages seem to come as a matter of course to Ezeulu and he assumes that his audience knows what he is talking about. The reader, however, cannot help noticing the irony in this and other numerous lessons the Chief Priest delivers to his community. Ezeulu surely must be that stubborn wrestler whose back never touched the ground. Indeed when he reenacts his rise to the'throne' of Chief Priest he recounts his experiences through the wrestling image; the personal god who seizes the wrestler with one hand and throws him on the stony earth must be Umuaro with whom Ezeulu admits he is engaged in a wrestling combat. The Chief Priest can thus be likened to the poor fly that has no one to advise it as well as to the slave who see another cast in a grave.

The equivocal nature of these tales, proverbs and wise sayings thus heightens the reader's interest in them. Their ambiguity is a modernist literary device which enables Achebe to let the characters speak for themselves but by so doing provide the reader with valuable tools with which to assess them. When Ofoka tries to analyse the nature of the confusion in which Umuaro is enmeshed he likens it to the predicament of 'the puppy in the proverb which attempted to answer two calls at once and broke its jaw' (p.188). The novel keeps displaying these sayings as if to challenge the reader to test their validity; they make *Arrow of God* read sometimes like a bad dictionary, introducing more words rather than defining the world of the novel. It is possible, however, to sift through the multiloquence and emerge with meaning. Nwaka's speech is a useful benchmark:

> The white man is Ezeulu's friend and has sent for him. What is so strange about that? He did not send for me... Did not our elders tell us that as soon as we shake hands with a leper he will want an embrace?.... What I say is this, a man who brings ant-ridden faggots into his hut should expect the visit of lizards. But if Ezeulu is now telling us that he is tired of the white man's friendship our advice to him should be: You tied the knot, you should also know how to undo it. You passed the shit that is smelling; you should carry it away. Fortunately the evil charm brought in at the end of a pole is not too difficult to take outside again. (pp.143–144)

Nwaka is not one to say anything good about the Chief Priest but his rhetoric often persuades Umuaro against Ezeulu. When the reader has decoded the vague references to lepers, lizards, ant-ridden faggots, knots and charms all of which must be familiar to Nwaka's audience, he must ask if there is any substance in any of these copious images. To answer in the affirmative is to compare Nwaka's position with that of other characters in the novel because Nwaka's value is in spite of himself. He can be taken seriously not because he is any more genuine than Ezeulu, for instance, but because he often brings out the worst and the best in people. He is one of several compilers, albeit the most versatile, of the Umuaro dictionary of values. Another useful contributor is a minor character, Nweke Ukpaka, whose verbal skills speak volumes for Umuaro. 'The white man,' he says:

> 'is like a hot soup and we must take him slowly slowly from the edges of the bowl. Umuaro was here before the white man came from his own land to seek us out. We did not ask him to visit us; he is neither our kinsman nor our in-law. We did not steal his goat or his fowl; we did not take his land or his wife. In no way whatsoever have we done him wrong. And yet he has come to make trouble for us. All we know is that our Ofo is held high between us and him. The stranger will not kill his host with his visit; when he goes may he not go with a swollen back. I know that the white man does not wish Umuaro well. That is why we must hold our Ofo by him and give him no cause to say that we did this or failed to do that. For if we give him cause he will rejoice. Why? Because the very house he has been seeking ways of pulling down will have caught fire of its own will...' (p85)

Nweke Ukpaka's song-like philosophy endears him to the reader and to the community whose values he puts forward with such a disarming touch. It sounds naive but its essential argument about the need for unity and the efficacy of dialogue with Umuaro's enemies is consistent with the world view expressed by other members of the community such as the forthright Ofoka. Nweke Ukpaka's speech is similar to the one made by one of the elders in *Things Fall Apart* to Rev. Smith. Such a speech provides an occasion for Achebe to allow the character to speak for himself. With his wise sayings and rich metaphors, Nweke Ukpaka demonstrates how verbal skills constitute the power of the community. Each of the characters in the novel uses these skills to present a case for the composite group. Gareth Griffiths is only partially right to insist that:

> Proverbial language is not a static repository of wisdom to which Achebe subscribes unquestionably and against which he measures the actions of his novel in an uncritical way. Rather it is one of a

range of rhetorical devices which serve to define response in a world in which increasingly all response is relative and inadequate.[17]

It is true that the language is not 'a static repository of wisdom,' indeed Achebe in this novel, as in *Things Fall Apart*, uses proverbial language to censure his community. He neither spares the community, nor he claims for it a monopoly of virtue or wisdom. But 'relativity and inadequacy of response' need qualification in any discussion of his two novels of Igbo cultural heritage. The process of extracting value from the legacy of his ancestors makes Achebe, like Faulkner, demonstrate love and indeed bias toward his community. Achebe is in these novels, to paraphrase Moreland who describes a similar situation in Faulkner, not a potential modernist author impatient to close out and leave Umuaro/Umuofia for the literary profession of exile and alienation but as undeniably an Igbo himself, author and victim both of his own version of their self-castrating, suicidal nostalgia and irony.[18]

If the task is so absorbing and sometimes very difficult it never makes the writers shirk their loyalty to a specific, likeable people and locale. Faulkner created Yoknapatawpha and provided his readers with a map of the County. Achebe similarly creates a convincing world through speech and a skilful use of locale.

The world which evolves in *Things Fall Apart* is a convincing one and it provides an authentic background for the characters. The setting is presented through a series of unfolding scenes which are depicted with a clear perception of history and milieu. Achebe views Umuofia on its own terms and allows the community its sense of place and time so that even if the reader is able to recognise, as Achebe himself does, that the distances being talked about in grandiose terms are only a matter of a few miles, they nevertheless represent the world for 'these people.' The reader is expected to take Uchendu seriously when he lectures Obierika and Okonkwo on the virtues of travel:

> People travelled more in those days. There is not a single clan in these parts that I do not know very well. Aninta, Umuazu, Ikeocha, Elumelu, Abame I know them all. (p.97)

Uchendu delivers his homily in a village called Mbanta, 'just beyond the borders of Mbaino.' There are also 'very distant places' such as Umuru on the bank of the Great River where the white man has his government and soldiers who have earlier 'wiped out' Abame, another distant place.

More fascinating, however, is the clan itself which Achebe creates with an uncanny intimacy as this early description in the novel demonstrates:

> Umuofia was feared by all its neighbours. It was powerful in war and in magic, and its priests and medicine-men were feared in all the surrounding country. Its most potent war-medicine was as old as the clan itself. Nobody knew how old. But on the point there was general agreement the active principle in that medicine had been an old woman with one leg. In fact, the medicine itself was called agadi-mwanyi, or old woman. It had its shrine in the centre of Umuofia, in a cleared spot. And if anybody was so fool-hardy as to pass the shrine after dusk he was sure to see the old woman hopping about. (p.8)

Myth and reality become indistinguishable. It is impossible to consider the cleared spot in the centre of Umuofia without thinking of the old woman and the passage is not one of those depicted by a sceptical narrator; here he gives the people's sense of place full play as he does with Evil Forest, that dreaded place 'alive with sinister forces and powers of darkness.' To know Umuofia is to be aware of this background of unknown forces represented convincingly by the Masks whose chief not coincidentally is called Evil Forest. Even the dead are not far away:

> The land of the living was not far removed from the domain of the ancestors. There was coming and going between them especially at festivals and also when an old man died, because an old man was very close to the ancestors. (p.85)

Portraits of Umuofia are sometimes drawn by a detached observer who begins with straight forward details, such as the numerous descriptions of the market place and of the ilo, but these soon merge into the observations of an insider whose knowledge of the facts defies any questions. The beginning of chapter six is perhaps the best example:

The whole village turned out on the ilo, men, women, and children. They stood round in a huge circle leaving the centre of the playground free. The elders and grandees of the village sat on their own stools brought there by their young sons or slaves. Okonkwo was among them. All others stood except those who came early enough to secure places on the few stands which had been built by placing smooth logs in forked pillars.

The wrestlers were not there yet and the drummers held the field. They too sat just in front of the huge circle of spectators, facing the elders. Behind them was the big and ancient silk-cotton tree which was sacred. Spirits of good children lived in that tree waiting to be born. On ordinary days young women who desired children came to sit under its shade. (p.33)

The realistic camera view which focusses on the participants and on their places in the scene soon gives way to an observer who is aware of custom and of the legend behind the silk-cotton tree where the eye of the camera stops suddenly. The symbolic function of the setting takes over from the authentic. The reader of *Things Fall Apart* is asked to make this shift in order to understand Umuofia for which all these scenes and their significance are very real. It is possible for the reader to make this shift because the narrator convinces him that he knows his terrain very well, as this description of the place of Okonkwo's suicide demonstrates:

There was a small bush behind Okonkwo's compound. The only opening into this bush from the compound was a little round hole in the red-earth wall through which fowls went in and out in their endless search for food. The hole would not let a man through. It was to this bush that Obierika led the Commissioner and his men. They skirted round the compound, keeping close to the wall. The only sound they made was their feet as they crushed dry leaves. (p.146)

This passage can be compared with an earlier one where the narrator sets the scene or clears the pathway to Ikemefuna's tragic rendez-vous:

The footway had now become a narrow line in the heart of the forest. The short trees and sparse undergrowth which surrounded the men's village began to give way to giant trees and climbers which perhaps had stood from the beginning of things, untouched by the axe and the bush-fire. The sun breaking through their leaves threw a pattern of light and shade on the sandy footway. (p.41)

Both passages reveal an informed and sensitive narrator whose topographic awareness is clearly one of an insider. The world is realistically portrayed through such passages. The narrator and ultimately the reader know Umuofia intimately.

The subtlety that reveals the community to the reader is also reflected in the way Achebe deploys time in the novel. *Things Fall Apart* sometimes reads like a timeless novel. The people trace their beginnings to a mythical past, to the time 'the founder of their town engaged a spirit of the wild for seven days and seven nights' (p.3). But the narrator soon brings the reader down to earth by counting the years of the story proper. Thus it is possible to calculate Okonkwo's age which by the time the story opens must be about thirty-eight. We are later unobtrusively reminded that the white people have a queen. It is also revealed that Okonkwo has spent seven years in exile but for a people who hardly make any distinctions between the living and the dead such a detailed chronological count is not helpful. Okonkwo's exile from Umuofia, for instance, is a technical device which highlights his alienation from his community. His absence from the village allows the people a breather. It is a moment of stock-taking for both characters but if the community has learned a few things, Okonkwo unfortunately hasn't. The change of place and time develops Umuofia but not Okonkwo who returns to the village as fiery and as misguided as he left it. His thoughts when he returns are still about 'those days when men were men.' Umuofia on the other hand 'has grown another tail' more attuned to the prevailing circumstances. The community lives.

Arrow of God presents an even more vibrant community for, though Ezeulu often seems to paint a gloomy picture, the dominant setting of the novel is that of a festival. Not surprisingly, some of these festivals such as the festival of purification defy spoilers and as Chief Priest who must supervise the activities Ezeulu cannot, as Okonkwo is able to do, remain in the background where he may commit an indiscretion. This is how the narrator describes the atmosphere at one festival:

> A stranger to this year's festival might go away thinking that Umuaro had never been more united in all its history. In the atmosphere of the

> present gathering the great hostility between Umunneora and Umuachala seemed, momentarily, to lack significance. Yesterday if two men from the two villages had met they would have watched each other's movement with caution and suspicion; tomorrow they would do so again. But today they drank palm wine freely together because no man in his right mind would carry poison to a ceremony of purification; he might as well go out into the rain carrying potent, destructive medicines on his person. (p.66)

There is much unity and conviviality because the gods have a lot to do with these occasions. One festival, the reader learns:

> brought gods and men together in one crowd. It was the only assembly in Umuaro in which a man might look to his right and find his neighbour and look to his left and see a god standing there perhaps Agwu whose mother also gave birth to madness or Ngene, owner of a stream. (p.202)

The narrator of *Arrow of God* identifies with these views which clearly belong to a member of the community. However, as in *Things Fall Apart*, a delicate shift can be recognised between the view point of a careful but detached observer who records his surroundings in great detail and a participating narrator who transmutes these details into symbol.

One of the most impressive scenes of the novel occurs in Chapter Seven. The setting is the market place which the narrator says hums with people 'as though all the bees in the world were passing overhead.' But attention is focused on Ezeulu at his best. The scene is set to demonstrate the link between him and his people and it also establishes the connection between the Chief Priest and his god. The narrator is a participant observer, a reliable witness of the events. His eye records details of the Chief Priest's appearance.

> He wore smoked raffia which descended from his waist to the knee. The left half of his body from forehead to toes was painted with white chalk. Around his head was a leather band from which an eagle's feather pointed backwards. On his right hand he carried Nne Ofo, the mother of all staffs of authority in Umuaro, and in his left he held a long iron staff which kept up a quivering rattle whenever he stuck its pointed end into the earth. He took a few long strides, pausing on each foot. Then he ran forward again as though he had seen a comrade in the vacant air; he stretched his arm and waved his staff to the right and to the left. And those who were near enough

heard the knocking together of Ezeulu's staff and another which no one saw. At this many fled in terror before the priest and the unseen presences around him. (p.70)

Achebe uses this scene to define Ezeulu's personality and to emphasise the social role which he plays in Umuaro. It is a comment on the nature of his authority and on the respect which is attached to his high office. His link with 'unseen presences' strikes terror, and the reader is told that 'those who were near to him were able to hear the knocking together of Ezeulu's staff and another which no one saw.' This is reminiscent of the scenes in *Things Fall Apart* where the power of myth and the effect of reality is often indistinguishable.

Umuaro, however, is often presented as a real world. The myth perhaps is even meant to add to the grandeur. The people have a sense of place which is similar to that which was observed in *Things Fall Apart*. Indeed their map is much bigger than that of Umuofia. It is a smaller clan comprising six villages where Umuofia had nine but its contacts with the outside world have, not surprisingly, been extended and even the Chief Priest who is prohibited by custom to travel outside his village answers the call of the white man to 'visit' him in Okperi. They talk about places in the same grandiose phrases as the Umuofians do but it all sounds credible since at this time even the 'iron horse' is for them not yet a mode of transport.

Changes in setting have a great influence on the plot of the novel. Ezeulu's imprisonment for two months is the straw that breaks the back of Umuaro. His absence, like Okonkwo's, gives the two warring factions time to take stock but as with Okonkwo's growth the Chief Priest does not change while Umuaro on its part has taken a hard look at its predicament and decided to alter the rules to suit the changing scene. The Chief Priest who initiated the change by sending his son to the missionaries regresses into conservatism.

Sometimes changes of scene enable the narrator to shift his perspective. Chapter two, for instance, ends with the war between Umuaro and Okperi. The war is presented from the point of view of the community and the mention of the breaking of guns triggers the introduction in chapter three of the views of Captain Winterbottom on the same war:

> This war started because a man from Umuaro went to visit a friend in Okperi one fine morning and after he'd had one or two gallons of palm wine its quite incredible how much of that dreadful stuff they can tuck away anyhow, this man from Umuaro having drunk his friend's palm wine reached for his ikenga and split it in two. (p.37)

Akukalia and his companions have a different view of the causes of the war which may have been unnecessary and perhaps absurd but was surely not a result of the man's drunkenness. This view tells more about Captain Winterbottom than the people he describes in such paternalistic terms.

Change of setting in *Arrow of God* often means a change in perspective. It works, to quote Ezeulu again, like a mask dancing. The movement from the festive market place to the fractious compound of the Chief Priest represents a change of point of view. The people celebrate while Ezeulu quarrels with his sons, Edogo and Obika, who in his eyes are still children. When the scene changes to the Government house, as demonstrated above, it also reflects a change in perspective. The differences between Captain Winterbottom and his superiors and even the quarrel between him and Clarke testify to the Umuaro wise saying that both sides 'cut grass': they should thus not call each other names. This equally applies to the missionaries who, like the Government officials, have their problems. The novel handles all these points of view through the rhythmic changes of setting. For some, like the composite of Umuaro, these changes represent growth but for others such as Ezeulu and Captain Winterbottom changes in scene merely highlight their limited perspective.

The time of the novel is both a time of myth and of history. The myth of origin identifies the Umuaro people who came to being in 'the very distant past, when lizards were still few and far between.' Because of their link with their ancestors who, as in *Things Fall Apart* are ever present, it often seems as if the novel is also timeless. But the world of Umuaro is real and is specified and history plays a significant part in the development of the novel's plot. The reader recognises the breaking of guns by Captain

Winterbottom and is able to place it as Charles Nnolim confirms, within a specific historical moment.[19] Even Ezeulu's otherwise timeless ritual of eating the yams to enable him declare the New Yam Feast has developed a sense of urgency. When he is arrested time literally stops. His inability to correct his 'clock' spells doom for him and for his god. The Umuaro calendar is marked by feasts and by market days. The numerous feasts, therefore, heighten their consciousness of time. Each provides something to which the people can look forward. Ezeulu's individualism makes him try to interrupt this rhythm. Umuaro people can relate with the new religion in time because it also talks about a feast. When they take their yams, therefore, they recognise that they are still taking part in a harvest festival. It can be assumed that many elders would have found it difficult to comprehend the new way without their reference to the time-honoured tradition of Umuaro. The novel begins with Ezeulu's meticulous concern with the new moon and ends when he eats his twelfth yam. When the ritual is over he announces that 'the New Yam feast would be eaten in twenty-eight days' but unfortunately he has got it all wrong. The demise of the community and its Chief Priest could be said to have been enacted through the skilful manipulation of time. It is a question of the difference between the precision of the ritual of the yams and the manoeuvres of the new time represented by Captain Winterbottom which coincidentially is precise, even more precise. Ezeulu's love of precision ironically ruins him.

Both *Things Fall Apart* and *Arrow of God* are intimate and sympathetic accounts of the communities which Achebe describes. The novels demand that we see them not as studies of individuals but as the careful analysis of the heritage of the author. Achebe deploys devices that make such a task possible. One of them, for example, is his skilful characterisation in which the community is clearly personified so that it is impossible for the reader to see it as mere background. This is a revolutionary innovation which Achebe introduces to the modern novel. In reading Achebe's early novels we need to be prepared for a modernist novelist's tendency to destroy our 'tidy categories of thought.' By consciously toppling linguistic systems thus disrupting grammar and creating a new set of linguistic and moral values Achebe is able to create new wholes as in Umuaro and Umuofia. Achebe's modernism led to further experimentation by Gabriel Okara in *The Voice* and Ayi Kwei Armah in *Two Thousand Seasons*.[20]

AYI KWEI ARMAH, *TWO THOUSAND SEASONS*

Two Thousand Seasons reads like an apocalyptic text which reveals a community under persecution. Like other texts of this nature it seeks to recreate the community and in the process give it a clearly identifiable character. The reader in search of 'a single memorable character' should, therefore, locate such a character in the pervasive but deliberately portrayed features of Anoa, the community that is the novel's central concern. This is the point Eustace Palmer misses when he locates such a memorable character in King Koranche and thus incorrectly declares the novel 'sadly deficient in characterisation.'[21] Izevbaye is partially right when he observes that '(even) the characters are not whole persons but active and passive senses,'[22] but, his observation is likely to lead the reader away from the true nature of the characterisation in the novel, since there is, in fact, a whole person and what he calls 'active and passive senses' are traits of the novel's major character. Criticism of *Two Thousand Seasons* should account for the experimentation which transfers wholeness from the individual 'person' to the communal 'personality.'

That the novel is centred around a community is evident in the first sentence: 'We are not a people of yesterday,' and in the way the communal voice pervades the narrative.

The novel could thus be said to be an answer to the question 'Who are we?' It pursues this answer meticulously by delineating the nature of the collective group through whose eyes the reader sees the story. The method allows the collective voice to portray the psychological and moral nature of the community in passages such as this:

> 'Our way, the way, is not a random path. Our way begins from coherent understanding. It is a way that aims at preserving knowledge of who we are, knowledge of the best way we have found to relate each to each, each to all, ourselves to other peoples, all to our surroundings... Our way knows no way is wholeness. Our way knows no oppression. The way destroys oppression. Our way is hospitable to guests... Our way produces before it consumes. The way produces before it consumes... Our way creates...' (p.39)

The communal ethic is communicated to the reader through this kind of litany which seems to go on endlessly; 'the way' appears fifty times in the first chapter alone. Armah's method creates the moral world of the novel by means of an anthology of virtues which the reader can easily locate each time the ubiquitous 'way' is used. The way becomes synonymous with all that is good in the community, and it is defined either positively as in the above passage or as in the following passage by contrast:

> 'A shrunken soul, shrunken from the way, may see the disaster of families cut off from the other families around and still think their fearful huddling together against others is some kind of love, not hate made visible... For souls reduced near death can see beauty even in the triumph of ugliness itself, can see love in all-pervading hate: So far is their vision cut off from any truth, so far are they from the way.' (p.183)

Both these passages are concerned with the dominant theme of the novel which is wholeness or unity. This theme is achieved through the strong links created among the characters and by the high degree of polarization which exists between the people of the way and those that seek to destroy them.

To understand the psychology of the community is to penetrate the two contrasting worlds where good and bad traits may be found in individuals who, by the novel's logic, cannot be understood apart. The narration 'stops' occasionally to fill in a good or bad trait as the case may be. The following passage is typical:

'Of those that journeyed most stopped close by, their new homes soon mere extensions of our old. A few went farther in the heat of some small anger or some unusual fear. Such, to PAUSE BRIEFLY HERE, was the hunter Brafo.' (p.5)

Every individual 'character' in the novel is introduced in this manner. This includes even the 'developed' characters such as King Koranche and the mystic Isanusi, who, in their various activities, only embody the worst and the best traits in the community. Koranche, for instance, emerges as a retarded child who is described by the narrators as a 'dead spirit.' He is projected at his worst when compared to other children of his age with whom he cannot compete in the community's initiation rites. As he grows up and becomes King his relationship with some of his subjects is presented as a conflict between 'skill and intelligence on the one hand' and 'on the other hand, those born mediocre, those inferior through no fault of their own' (p.74). The crisis between these irreconcilable poles results in what the narrators call the 'schism' in the community. While Isanusi and the twenty young men present the proper behaviour which in this novel also means the way or the spirit of the community, the group represented by Koranche stands for all that is bad; Koranche is a symbol of oppression and despair. There is no middle ground, no possibility of mediation or reconciliation between the two poles.

This is the background against which the racial war in the novel is executed. The irreconcilable divisions are amplified by the arrival of 'predators' from the desert, who are followed years later by 'beasts' from the sea. The novel's eschatological ethic reduces all the forces of history, which in this case reads as the colonial past, to their outstanding characteristics, thus making the participants in the colonial incursions appear as dangerous and often unnaturally degenerate beasts. Anoa's prophecy often sounds like Jeremiah's announcement of wild beasts from the North who would tear Israel to pieces.[23] The tensions already created within the group are heightened by persecution and as they reach a peak the young men and women find that their bonds become stronger:

'Listening minds began to grow connections, the remembrances were separate, but underneath them all ran connected meaning: Our common captivity now, our broken connectedness before the onslaught of predators and destroyers and for the time to come our common destiny.' (p.125)

The reader never gets to know any individual in this powerful group. Abena, who is reasonably portrayed, reads like another version of Anoa, the woman who not only gives the community its name, but who may also be seen as the community itself. Both women, and others such as Noliwe, Idawa, Nigome and Ndola, represent the essence of the community. 'In their general condition of pain' the narrators say, 'there was no occasion for anyone to draw attention to his particular affliction' (p.55). This is the way much of the characterisation is handled. Most of the time there is a roll-call involving a cluster of names which the reader need not bother to remember. It is more than half way through the story that the reader gets to know about Isanusi and King Koranche. The reader, however, becomes acquainted with the community's history, its customs, its movements, and with its problems and the ways it has gone about solving them. Even the names, as Isidore Okpewho and Emmanuel Ngara have pointed out, are carefully chosen to represent an African community.[24] To go through the list is to make a journey across Africa. The community is the body where all the other 'characters' are only parts:

'How infinitely stupefying the prison of the single, unconnected viewpoint, station of the cut-off vision. How deathly the separation of faculties, the separation of people. The single agent's action is waste motion; the single agent's freedom useless liberty. Such individual action can find no sense until there is again that higher connectedness that links each agent to the group. Then the single person is no cut-off thing but an extension of the living group, the single will but a piece of the group's active will, each mind a part of a larger common mind. THEN EACH EYE INSPIRES ITSELF WITH VISIONS SPRINGING FROM GROUP NEED, THE EAR IS OPEN TO SOUNDS BENEFICIAL TO THE LISTENING GROUP, THE LIMBS MOVE AND THE HANDS ACT IN UNBROKEN CONNECTION WITH THE GROUP.' (p.134) (My emphasis).

There is an incredible growth pattern in the way any 'diseased' part seems easily replaceable. The novel thus leaves the reader in no doubt about who has the last word; people are only 'memorable' when seen in the context of the community. This is the point Isanusi makes when he is putting forward his alternative religion to the white missionary.

> 'There is indeed a great force in the world, a force spiritual and able to shape the physical universe, but that force is not something cut off, not something separate from ourselves. It is an energy in us, strongest in our working, breathing, thinking together as one people; weakest when we are scattered, confused, broken into individual, unconnected fragments.' (p.50)

'There is no beauty but in relationships,' the narrators insist, 'nothing cut off by itself is beautiful' (p.206). Wholeness is more than a slogan, it is worked into the novel's concept of a millennium. The technique provides the community with an opportunity to live its future in the present but in such a future only one community stands out, not single individuals. The central character of *Two Thousand Seasons* is Anoa or the black race, not Isanusi, not even the King, Koranche.

The language of *Two Thousand Seasons* both sustains and mars the novel. Its incantatory and abrasive tone advances the reader's interest but it also repels and at times even bores. The litany of virtues, for instance, often sounds more appropriate for worshippers at a religious ritual than for an uncommitted reader for whom the novel may sound rather heavy and monotonous. The novel, however, speaks in many voices and interest is maintained if the reader keeps a close ear to these as they emanate not from the communal narrative voice as it ostensibly claims, but from an 'implied author' who is looking over the shoulder of the twenty narrators and directing the reader's attention to the communal perspective and to its message of wholeness or unity.

There is what may be called, for want of a better term, a name-calling voice, identified by the narrators when they reflect on the prophecies of Anoa, as 'a harassed voice shrieking itself to hoarseness.' The language which this voice uses is evocative, contemptuous and sometimes vulgar. The first five chapters are dominated by this voice and the prologue sets the denunciatory tone:

'Woe the race, too generous in the giving of itself, that finds a road not of regeneration but a highway to its own extinction. Woe the race, woe the spring. Woe the headwaters, woe the seers, the hearers, woe the utterers. Woe the flowing water, people hustling to our death.' (pp.xii–xiii)

Armah's community is different from that of Achebe; it speaks neither in proverbs nor in folk tales. The language is directed against enemies identified in the book as 'predators, destroyers, askaris and zombis' and the abuse can be blunt:

'We are not stunded in spirit, we are not Europeans, we are not Christians that we should invent fables a child would laugh at and harden our eyes to preach them daylight and deep night as truth. We are not Muslims to fabricate a desert god chanting madness in the wilderness, and call our creature creator.... We have thought it better to start from sure knowledge, call fables fables and wait till clarity. But from the desert first, then from the sea, the white predators, the white destroyers came assailing us with the maddening loudness of their shrieking theologies.' (p.3)

The same voice also describes some bizarre incidents such as the orgies which the reader is to associate with the sexual depravity of the Arabs in the story. The world of the novel divides into two irreconcilable groups and each has a language to match. In contrast to the vehemence and abuse described above there is an accompanying second voice also identified by the narrators as 'calmer, so calm it sounded to be talking not of matters of (our) life and death but of something like a change in the taste of the day's water' (p.16). If the first voice is notorious for its name-calling, this one is full of praise for 'the people of the way.' This is evident when any of the women who emerge as the essence of the group is described. This portrait of Idawa is typical:

'Idawa had a beauty with no (such) disappointment in it. Seen from a distance her shape in motion told the looker here was coordination free, unforced. From the hair of her head to the last of her toes there was nothing wasted in her shaping. And her colour; that must have come uninterfered with the night's own blackness... But Idawa's surface beauty, perfect as it was, was nothing besides her other, profounder beauties; the beauty of her heart, the way she was with

people, the way she was with everything she came in contact with;
and the beauty of her mind, the clarity with which she moved past
the lying surfaces of the things of this world set against our way, to
reach judgement holding to essences, free from the superficies.' (p.70)

The contrast between beauty and ugliness is extended to
depth and 'superficies,' harmony and chaos, 'clarity' and
darkness and the oscillating nature of the 'twin voices' maintains
the consistent and at times too repetitive rhythm of the prose. It
also helps to sustain the major battle between 'us' and 'them.'

In trying to draw the lines of the struggle, however, the
implied author gives a great deal away. The people of the way are
meant to speak a very simple, direct and straight-forward
language and the author succeeds when he translates such words
as castle into 'the stone palace' or when east and west read as 'the
falling' and the 'rising' or in the useful transfer of years into
seasons (dry and wet). The effort is to present an African point of
view but Armah's simplicity, unlike Achebe's, is its own enemy.
The implied author in Achebe's novels, especially in *Things Fall
Apart* and *Arrow of God* distinguishes himself unobtrusively from
the communal voice. In Armah's novel, however, the voice of the
implied author is ostensibly submerged in the communal
perspective. But if the effort is aimed at portraying a people with
a simple language and an uncomplicated way of looking at life,
the reader is taken aback when he is suddenly confronted with
such words and expressions as 'discombobulation,' 'catatonia,'
'vatic time,' 'translucent threads,' 'a cataclysm of anger,' 'brazen
cacophony,' 'propitious,' 'plethora of warnings,' and many more
(pp.31, 32 ff). Indeed it is tempting to declare at such moments
that the novel has only one narrator and that the communal voice
is a trick to enable the writer to recreate his own version of
African history.

Such a conscious effort can be seen in the way symbols and
metaphors are deliberately reversed:

'Our people had prepared themselves for the coming confusion by
choosing a cry of recognition, the call of the black vulture. Afterwards
those who had been directly in the fight adopted the vulture as their
double. Let the ignorant laugh at such identification. We listen to
their mindless laughter, see their brainless faces. Of the vulture what

is it they know? That bird that lives off carrion but never kills a living thing that has not first attacked it, that bird is also of the way.' (p.43)

There is thus a tribe of the vulture and later mention is made of vulture cries and 'signs of the vulture' (p.153). Similar reversals may be recognised in the positive use of the forest which never appears as a jungle. On the contrary, all the best people live there and whatever predatory animals the reader comes across emerge instead from the sea and from the desert. The forest provides the proper environment for the guerilla activities planned by the twenty revolutionary young men and women. Sometimes the language goes beyond these deliberate reversals and breaks the narrative to argue a thesis. One such long thesis on 'cripples' concludes thus:

'The cripple regrets the disappearance of the first distance, imposed by others shrieking, now remembered as useful insulation for himself. The cripple dreams of such a distance no longer merely a defensive distance but a distance to turn the contempt of others into contempt against others. This kind of cripple, his deficiencies are inner. But an inner reparation lies beyond his long despair. The external, the superficial, the manipulable: On such he must depend in his ambition to distinguish himself. The world of tinsel, the superficies, come as perfect clothing to cover the cripple's deformity from recoiling sight. In the fullness of the ostentatious cripple's dreams the spirit of community is raped by worshippers of impressive trash...' (p.63)

Two Thousand Seasons often reads like a *roman à thèse*. It attempts to demonstrate a thesis on 'solidarity' by persistently distancing the chosen group from any contact with the others. But the impression of simplicity which is portrayed, especially when the wise old Seer Isanusi speaks, is betrayed when the reader confronts the other denunciatory voices whose words and phrases clearly emanate from an experience which is different and more complicated than the black and white picture which the communal narrators try to paint. If the aim is to imitate and translate the language of a 'simple' community then the effort has failed. When the narrators depict their experiences at initation they remark that 'each season had its riddles, its proverbs and its songs,' but the reader never gets the feel of these and, with Achebe in mind, must regret the scanty references to 'full-moons,' 'fundis' and of time measured in the space 'it takes a person to swallow his saliva seven times' (p.66).

Two Thousand Seasons creates a sense of community through a careful manipulation of space and time. The method first reveals general characteristics and then relates these to the mood and character of the community. There is also an attempt, though not a very successful one, to set the community in a solidly constructed environment. The landscape, however, is not as vague as it would first appear, and it is not true, as Palmer claims, that 'Armah makes little attempt at the evocation of setting or creation of local colour.'[25] The novel's aim is to create a garden of Eden where 'the people of the way' can live. Background description thus serves two purposes, first to highlight this ideal, then to set it into a context:

> 'With what shall the utterers' tongue stricken with goodness, given silent with the quiet force of beauty, with which mention shall the tongue of the utterers begin a song of praise whose perfect singers have yet to come...? Who saw mountains flung far to the falling, so far they in the end seduce the following eye and raise it skyward, when the return to the source, to you. Descending slopes, unhurrying even at the long curve of the water falls, descending into the gentleness of land, of earth so good it is seldom visible itself, earth covered under your forests: Who would have known, coming from so near the desert, who would have known there was in this world such a variation, such a universe of Green alone?' (p.56)

The 'universe of green' has a name, Anoa. It is also 'washed' by two rivers, Esuba and Su Tsen. Similarly as the people migrate they identify deserts, plains, mountainsides and forests. The reader is reminded of Poano where there is a 'stone palace' and names of neighbouring towns such as Simpa, Anago, Bomey and Ahwei. The towns of Edina and Enchi have suffered an invasion. There are also towns such as Fulani, Gao and Kedia. The towns, like the names of the characters, reflect the pan-African thrust of Armah's argument. The specifics may result in a useful map of the country but more than this is a qualitative divide between beautiful places where the people of the way live and unpleasant places which are remnants of what their enemies have left. The former is usually described in language that is enchanting and rhetorical:

'We had thought, from seeing the waters of Anoa water suspended bubbling at the lip of its forest fountain, water falling like long, translucent threads airing in the wind before the masters of the waving art take them for their use, water flowing, rushing, water slowed down behind new obstacles, water patiently rising till it overflows what can never stop it, water calm, immobile like the sky in a season starved of rain we had thought, from seeing Anoa's waters from hearing their thirty different sounds, that there was nothing of beauty in water we had yet to see, no sound of its music we had not heard. But the last of our open initiations took us to the coastland. There we saw in the same water we thought we knew so well a different beauty.' (p.75)

The sense of calm, music and beauty is contrasted with the desolation inflicted by the enemy:

'That eighth day we came to a large town, larger than where we had stopped among the gentle people. But here only the physical place was left, and of that merely the charred husk... There was not one living creature there. Death had visited this place and time had passed over it. There were no corpses, only skeletons. From these too the bones were being removed by which night creature we could find no indication... In the centre stood a huge baobab, leafless, all its branches dead.' (p.79)

Images of towns reduced to 'charred husks' and of skeletons and shrunken baobab trees contrast sharply with the beauty of Anoa's waters. Just as the characters and the language fall into two distinct categories, the setting is also depicted in such a way that one terrain stands for oppression and despair while the other stands for beauty. The symbolic use of the setting is the novel's strong point. A description such as the movement of the young men through a cave enacts their present predicament and shows the possibilities for the future:

'In the middle of a long stretch of calm sea and rock there was this whirling turbulence, pushing itself forward down a tiny opening in the rockface, its movement giving off a low sound like a moan. The space through which the water rushed in its disappearance was large enough to take the width of one canoe, no more... We were amazed. Here was beauty to madden the soul with happiness. Here was space for wandering, here was cool darkness to soothe each spirit seeking quiet. Here also was light reaching rock and water from hidden, subtle openings above.' (p.102)

Their path through the turbulence, into the cave, and eventually into light is reminiscent of their capture and their experiences in the slave ship out of which they finally liberate themselves. The 'fifth grove' serves a similar symbolic function. The narrators say that it is not a place of visible paths: 'Dwellers there have always been quiet movers, disturbing nothing they need not disturb. Yet even here the eye searching for easy access is drawn naturally to openings between plants, openings that would be, the beginning of paths...' (p.186).

The novel's persistent concern with the future offers the reader a way to examine the way time functions. There are two time schemes in the novel. The twenty narrators take the reader from the moment King Koranche assumed power (chapters 4–7) through their capture and finally to their liberation. Events do follow in an ordered sequence of days and seasons though they get a bit blurred when the reader confronts biblical expressions such as 'the thirty days and thirty nights' in which the narrators find their way to the fifth grove. The second scheme (chapters 1–3) is more fascinating as it exposes the presence of the other narrator already mentioned. This second time scheme cannot be measured even though as the title suggests it could be a period covering 'two thousand seasons.' The truth about this second scheme is, however, explained by the novel's narrator masked in a communal voice:

> 'We lost count of stable seasons, lost count of drought, lost count of good rains and in the ease of thirty thousand seasons forgot all anxiety.' (p.141)

This is the voice of tradition evoking the mythical background by taking the community back to its primordial times. The novel erects two poles of perfection within this background. The past which can be identified as a mythical Eden is 'interrupted' by a concrete situation (colonialism) which leads the seer to construct a Heaven which his persecuted community will inherit. Glimpses of the 'new heaven and new earth' are enacted thus enabling the people of Anoa to live their future in the present. In such a scheme time is momentarily suppressed. When Isanusi sees the twenty young men and women who have

broken from their past he remarks that it is 'a new day beginning.'
All their activities are part of this new day:

> 'Endless our struggle must seem to those whose vision reaches only
> to the end of today. But those with ears connected to our soul will
> hear a message calling us to a better life, to a life closer to our ancient
> way.' (p.153)

For the twenty 'narrators' such a life began with their
liberation.

Richard Bauman defines performance as 'a mode of spoken
verbal communication which consists in the assumption of
responsibility to an audience for a display of communicative
competence.' This competence, according to Bauman, 'rests on the
knowledge and ability to speak in socially appropriate ways.'[26]
Bauman also draws attention to a list of communicative means
through which such competence operates, namely: special codes,
figurative language, parallelism, special paralinguistic features,
special formulae, appeal to tradition and disclaimer of
performance.[27] These features are relevant to a discussion of Ayi
Kwei Armah's *Two Thousand Seasons* and Gabriel Okara's *The
Voice*. Even more useful is Burke's point that performance arouses
an attitude of collaborative expectancy. 'Once you grasp the trend
of the form,' says Burke, 'it invites participation.'[28] Both novels
appeal to a participating 'audience.'

Two Thousand Seasons is addressed to two audiences. One
audience is identified in the prologue and it consists of 'hearers,
seers, imaginers, thinkers, rememberers and prophets' (p.xi). They
are enjoined by the narrator, who claims to be one of them, 'to
make knowledge of the way.' The second set is identified first in
general terms as 'listeners' but specified in the course of the story
as the community of Anoa, or 'all the black people.' The narrator
of the prologue surrenders his authority in much of the novel to a
group of twenty revolutionary young men and women who start
as would-be 'seers and imaginers' but attain their dream as the
story unfolds. But, for these young men and women the story
should begin from chapter four because it is at this stage that they
reach an age which would allow them to communicate their

experiences to an audience. As they themselves confirm at the end of chapter three:

> 'It was in Koranche's time as King that the children of our age grew up. It was also in his time disastrous time that the white destroyers came from the sea.' (p.74)

The first three chapters, therefore, are dramatizations of the communal ethic, designed to be chanted, the reader can assume, by a group of faithful followers of the way. These chapters are supposed to express the mood of its listeners who are invited to participate in the re-enactment of history and myth. A sense of community and participation is emphasised by the pervasive use of the pronouns 'we,' 'us,' 'they,' and 'them.'

> 'WE are not a people of yesterday. Do THEY ask how many single seasons WE have flowed from OUR beginnings till now? WE shall point THEM to the proper beginnings of THEIR counting. On a clear night when the light of the moon has lighted the ancient woman and her seven children, on such a night tell THEM to go alone into the world. There, have THEM count first the one then the seven, and after the seven all the stars visible in THEIR eyes alone.' (p.1) (My emphasis)

Sometimes specific questions are addressed to a group within the group because the method seeks to challenge as well as to differentiate the audience. Questions are asked of sections of the audience who apparently are not sure about the events being described:

> 'Who is calling for examples? You do not understand how the destroyers turned earth to desert? Who would hear again the cursed names of the predator Chieftains? With which stinking name shall we begin.' (p.7)

Part of the audience, the narrators say, is still 'fascinated by glittering death.' Often the audience is asked to hear something 'for the sound of it' and some events have become so well-known, the narrators claim, that 'it would be wasted breath repeating them.' Participation and shared beliefs are crucial to the novel but that may also explain why it has alienated more readers than it has enchanted.[29] The reader who is not part of this eschatological vision is bound to feel bored and frustrated and it can be assumed that even the 'faithful' could find the drama outrageous.

Armah, however, makes good use of parallelism and at times some fascinating figure of speech to keep the interest of the reader. If parallelism, as Geoffrey Leech describes it, consists of variant and invariant units,[30] then 'the way' is the invariant unit, not just of specific passages but of the whole novel. It provides, to use Leech's phrase, 'the foregrounded regularity' which gives the novel its rhythm. Every other part of the novel is the variant unit providing definitions and means of arriving at the communal message of the novel.

In keeping with the skill of the performer, the narrators do resort sometimes to what Bauman calls 'disclaimer':

> 'With what shall the utterer's tongue stricken with goodness, river silent with the quiet force of beauty, with which mention shall the tongue of the utterers begin a song of praise whose perfect singers have yet to come?' (p.56)

This, of course, is only a pose by the 'utterer' who looks forward to his audience to applaud his efforts. 'The people using all things to create participation, using things to create community' the narrators assert, 'have no need of any healer's art, for that people is already whole?' Community and wholeness constitute the major theme; the narrative design of the novel and the attempt to perform before an audience by using some well-known codes or indeed by creating new ones provides the novelist with the opportunity to realise his objective.

The communal perspective has been used to good effect by Ayi Kwei Armah even though its effect in *Two Thousand Seasons* needs qualification. The method provides Armah with a tool which enables him to tackle such issues as pan-Africanism which have always been his subject.[31] In pursuing his dream of a unified Africa, Armah delineates the character of the community from its primordial times through its present and even gives the reader a glimpse into what the future would look like.

GABRIEL OKARA, *THE VOICE*

Community is at the centre of Gabriel Okara's experimental novel, *The Voice*.[32] Much of the story emerges through the point of view of Okolo who is also the voice of the title. But Okolo is only the eyes through which Okara scrutinizes his community which emerges as the novel' s centre of dramatic action and as its major character. His 'silence' enhances his role of the narrator as observer and it also triggers much of the activity that takes place in the novel; the reader comes to appreciate his dilemma but only against the background of the dramatic relationships in which he engages with different sections of the community. He often seems to loom large because his community, like that of Densu in Armah's *The Healers*, is after strange gods and is thus recognisable more in terms of what it might have been than in its present state of anarchy. Both novels define their communities through series of vices which are then juxtaposed against a background of virtues, but they both reveal a passionate need on the part of the participant observers, who are both orphans, to seek relationships in spite of the serious shortcomings of their respective communities.

The Healers represents the quest, to borrow a term from *Two Thousand Seasons*, as a search for 'the way.'[33] Similarly, Okolo is searching for 'it' but he will not give it a name because, as he says, 'names bring divisions and divisions, strife' (p.25). He is looking, he claims, 'for belief and faith in that something (we) looked up to in times of sorrow and joy (p.89), which really is another phrase for community.[34] The community, and not Okolo, is thus the centre of interest in the novel. Okolo penetrates the psychology of the twin communities of Amatu and Sologa, which have both refused to adopt him, in order not only to understand the reasons for this refusal, but also to analyze the causes of their general malaise. The malaise, as he demonstrates so well stems from the excessive worship of the shadow-devouring trinity, of gold, iron, and concrete' (p.89). Each 'character' is seen as one of the many images which could develop the composite picture of Amatu and

Sologa; each is a trait of the larger character. The tendency among critics such as Emmanuel Obiechina, Eustace Palmer and Solomon Iyasere, to treat the novel as a clash between the individualism of Okolo (and Tuere) against the community is justifiable but it ignores the fact that Okolo only provides a point of view on the community and that 'they' and not he constitute the novel's centre of dramatic interest.[35] Their follies, and their crass materialism, expose them as a community without a core but one which is powerful nevertheless. That is why at the end of the novel the water rolls over Okolo and Tuere 'as if nothing had happened' (p.127).

Emmanuel Ngara's observation is more accurate. 'Okolo,' he says, 'has used what little education he has to acquire real knowledge about his society and its predicament.'[36] Okolo's knowledge is the reader's gain, for, much as one sympathises with his predicament, it is the community which outlasts him that fascinates the reader. Okara deploys many devices to give the reader the feel of this community, one of them being the device of using a silent but thoughtful character as a benchmark from which to survey the community. But more than this, he speaks the language of the people and allows them to express themselves in their own idiom. He places them within a convincing setting so that their performance, as it were, may be watched by the reader. Okolo is the device that records the performance but sometimes the actions of individual characters speak for themselves and the reader can dispense with Okolo's point of view which tends to be tinted by his depressing experiences.

Eighty odd voices in *The Voice* form the 'dark cloud' which suffocates Okolo who would otherwise have been a 'bright star' (p.26). The metaphor is used early in the novel and it is crucial to an understanding of the management of its point of view and of the nature of the relationship between Okolo and his community. Okolo is isolated in such a way that his morality sharply contrasts with the amoral communities of Amatu and Sologa. His Spartan existence contrasts with the exhibitionist display by the people of their new-found gods of gold, iron and concrete. Consequently, they cannot understand or appreciate his search for 'it.' He is thus 'smothered' so that the people may 'shine.' The shine, of course, is purely a narrative device since the reader comes to know corrupt, irresponsible, and apathetic communities. Okolo is submerged so that the reader may see these shortcomings in their full perspective. His predicament offers the reader a perspective from which to evaluate the character of the twin communities.

Okolo's role as observer and recorder is highlighted from the beginning:

> It was the day's ending and Okolo by a window stood. Okolo stood looking at the sun behind the tree tops falling. The river was flowing, reflecting the finishing sun, like a dying away memory. It was like an idol's face, no one knowing what is behind. Okolo at the palm trees looked. They were like women with their hair hanging down, dancing, possessed. Egrets, like water flower petals strung slackly across the river, swaying up and down, were returning home. And, on the river, canoes were crawling home with bent backs and tired hands, paddling. A girl with only a cloth tied round her waist and the half-ripe mango breasts, paddled, driving her paddle into the river with a sweet inside.... To the window he went once there and looked at the night... Larger and darker clouds, some to frowning faces, grimacing faces changing, were skulking past without the moon's ring, suffocating the stars until they too lost themselves in the threatening conformity of the dark cloud beyond. (p.26)

The window serves as a useful observation point from which Okolo's metaphoric mind scrutinizes the environment. The links between nature and man, in which palm trees dance like frenzied women or in which clouds look grim and frown, can be seen as a reflection of his colourful mind but they also enact and forecast his future that is suggested by that ominous metaphor of the stars, which, like Okolo, lose themselves in 'the threatening conformity of the dark cloud beyond.' The dilemma not withstanding, Okolo never abandons his role of an onlooker and recorder of the activities of the people around him. The passage is a good illustration of the faithfulness to detail which characterises this task. Such details accumulate until they become the 'mysterious might of tradition.'

The tradition maintains its might by sheer force of numbers. Size, not quality, explains its dominance over Okolo. When the novel opens, the reader is introduced to three messengers who, as they approach Okolo, multiply into 'a thousand hands, the hands of the world,' then into 'a million pursuing feet, the caring-nothing feet of the world,' (p.28). Indeed to say that Okolo is overwhelmed by this mass of people is an understatement, for, even if the reader sees these figures as a figment of Okolo's persecuted imagination, it is difficult to ignore the manner in which he has been reduced to a 'rat' small enough to 'escape through a hole' (p.28). As the reader's attention is shifted from one community to another the dominance of the other voices over that of Okolo is maintained. In Amatu, the corrupt Abadi insists that 'all the voices must be one.' These voices 'drown Okolo's voice asking, is it here?' The experience is duplicated in Sologa where he finds 'frustrated eyes, ground-looking eyes, cold eyes, bruised eyes, despairing eyes nothing caring eyes, hot eyes,... grabbing eyes and aping eyes' (p.80). Even in the boat which takes him to Sologa, Okolo experiences isolation and dimunition amidst the voices which 'tear up the engine's sound to pieces.'

Okolo's communities are, however, not mere undifferentiated masses as these first impressions suggest. Okara's dramatic method allows the reader to go beyond Okolo's perception so as to record the diversity of traits which eventually cohere around the communities whose character is the subject of the novel. Their character is successfully created through a series of traits which are similar but which at the same time reveal remarkable differences.[37] No where is this better illustrated than in the scene in chapter seven in which Chief Izongo calls his Council of Elders to deliberate on the aftermath of Okolo's expulsion:

Izongo:'One-man-one-face!'

First Elder:'Yes,' No two persons have the same face, and no two persons have the same inside. What is yours?'

Izongo:'You are asking me? I am lightning!'

First Elder:'Lightning!'

Izongo:'Yes. I am lightning. Nothing stands before lightning. What is yours?'

Second Elder:'Yes! I am water. Water is the softest and the strongest thing to be. What is yours...?' (pp.98–99)

The first Elder's wisdom about differences in human nature is, presumably, a residue of a culture that is now gone but their list of praise names provides a useful guide to the diversity that exists in the community. What the scene illustrates is the way this diversity which in the past served useful communal objectives is now being misused by Chief Izongo for his own selfish ends. Water, fire, and pepper, which each of the elders selects as a praise name, are different but complementary. It is also true as one of them later claims that 'many ants gather together and crumb bigger than themselves they carry' (p.99) but such metaphors now bear little value because what the chiefs carry is only the burden of Chief Izongo. Okara's method works by implication. The reader knows the community by what it might have been and such 'reminiscences' which the Elders enact are reminders to the reader of the way things were. Similar violations of tradition are shown in Sologa where 'good old' methods of judgement are replaced by a Kangaroo court which forces a young girl to confess a crime she clearly has not committed.

These vignettes of the past crop up very often; Okolo keeps recalling the past as a means to understand a chaotic present:

> Seeing only darkness in front like the wall, Okolo looked back at his early days when he was a small boy, a small boy going to the farm with his mother in a canoe and making earth heaps to receive the yam seedlings. How sweet his inside used to be when at the day's finishing time with the sun going down, they paddled home singing; and how at harvest time when the rain came down almost ceaselessly, they returned home with the first yams, only for small boys, like him, to eat first. How in expectation of the first yams he went through the long planting time.. then the death of his mother and then his father. (p.105)

The passage is symbolic. The loss of his parents, especially his father whom he portrays as the embodiment of tradition, is a sign of what the people as a whole have lost: the singing and the joy of harvest are cut short by the 'death' of the community (his father and mother).

The past may be seen by implication but the present displays its vulgarity and chaos in individuals ranging from Chief Izongo to his confused messengers in Amatu, and from the Big One to the policeman in Sologa. Each of these people exhibits the traits which have negated the community. To indicate how bad things have become Okara draws profiles of two individuals, Abadi, and the white man in the service of the Big One, who should 'know' but who are as bad as the mob. Abadi, the reader is told, has his M.A. and Ph.D. but does not have 'it.' Indeed the reader need not learn this from Okolo because Abadi's abuse of language speaks for itself.[38] His perversion is shown in the way he turns words like 'collective responsibility' to translate as dictatorship, all in the interest of 'our leader.' For him, anything is right especially if it is done to `toe the party line'. Similarly, the white man in Sologa recommends the asylum for Okolo when the latter is convinced that, 'at least,' he will understand.

Very short sketches usually suffice to show the motivations and activities of most of the 'characters' in the novel. The second messenger, for instance, says:

> Any way the world turns I take it with my hands. I like sleep and my wife and my son, So I do not think. (p.25)

Similar sentiments are expressed by Tebeowei and it can be assumed that most of the people of Amatu and Sologa have come round to this pseudo-philosophy of 'live and let live.' Some of the people Okolo encounters on his journey go even a step further in seeking dubious ways by which they can become rich. It is charitable to say that the 'characters' in the story constitutes a community. They have lost those 'ties of blood and kinship' which bind people to a land and which ensure bonds of friendship, of shared feeling and common belief, unless we see their excessive concern with money and 'concrete' as a common belief.[39] The novel, however, does not allow us to do this. Okolo, who still loves those who would persecute him, cries out in anguish:

> 'All I want... is to revitalise my flagging faith, faith, in man, belief in something,' he said with all his inside and his shadow. 'Believe and faith in that something we looked up to in times of sorrow and joy have all been taken away and in its stead what do we have? Nothing but a dried pool with only dead wood and skeleton leaves. And when you question they fear a tornado is going to blow down the beautiful houses they have built without foundations.' (p.89)

Okolo finds a bit of what he is looking for in Tuere who, like him, has also been rejected by the community. When both of them are condemned to death, the cripple, Ukule, vows to continue where they have left and the doubts that are beginning to manifest themselves among some of the messengers and possibly even in Abadi show that some sense of community might have been cultivated after all. Okara creates this sense of a community by showing its vices depicted in individuals within it and then contrasting them with a few like Okolo and Tuere who are virtuous. The emphasis, however, is never on these individuals. They form, instead, a network that helps the reader to understand the community. This applies even to Okolo whose presence in the story cannot be easily ignored. Okara's point seems to be that community is not only prior to the individual, it normally out-lasts him. What Okolo has left behind is a potentiality, a real possibility of producing 'individual as communal which the vicious 'characters' in the novel seem unable to grasp.'[40] The novel leaves the reader with a self-destructive character (the community) but one full of energy which express itself through a vigorous use of language.

The language of *The Voice* is babelish. It is, therefore, not surprising that readers of the novel are often irritated by its 'strange Ijaw rhythms and syntax.'[41] But as in Armah's *Two Thousand Seasons*, this curious language both sustains and mars the novel. Its variety fascinates the reader who may also feel that it is perhaps too varied. The movement from character to character with its accompanying shifts in register and idiom makes great demands on the reader's attention and it is often difficult to determine the criteria for some of the shifts especially those between the third-person narrator and Okolo, the novel's main narrator. The latter often speaks what must be the trad-itional language but he appears to be so much at home with all the 'languages' that it is tempting to charge Okara with a false attempt at translation, a 'crime' which is more obvious in Armah's *Two Thousand Seasons* but which is always threatening to occur in *The Voice* as well. It can, however, be argued that language and theme are indistinguishable in the novel and that Okara with a modernist's awareness, successfully creates a Tower of Babel as an index of the anarchy into which the communities of Amatu and Sologa have plunged themselves.

There is plenty of evidence in the text to support this argument. In the first place, the implied author always appears in complete control of the material, so that, even if we quarrel with him for making us adjust too often, we cannot fault him for the dexterity which he moves from one "language" to the other:

> "You have your M.A., PH.D., but you have not got IT," Okolo interrupted him, also speaking in English. All eyes, including Chief Izongo's left Abadi and settled on Okolo, Abadi's face became twisted in rage but he held himself.

> "As I was saying, I have my M.A., PH.D., degrees," he continued and all eyes left Okolo and settled again on Abadi, "But I, my very humble self, knew where my services were most required and returned to Amatu to fight under the august leadership of our most honourable leader. I cannot therefore stand by when I see our cause about to be jeopardised by anyone... We are fighting a great fight and this is not the time to split hairs."

> "Whom are you fighting against?... Are you not simply making a lot of noise because it is the fashion in order to share in the spoils. You are merely making a show straining to open a door that is already open..."

> "Listen not to him, fellow Elders. His mouth is foul." As Abadi ended, there arose a great shout of applause, feet stamping and hand-clapping. Then with his voice quavering with emotion he (Izongo) began to speak in the vernacular... (pp. 44-45).

Two main languages are identified here, the vernacular and English. The former is spoken by Chief Izongo and his Elders while the latter is the language of the third person narrator or the implied author and it is also the language which both Okolo and Abadi speak. There is, however, a close link between the observation of Okolo and the third person narrator. Their language is distinguished from the pompous, almost meaningless, expressions of Abadi who has his M.A. and PH.D. An indication is given of a further attempt to speak in another language when Abadi switches from such expressions as 'the unparalleled gallantry of our leader' to 'Listen not to him, fellow Elders.' Similar awareness of audience is responsible for the constant shifts from Okolo's impeccable English, as when he communicates with the whiteman in the service of the Big One, or at moments when he is soliloquising on the possibilities of his search for 'it,' to the colloquial speech of the people of Amatu and Sologa. The reader is often reminded that this is the 'vernacular.' What emerges is thus a translation which is carried out sometimes by Okolo, as when he is recalling the conversation in the boat, or by the third-person narrator who, like Okolo, is quite capable of moving from one language to another.

The technique of the novel suggests, however, that it is not so much a matter of who says what at any given time, rather it is a question of who shouts most. The novel reveals eighty-three voices which invariably 'sing out' or 'shout' or 'threaten' or, like Okolo's, are just 'silent.' Readers who are irritated by the style can take comfort in the fact that what they are witnessing is a 'shouting' contest whose inevitable winners are the communities of Amatu and Sologa. Attention has so much been centred on the strangeness of the language that it is too often forgotten that the novel deliberately draws the reader's attention to the problem of language as a way of showing the complete breakdown of values in the community. This breakdown is not simply a case of Okolo's clarity against the people's confusion, it is also an indication of Okolo's own dilemma which stems from his unsuccessful efforts to try and discover his tradition and the reasons for its collapse. The people's struggle with proverbs and praise-names, which they now completely misuse, his own inability to capture the essence of a forgotten culture, are all enacted through language. The facility with which Achebe captures the idiom of his people, for instance, cannot be found in *The Voice* and this is because, while Achebe worships his ancestors and celebrates the past, Okara chastises his contemporary society and asks it to find ways of recovering that past. The reader, however, leaves the novel with the impression that this is neither possible nor desirable.

The last paragraph of the novel perhaps supports such a claim:

When day broke the following day it broke on a canoe aimlessly floating down the river. And in the canoe tied together back to back with their feet tied to the seats of the canoe, were Okolo and Tuere. Down they floated from one bank of the river to the other like debris, carried by the current. Then the canoe was drawn into a whirlpool. It spun round and round and was slowly drawn into the core and finally disappeared. And the water rolled over as if nothing had happened. (p.127)

The ease and clarity with which the third-person narrator handles this sad event is a sharp contrast to the confusion that the reader has witnessed so far. Community endures in spite of all its shortcomings and it is this endurance, and not Okolo's rather naive approach to tradition, which shows signs of hope. No one doubts his moral earnestness but it seems that he is as irrelevant as some of the new things which he so vigorously opposes.

Okara's use of language thus presents a paradox. He muddles it in order to clarify the theme. The 'translations' are better than those of Armah in *Two Thousand Seasons* but they are not an end in themselves. Critics who praise him for finding an idiom which combines the 'devices of his native language with Modern English syntax' do not do him much justice, for the combination of such odd phrases as 'hunger-killing beauty,' 'wrong-doing inside,' 'inside smelling with anger,' 'surface-water-things' and all the numerous misapplied proverbs which run concurrently with such fine passages of beautiful prose as that in the paragraph just quoted, do not reveal a contented implied author. On the contrary, the babelish language is a measure of the modernist anguish of both the third-person narrator and of Okolo who is the main narrator of the story. As with characterisation, Okara's management of point of view works by implication. The reader can only imagine what might have been if he is able, as Okolo cannot, to survive the chaos.

Okara's management of setting in *The Voice* is convincing. He manipulates landscape to suit the emotions of the 'characters' and it works best at this symbolic level, but consciousness of a specific, recognisable environment is also carefully maintained. The village of Amatu is identified by its palm trees, its nearby forest, its drums, and by its huts with mat doors. The reader is also reminded of the gatherings in Chief Izongo's compound. Similarly, the town of Amatu is identified by its streets, and by 'honking' cars, by 'eating houses' and the Constable on his beat. It can be said that Okara successfully localises the characters in an environment within which they can act out their stories. As Okolo moves from village to town and back the reader notices the care with which these two communities are delineated, but since both communities are corruptions of an ideal, they both are raised to the level of symbols and thus stand for more than their specific descriptions allow.

The novel is marked by several observation points such as Okolo's window already mentioned. These guideposts help to establish Okolo as the novel's main observer of the events but they also provide the setting from which these events derive their significance. Many of the activities in the first part of the novel, for instance, take place in or around Tuere's hut which is both a specific, geographically identifiable place, and a symbol of the community's abuse of tradition. She has been condemned to this hut near the forest because the people claim that she is a witch. Yet her fate and that of Okolo have become so identical that it is obvious there is more to it than the community is prepared to admit. Okara sets the scene in symbolic terms:

> As Okolo stood thus speaking with his inside, a voice entered his inside asking him to bring some firewood from the corner of the hut. With a start, he moved towards the corner with hands extended in front. Soon his hands touched the wall. Then he lowered them slowly until he touched the splinters of firewood propped against the wall. He took them and moved back. As he moved back unseen hands took the firewood from his hands and crossed them on the embers. Then there were more blowings. Then suddenly a twin flame shot up. The twin flame going into one another and becoming one, grew long and short, spread, twisted and danced, devouring the essence of the firewood like passion. And the face of Tuere was satisfaction, for her breath and shadow had gone into the flame. She remained kneeling before the dancing flame with face intent, looking at the flame, looking at what is behind the flame, the root of the flame. (p.33)

The effort to light a fire in a dark hut is realistically portrayed, but, as the twin flame shoots up, it becomes clear that this scene symbolically unites Okolo and Tuere whose face now beams with satisfaction because, as she says, 'her breath and shadow (had) gone into the flame.' It is possible to see the firewood as the tradition whose 'essence' is now being 'devoured' by the twin flame. Tuere's desire to see what is behind the flame, the root of the flame, coincides with the desire of Okolo to understand the meaning of 'it.' This scene also highlights the paradox in the novel because it is the flame which symbolises both characters that also destroys them. What they enact in the hut foreshadows their fate in a community which no longer appreciates their search for meaning. The common humanity which has produced their flame is lost by the world outside and as Okolo surrenders to the mob the reader is treated to an evocative setting in which sub-human creatures dominate:

> The people snapped at him like angry dogs snapping at bones. They carried him in silence like the silence of ants carrying a crumb of jam or fishbone. They put him down and dragged him past thatched houses that in the dark looked like pigs with their snouts in the ground; pushed and dragged him past mud walls with pitying eyes; pushed and dragged him past concrete walls with concrete eyes; pushed and dragged him along the waterside like soldier ants with their prisoner. They pushed and dragged him in panting silence, broken only by an owl hooting from the darkness of the orange tree in front of Chief Izongo's house. (pp.38–39)

The inhumanity of the community is evoked in this scene in which houses look like 'pigs with their snouts in the ground.' The passage also shows how Okara successfully transmutes specific details about the environment such as the thatched houses with mud walls, the yams, the waterside and the owl, into symbols. The reader gets a good picture of a village setting but attention is also drawn to the inhumanity and superstition that are part of the village of Amatu. The unequal relationship between Okolo and his community is also highlighted; the 'beasts' overwhelm the silent, helpless, Okolo. *The Voice* sometimes reads like a novel of terror and in scenes such as the one quoted above, this terror manifests itself through external violence. In the city of Sologa such terror is depicted in the mind of Okolo:

> His thoughts in his inside began to fly in his inside darkness like frightened birds hither, thither, homeless... Then the flying thoughts

drew his hand but the hands did not belong to him, it seemed. So Okolo on the cold, cold floor lay with his body as soft as an overpounded foo foo. So Okolo lay with his eyes open wide in the rock-like darkness staring, staring. (p.76–77)

The terror of this darkness 'expands his head' until he begins to touch objects within the cell. What he touches is a skull but no one will believe him and his terror only intensifies. The town turns out to be a worse form of terror than the village from where he was exiled. But even in the description of this state of terror vignettes of village life can be recognised. Okolo's body, for instance, is 'as soft as an over-pounded foo foo.' Earlier we learn that 'his legs were as heavy as a canoe full of sand.' Such subtle hints give the reader a feel of the community which is being studied. The people gather in the city in the same ways as they do in the village and Okara's description highlights the similarities:

> Night had fallen and in one of the unpaved streets in the slum areas of Sologa the darkness was more than darkness because it had been forgotten. In the forgotten street stood a house with corrugated iron sheet walls and roof held together with nails and sticks. And in the house, sitting round an oil lamp, were the mother-in-law and her son, Ebiere, the bride; and her brother, and a group of men and old women. (p.107)

The oil lamp, the rickety building, and the crowd which has assembled to 'try' Okolo are reminders of his previous experiences in Amatu; indeed, this trial is a prelude to the final trial in Amatu in which Okolo (with Tuere) is condemned to death.

The Voice ends where it began, in the village of Amatu:

> The drums were beating in Amatu. They had been beating bad rhythms since the finishing of the day and the night had fallen. It was a night that the moon did not appear and it was darkness, proper darkness. Still the drums continued to beat in the compound of Izongo. And the people continued to dance, the men and women knowing nothing, dancing like ants round a lamp hung on a pole. They continued to dance drink and eat goat meat, for today was the day to remember the day Okolo left the town. (p.113)

The village lives, but only just. The rhythms of their drums are 'bad rhythms' and they dance like ants round a lamp hung on a pole. On such a moonless night, the narrator implies, the idea of a dance in the Chief's compound is absurd. But things have changed; the Chief now wears 'a black suit with brown shoes and on his head a pith helmet in the dark night.' It can be assumed that such a grotesque appearance and other perversions of 'tradition' heighten the antagonism between Okolo and the community. In outlining the details of this antagonism, however, the narrator pays greater attention to the community than to Okolo who himself, as narrator, adds to our knowledge of his community. One of the messengers significantly remarks that 'Okolo has no wife, no children and his father and mother are dead' (p.25). No wonder, then, that he should go the lengths he does in search of a community. What he finds is chaotic but dominating and the reader is not surprised that he feels terrorised and is eventually eliminated by it.

Okara's modernism gives the reader a full picture of a world at odds with itself. As we move with Okolo, his modernist rebel, from his window, to Tuere's hut, through the boat, and into the town, we come across various traits which contribute to our knowledge of the novel's main character.

Okara is equally a story-teller in the real sense of the word. *The Voice* shows an awareness of audience and is everywhere marked by a sense of performance. It has, as Palmer remarks, 'the directness of folk-lore, the mystery of a fairy-tale and the symbolism of a fable.'[42] As in a folk-tale the characters 'live' and act their stories rather than just tell them. The reader is able to recognise the various traits of the community by the way the numerous individuals present them. The novel begins on an evocative note:

> Some of the townsmen said Okolo's eyes were not right, his head was not correct. This they said was the result of his knowing too much book, walking too much in the bush, and others said it was due to his staying too long alone by the river.
>
> So the town of Amatu talked and whispered; so the world talked and whispered. Okolo had no chest they said. (p.23)

The town of amatu is evoked as a purveyor of gossip. This sense of common knowledge is a hallmark of the folktale where most of the events relayed are usually assumed to be part of a well-known tradition. Everyone in the community knows about Okolo and his 'dangerous' search for 'it.' That is why they all come out in large numbers to arrest him when he takes refuge in Tuere's hut.

No one, it appears, wants to miss any of the excitement generated by Okolo. Thus his pursuit is started by three messengers whom Okara introduces as if on stage, then the group is expanded to include many people that they all can only be identified as 'voices,' 'hands,' and 'feet.' As the story progresses, however, it is possible to identify many of the voices. Tuere, for instance, notices the voice of Seitu who was responsible for her banishment. But the people love a performance whether as spectators or as actors. Chief Izongo's gestures which sometimes tell them to laugh, scream or simply keep quiet, suit many of them, but when they do get a chance they prove to be very good performers, as Abadi, the Chief's spokesman shows. The scene in chapter seven where each of the Elders takes pride in enacting their praise names shows them at their best.

It can be argued that *The Voice* has no continuous line in its narrative and that the novel, typically modernist, presents a series of dramatic episodes performed by the various 'characters.' The structure of the book supports this argument. There are constant shifts from village to town. The first two chapters take place in Amatu and end with the expulsion of Okolo. Chapter three is the boat scene where the curious but lively passengers enact what may be seen as a microcosm of the activities of the larger communities of Amatu and Sologa. Chapter four takes the reader back to Amatu, specifically to Chief Izongo's compound where a mini-celebration is already going on to mark the departure of Okolo. The reader is again taken to Sologa in chapter five where Okolo's other nightmare begins, only to be returned to the village in chapter six where a bigger celebration is being planned by the Chief. There is another boat-scene (chapter ten) which records the return of Okolo. The remaining chapters dramatize Okolo's final return and its consequences. These shifts sustain the reader's interest. Repetition as used in the other novels discussed above also enhances performance in the novel. Mention has already been made of the numerous voices in the story for which Okolo's voice is no match. The reader's attention is also drawn to 'spoken words' (eleven times), and 'teaching words' (twelve times) all of which are reminders to the reader of the significance of speech in the novel. Repetition is a pervasive feature of the novel. The following passage is typical:

> Okolo opened his eyes and looked in front of him. The people were sleeping. He looked towards his left. The people were sleeping. He looked towards the right. The people were sleeping... Okolo at the rising, falling rising, falling cheeks looked. They were rising, falling, rising, falling, like the cheeks of a croaking frog. (p.58)

The scene reveals Okolo as the only 'watcher' and the technique of repetition emphasises this role which enables Okolo to recall and describe accurately the words and actions of the people in the boat.

Proverbs and wise-sayings, though largely but consciously misused, form part of the repertoire of the community and for the Elders, and sometimes for Okolo, they are a useful way of encapsulating the essence of the group. They, however, use them as badly as they use their drums and their dance. But in each case these shortcomings are highlighted to show what has been lost by the people. If they can no longer dance properly it is because they have become too busy to recapture the rhythm.

The title of *The Voice* suggests a situation of dominance on the part of the titular character over the events which take place in the novel. This is, however, not the case because Okolo is only one voice among many voices; he merely provokes the other voices into action during which he becomes a mere 'watcher' or 'hearer.' Okolo, like the reader, watches and analyzes the community of the novel. The eighty odd voices provide the basis for an assessment of the group and the initial response which does not need revision is one of anarchy. Criticism of the novel has so far centred on Okolo and his predicament and it has missed the central focus which is the community. The character of Okolo is a tool which should help the reader to understand the 'tradition' which Okara is trying to describe. It is true that what appears in the novel can hardly be called a community but this is precisely the point of the story: Where has the community gone?

Okara has made efforts to recover his tradition but he has also shown how difficult such retrieval can be. Nowhere is this better shown than in his use of language which can at best be likened to the tower of Babel. Okara has been praised for being able to reconcile the 'syntax' of a traditional African language with the European form of the novel but this is only half the story. The effort is unsuccessful but the narrator shows us that the lack of success is deliberate. It is meant to show the present chaos in the society and the difficulty which the Modern African experiences when he tries to recover the past. Okara argues that it is community that endures, not brave individuals within it, no matter how earnest or well-intentioned.

An effective use of setting gives the community a credible and realistic environment. The reader also finds that background description quickly rises to the status of symbol and the place becomes more important for what it stands for than its current diminishing form. Subtle methods are, however, introduced to give the reader a feel of what village life used to look like before it was violated by the new-found gods of gold, iron, and concrete. The reader comes to know this through reminiscences of individuals such as Okolo who keeps referring to his father as a standard bearer of the tradition. Even the corrupt and apathetic elders do sometimes show what it was like. They do misapply their proverbs and wise saying but they are still reminders, for Okolo at least, of the 'good old days.' The novel is also told in the manner of folk-tales and it is successful in its attempt to draw the attention of an audience. Participation is required since each 'character' appears only in a group. Okolo's isolation is more a psychological, self-inflicted, affair than a dramatic one. No one leaves him alone even if this seems to be what he demands.

The Voice differs from the novels of Chinua Achebe and Ayi Kwei Armah which have been discussed under the title of 'the communal perspective' but it bears resemblances with them as well. It differs from the other novels because it defines its community by implication and suggestion. There are, however, similarities with Achebe's *Things Fall Apart* and *Arrow of God* in its use of language as a theme. The language of the community does not come out as clearly as it does in Achebe but this is because Okara seems to suggest that such a retrieval is neither possible nor desirable. Characters in all the novels by these three writers always have to give way to a large community figure which, in Achebe, more than in the others, reveals a shrewdness and a humanity which demands the reader's attention. This technique adds a new dimension to characterisation and the management of point of view in the modern novel.

CHAPTER SEVEN

CONCLUSION

In *Comparative Literary Studies: An Introduction*, S.S. Prawer defines 'placing' as:

> The mutual illumination of several texts or series of texts, considered side by side; the greater understanding we derive from juxtaposing a number of (frequently very different) works, authors and literary traditions.[1]

Placing is the essence of this study. Thirteen novels by British, American and African writers are described in the preceding chapters with the aim of allowing them to illuminate one another and the modernist's handling of point of view is used as an instrument to achieve this aim.

The communal perspective discussed in the final chapter shows that views about character in the novel need to be revised to account for a human referent which is larger than the individuals to whom we have become accustomed. Such attributes as 'proper name,' 'physical and moral nature' need to be transferred from the individual to the community. Rather than ask who is he? and what does he stand for? We should instead ask who are they? And what do they stand for? These questions suggest a revolutionary approach to an understanding of the presentation of character in some novels written by Africans. With such questions in mind we may no longer accuse Armah, for example, of failure in presenting character in *Two Thousand Seasons* since the dominant character in the novel is the community of Anoa and individuals in the novel are only traits of this character. To recognise this method is to notice at once that ideas held about novels such as *Things Fall Apart* and *Arrow of God* are suspect. Umuaro and Umuofia are not just backgrounds against which the tragedies of Okonkwo and Ezeulu are enacted. Both communities are characters in the novels.

Achebe creates them as characters and the reader must understand them in order to appreciate the proper roles of Okonkwo and Ezeulu. It is justifiable, as critics have done so far, to see these characters as central to both novels but such a view should not make us forget the protagonists, Umuofia and Umuaro, who upstage both these men. This argument can be extended to Gabriel Okara's *The Voice* where Okolo serves a similar function to that of Okonkwo and Ezeulu. In all the four novels the communities tower above individual characters.

This is the unique contribution the novel in Africa has brought to modern fiction. In order to appreciate this innovation, we need to compare their novels in this mode with the novels of a writer like Faulkner who is as concerned with his folk as Achebe, Armah and Okara. Much as Faulkner's community leaves lasting impressions on the reader it is still a chorus, a background against which the inimitable characters, such as Thomas Sutpen, may be understood. Faulkner shares with these novelists a need to extract value out of a dubious heritage but where he defines these values, such as honour, truth and respectability, through individual sensibilities and enacts their drama as they confront their communities, the African novelists define similar values through a powerful communal presence displayed in Achebe especially by a skilful use of language and setting.

What we are led to know is a people not individuals. We may further appreciate this technique if we see how in Achebe's other novels this sense of community is lost and attempts by the characters to enforce it fail. The Umuofia Progressive Union in *No Longer at Ease*, for instance, is a pale, almost unrecognisable shadow of its past. In 'those days' the community had character but things have changed and these changes are reflected in the quality of the novels; it is not surprising that many readers miss the vibrant communities of Umuofia and Umuaro.

The critic, however, can go beyond this distinctive feature and establish the common ground between the African novelist and his British and American counterpart. The process reveals similarities and differences in theme and technique between the novelists which should make the novels on both 'sides' worth re-reading. The Western reader for whom the discovery of African literature, according to Thomas Hale, may be as 'unexpected as the appearance of an extra-terrestrial being at the podium of an ACLA meeting to compare Martian and Venusian epics'[2] is offered an opportunity to re-read African novels along with more familiar novels. For the African literary nationalists for whom the notion of borrowing conceptual tools constitute a blow to their pride, this work represents our common interest in establishing the contribution that the African novel has made to world fiction.

The tendency of modernist writers to break with all traditions, has an attraction for the African novelist who is strategically placed to witness what may be described as the apocalyptic moment of transition into the new. By 1958 when *Things Fall Apart* was published, modernism may be said to have passed its point of intensity but for the African novelist, colonialism became that apocalyptic moment that had spurred writers of Europe and America a few decades back. Consequently, for them, modernism is far from exhausted.

Its unique response to chaos is just what they need to address the African condition. It can indeed be argued that for most contemporary artists, modernism is still their essential art and that African novelists are engaged in writing that is 'fully contemporary.'[3] This book tries to show that a profound interaction and appropriation has taken place and the African novelist deserves to be read more seriously as an artist who is accessible to all readers. There is, as Rene Wellek argues, 'a common humanity that makes all art, however remote in time and place, accessible to us.' Wellek suggests further that:

> We can rise beyond the limitations of traditional tastes into a realm, if not of absolute, then of universal art, varied in its manifestations but

still amenable to description, analysis, interpretation and finally inevitably, to evaluation.[4]

The state of African poetics so far suggests that we will do well to heed Wellek's call.

NOTES

1   I might add here that I am aware of the new paths literary criticism has taken in recent years. Modernism itself is probably out of fashion with the advent of post-modernism, of deconstruction, post-structuralism, semiology, etc. I still hold though that many of the basic ideas and motifs of modernism were distilled over an extended time-span and in a variety of different circumstances and are therefore still useful. My periodization starts from Henry James's novel of 1890 to African novelists who are still writing. The fact that similarities abound show that we have not yet heard the last word on modernism and that the possibilities which it offers are not yet exhausted. Needless to add that this study is of the African novel written in English. Its frame of reference includes an international phenomena but it is impossible to extend this work to cover writers of French-speaking and Portuguese-speaking Africa. I hope though that its essence will be applicable to this arm of our literature.

2   Malcolm Bradbury and James McFarlane, eds., *Modernism*, (London: Penguin, 1976), p.26.

3   Cited in Neil McEwan, *Africa and the Novel* (London: Macmillan 1983, p. 1. McEwan's book is very useful. He remains one of the few critics who argue that African writers

are innovative in their use of technique in the novel, a view which is clearly not yet common.

4   Kole Omotoso, *The Form of the African Novel: A Critical Essay* (Akure: Fagbamigbe Publishers, 1979), p.V.

5   Theo Vincent, 'Black Aesthetics and Criticism of African Literature.' *West African Journal of Modern Languages* Vol. 14, No. 1 (1976) p.23.

6   Modernism is discemible in many other African novels. This is only a representative sample.

7   Three main approaches are discernible, the 'Eurocentric,' 'the Afro-centric' and 'the syncretic' each approach curiously arguing for the uniqueness of the African writer. Simon Gikandi's *Reading the African Novel* (London: James Currey and Heinemann, 1987) is a new book though that is refreshingly different from these 'approaches.'

8   If there is a modernist identification parade these five writers would stand out as useful samples of the tendencies that are discussed in this book.

9   Percy Lubbock, *The Craft of Fiction* (London: Jonathan Cape, 1921) p.251.

10   Gerald Genette, *Narrative Discourse* (Oxford: Basil Blackwell, 1982) p.246.

11   Susan Sniader Lanser, *The Narratiev Act: Point of View in Prose Fiction* (New Jersey: Princeton University Press, 1981) p.60.

12   Boris Uspensky, *A Poetics of Composition: The Structure of the Artistic Text and Typology of a Compositional Form* trans. V. Zavarin and Susan Wittig, (Berkeley: University of California Press, 1973) p.127.

13   *The Art of Fiction* ed. R.P. Blackmur (London: Charles Scribner's Press, 1934) p.141.

14   Ibid., 186.

15 R.W. Short, 'Some Critical Terms of Henry James.' *PMLA* L & V (1950) pp.668-679.

16 Information obtained from James Gibbs through correspondence.

17 Sallie Sears, *The Negative Imagination: Form and Perspective in the Novels of Henry James.* (Ithaca: Cornell University Press, 1968) p.39.

18 Derek Elders, 'James Ngugi: A Grain of Wheat.' *African Literature Today* No. 1 (1968) p.52.

19 *African Writers Talking* eds. Dennis Dueden and Cosmo Pieterse, (London: Heinemann, 1972)

20 Ernest Baker, *The History of the English Novel,* ix (New York: Barnes and Noble, 1936) p.257.

21 *The Tragic Muse* p.510 and *The Interpreters* p.178.

22 *Palaver: Interviews with five African writers.* (Austin: African and Afro-American Research Institute, 1972) p.61.

23 Richard Priebe, 'Kofi Awoonor's *This Earth, My Brother....* as an African Dirge.' *Benin Review* 1, (1975) p.95.

24 Kofi Awoonor, 'The Poem , the Poet and the Human Condition.' *Asemka*, No. 5 (1979) p.20.

25 George Moore, *The Lake* (London: Heinemann, 1905) p.334.

26 G. Jean Aubury, *Joseph Conrad: Life and Letters* (Garden City: Doubleday, 1927) p.204.

27 *African Writers Talking* Op. Cit. p.124.

28 Thomas Moser, *Joseph Conrad: Achievement and Decline* (Connecticut: Anchor Books, 1957) p.43.

29 Warren Beck, 'William Faulkner's Style' in *Four Decades of Criticism* ed. Linda Wagner, (Lansing: University of Michigan Press, 1973), p.153.

30 Richard Poirer, 'Strange Gods in Jefferson' in *Twentieth Century Views on Absalom, Absalom!* ed. Arnold Goldman, (Englewood Cliffs, New Jersey: 1971), p.14.

31 Albert Guerard, *The Triumph of the Novel: Dickens, Dostoevsky Faulkner* (New York: Oxford University Press, 1976), p.322.

32 *Why Are We So Blest*; p.231.

33 Richard Moreland, *Faulkner and Modernism: Rereading and Rewriting.* (Madison, Wisconson: The University of Wisconson Press, 1990), p.4.

34 *Absalom, Absalom!* p.6.

35 M.J.C. Echeruo, *Poets, Prophets and Professors* Inaugural Lecture, (Ibadan; 1977), p.15.

36 Chinua Achebe, The Novelist as Teacher' in *Common wealth Literature* ed. John Press, (London: Heinemann, 1965), p.279.

37 Mark Schorer, 'Technique as Discovery' in The Theory of the Novel, ed. Philip Stevick, (New York: The Free Press, 1967), p.66.

38 Stephen Cohan, 'Readable Character,' in *Novel: A Forum on Ficion* Vol. 17, No.1 (1983) pp.6-7.

39 Shloith Rimman Kenan, *Narrative Fiction: Contemporary Poetics* (London: Methuen, 1983), p.64.

40 For detailed discussions of the politics of these novels see Arthur Shatto Gakwandi, *The Novel and Contemporary Experience in Africa* (London: Heinemann, 1977) and Abdul Jan Mohammed, *Manichean Aesthetics: The Politics of Literature in Colonial Africa* (Amherst: The University of Massachusetts Press, 1983, 1988). Generally the study of the politics of the novel has been very detailed and useful. Gikandi's (1987) recent study is one of the few studies that treat in detail the narrative strategies of some African novels. He gives a few pages to a discussion of modernist tendencies in the African novel. If this study is heavily biased towards technical strategies in the novels at the expense of their history and

politics, it is in a way redressing a bias that already exists in the field.

41   Bill Ashcroft et al., *The Empire Writes Back: Theory and practice in Post-Colonial Literatures*. (London: Routledge, 1989), p.37.

42   Ibid., p.38.

43   Chinua Achebe, *Morning Yet on Creation Day* op. cit., p.54.

CHAPTER TWO: THE DRAMATISED PERSPECTIVE

1   Mark Kinkead-Weekes, *Samuel Richardson: Dramatic Novelist* (London: Methuen, 1973), p.413.

2   Edwin Muir, *The Structure of the Novel* (London: Chatto and Windus, 1928, 1957) pp.59-60.

3   Eldred Jones, *The Writing of Wole Soyinka* (London: Heinemann 1983) 189-200).

4   *Some Observations on the Art of Narrative*, (London: Home and Van Thal, 1946) p.12.

5   Cited in *Henry James and the Comic Form*, (Ann Arbor: Universitty of Michigan Press, 1975), p.154

6   *Richardson: Dramatic Novelist* op. cit., p.411.

7   *Art of Fiction* op cit., p.171.

8   Cited in F.O. Matthiessen, *Henry James: The Major Phase* (New York: Oxford University Press, 1963), p.17.

9   R.W. Short, op. cit., p.675.

10   *The Air of Reality: New Essays on Henry James*, ed. John Goode. (London: Methuen, 1872), p.107.

11   'The Interpreters: A Form of Criticism,' in *Critical Perspectives* ed. John Gibbs, (London: Heinemann, 1982), p.229.

12　Cited in Miriam Allott, *Novelist on the Novel* (London: Routledge and Kegan Paul, 1965) p.296.

13　*Novelists on the Novel* op. cit., p.181.

14　*Time and the Novel* (New York: Humanities Press, 1972) p.63.

15　*Myth, Literature and the African World* (Cambridge: Cambridge University Press, 1976) p.10.

16　'Simple Novels and Simplistic Criticism...' *Asemka* No.5 (1979), p.32.

17　'The Interpreters: A Form of Criticism,' op. cit., p.219.

18　*Henry James and the Comic Vision* op. cit., p.156.

CHAPTER THREE: THE INWARD PERSPECTIVE

1　Kofi Awoonor, 'Interview' in *Kunapipi* vol.1 No. 2 (1979) p.78.

2　Virginia Woolf on Proust in Reuben Brower, 'The Novel as a Poem,' *The Interpretation of Narrative: Theory and Practice* ed. Morton W. Bloomfield (Cambridge: Harvard University Press, 1970). p.244.

3　Achebe, Soyinka, Armah have among others depicted this type of character.

4　Kofi Awoonor, 'The Poem, the Poet and the Human Condition,' *Asemka* No. 5 (September 1970), p.21.

5　Virginia Woolf op. cit., p.80.

6　Shiv Kumar, *Bergson and the Stream-of-Consciousness Novel* (London: Blackie, 1962), p.25

7　Susan Gorsky, 'The Central Shadow: Characterisation in The Waves,' *Modern Fiction Studies*, 18:3 (1977) p.450.

8   In A.A. Mendilow, *Time and the Novel*, (New York: Humanities Press, 1972), p.174.

9   *Palaver: Interview with Five African Writers*, op. cit. p.61

10   Kofi Awoonor, 'Comes the Voyager at Last,' *Okike*, 4 (1975).

11   *Palaver* op. cit., p.60.

12   Kofi Awoonor, *The Breast of the Earth* (New York: Doubleday, 1975) p.347.

13   Ibid., pp.352-353.

CHAPTER FOUR: THE MULTIPLE PERSPECTIVE I

1   Umberto Eco, *The Role of the Reader: Explorations in the Semiotics of Texts* (London: Hutchinson, 1979), p.47.

2   Lewis Nkosi, for instance, begins a study of *A Grain of Wheat* by asking if it is a Socialist novel. His answer is in the affirmative. Other Marxist critics such as John Chileshe similarly seek to impose a single meaning on Ngugi's novels.

3   Information confirmed in discussions with Ngugi himself.

4   It is quite possible to dispense with Captain Mitchell's accounts as they do not add much to the reader's knowledge about the characters and the situations they describe.

5   Eugene Ted Boyle, *Symbol and Meaning in the Fiction of Joseph Conrad* (The Hague: Mouton, 1965), p.175.

6   *Symbol and Meaning*, op. cit., p.164

7   *Symbol and Meaning*, op. cit., p.177

8   This question is implied in much of the novel.

9   Gerald Moore, *Twelve African Writers* (London: Hutchinson, 1980), p.285.

10   Eustace Palmer, *The Growth of the African Novel* (London: Heinemann, 1979), p.294.

11   Douglas Killam, *An Introduction to the Writings of Ngugi* (London: Heinemann, 1980), p.100.

12   I am thinking here in Wayne Booth's terms in *Rhetoric of Fiction* (Chicago: Chicago University Press, 1961).

13   D. Killam, op. cit., p.107.

CHAPTER FIVE: THE MULTIPLE PERSPECTIVE II

1   Karl Zink, 'William Faulkner: Form as Experience,' *South Atlantic Quarterly*, Vol. LIII (1954), p.382.

2   Donald Kartiganer, *The Fragile Thread: Form in Faulkner's Novels* (Amherst: The University of Massachusetts Press, 1979), p.147.

3   In Malcolm Cowley, *The Faulkner-Cowley File: Letters and Memoirs 1944-62* (London: Chatto and Windus, 1966) p.141.

CHAPTER SIX: THE COMMUNAL PERSPECTIVE

1   The Critical Perspectives volume edited by Bernth Linfors and Lyynette Innes is a record of some of the best studies of Achebe's novels but none of the writers included in the book mentions Achebe's innovation. It is more fashionable to see Okonkwo and Ezeulu as tragic heroes with flaws.

2   Nelson Wattie, 'The Community as Protagonist in the Novels of Chinua Achebe and Witi Thimaera,' in *Individual and*

Community in Commmonwealth Literature ed. Daniel Massa, Malta, The University Press, 1979, p.70.

3   Lewis Grassic Gibbon, *Sunset Song* (London: Longman, 1971), 275. I am grateful to Grahame Smith for drawing my attention to the possible links between *Sunset Song* and Achebe's novels.

4   Roger Fowler, *Linguistics and the Novel* (London: Methuen, 1977), p.35.

5   See Lindfors and L. Innes, op. cit. for a detailed analysis of these traits.

6   Kenneth L. Schmitz, 'Community: The Elusive Unity,' in *The Review of Metaphysics* vol. XXXVII No.2 (December 1983). p.243.

7   Most studies of the novel see Okonkwo as representative of his clan and thus read his end as equivalent to the downfall of Umuofia. See, for example, Eustace Palmer, *An Introduction to the African Novel* (London: Heinemann, 1971) p.54.

8   See Chapter IV for a discussion of Sutpen's character.

9   Gerald Moore, *Twelve African Writers* (London: Hutchinson, 1980), p.127.

10   David Caroll, *Chinua Achebe* (London: Macmillan, 1980), p.94

11   See Lindfors and Innes, op. cit., pp.170-245

12   See discussion on Okara below.

13   Eustace Palmer, *The Growth of the African Novel* (London: Heinemann, 1978), p.100.

14   Neil McEwan, *Africa and the Novel*, op. cit., p.23

15   Charles Nnolim in 'Folk Tradition in Achebe's Novels,' *Ariel*, vol. 14, No.1 (January 1983) has analysed this tale in a similar way.

16   Quoted in Nnolim, op. cit., p.47.

17   In Lindfors and Lynette Innes, op. cit., p.77.

18   Richard Moreland, op. cit., p.78.

19   In Lindfors and Lynette Innes, op cit, p.240.

20   I have borrowed this idea from Bradbury and McFarlane who see the process as a high point of modernist writing.

21   Eustace Palmer, *The Growth of the African Novel*, op cit, p.234.

22   Dan S. Izevbaye, 'Ayi Kwei Armah and the 'I' of the Beholder' in B. King and K. Ogungbesan eds. *A Celebration of Black and African Writing* (Oxford Zaria: OUP ABUP, 1975), p.232.

23   Paul Hansen ed. *Visionaries and their Apocalypses* (London: SPCK, 1983) p.23.

24   Isidore Okpewho, 'Armah's *Two Thousand Seasonss*' in *African Literature Today*, 13 (1983) 13; Emmanuel Ngara, *Stylistic Criticism and the African Novel* (London: Heinemann, 1982), p.134

25   Palmer, op. cit., p.234

26   Richard Bauman, *Verbal Art as Performance* (Mass: Newbury House Publishers, 1977), p.10.

27   Ibid., p.16.

28   Ibid., p.17.

29   The publishing record of the novel has been well-documented by Armah himself in the essay, 'Larsony or Fiction as Criticism of Fiction,' *Asemka*, 4 (1976) pp.1-14.

30   In Bauman, op. cit., p.17

31   All Armah's novels have this idea either as an implicit or as an explicit theme.

32   Gabriel Okara, *The Voice* (London: Heinemann, 1970; first published, 1964). All references are to the 1970 edition.

33   'The Way' is Armah's all-embracing term for the 'essence' of the African. It is used ad nauseam in *Two Thousand Seasons*.

34   In a recent study, 'Community: The Elusive Unity,' Kenneth L. Schmitz defines it in exactly the same terms as Okara and

Armah apply it. See *The Review of Metaphysics*, Vol XXXVII, No.2 (1983), pp.243-264.

35 Emmanuel Obiechina, *Culture and Society in the West African Novel* (Cambridge: Cambridge University Press, 1975), 147-9. Eustace Palmer, *An Introduction to the African Novel* (London: Heinemann, 1972), 155-167. Solomon Iyasere, *African Literature Today*, Vol. 12 (1982), p.11.

36 Emmanuel Ngara, *Stylistic Criticism and the African Novel* (London: Heinemann, 1982), p.52.

37 The 'Sameeness' which Iyasere has observed is only on one plane, their new found gods. They do, however, display appetites which are remarkably different even in this aspect. See especially the boat ride.

38 See below for a further discussion of language in the novel.

39 K. Schmitz, op cit., p.243.

40 See Schmitz, op. cit p.256.

41 Palmer, op cit, p.156.

42 Ibid, p.166.

CHAPTER SEVEN: CONCLUSION

1 S.S. Prawer, *Comparative Literature Studies: An Introduction* (London: Duckworth, 1973) p.144

2 Thomas A. Hale, 'Africa and the West: Close Encounters of a Literary Kind.' *Comparative Literature Studies* Vol.20, No. 3 (1983) p.262.

3 Neil M'Ewan op. cit., p.1.

4 Rene Wellek, *The Attack on Literature and Other Essays* (Brighton: The Harvester Press, 1980) p.63.

BIBLIOGRAPHY

The place of publication is London unless otherwise stated.

Ayi Kwei Armah, *Fragments* (Heinemann, 1974. First published New York: Houghton Mifflin, 1969)

_____. *Why Are We So Blest?* (Heinemann, 1974)

_____. *Two Thousand Seasons?* (Heinemann, 1979. First published in Nairobi: East African Literature Bureau, 1973).

_____. *The Healers* (Heinemann, 1979. First published Nairobi: East African Literature Bureau, 1978).

Chinua Achebe, *Things Fall Apart* (Heinemann, 1958)

_____. *Arrow of God* (Heinemann 1964).

Gabriel Okara, *The Voice,* (Heinemann, 1964).

Henry James, *The Tragic Muse* (Macmillan, 1890)

_____. *The Ambassadors* (Methuen 1903).

James Joyce, *A Portrait of the Artist as a Young Man* (Jonathan Cape, 1916).

Joseph Conrad, *Nostromo* (J.M. Dent & Sons, 1904).

_____. *Under Western Eyes* (Methuen, 1911).

Kofi Awoonor, *This Earth, My Brother* (Heinemann, 1972).

Ngugi Wa Thion'o, *A Grain of Wheat* (Heinemann, 1967).

_____. *Petals of Blood* (Heinemann, 1977).

William Faulkner, *As I Lay Dying* (Chatto and Windus, 1935).

_____. *Absalom, Absalom!* (Random House, 1936).

Wole Soyinka, *The Interpreters* (Heinemann, 1970. First published by Andre Deutsch, 1965)

_____. *Season of Anomy* (Thomas Nelsonn, 1980. First published by Rex Collings Ltd., 1973).

Virginia Woolf, *The Waves* (The Hogarth Press, 1931).

I BOOKS

Chinua Achebe, *Morning Yet on Creation Day* (Heinemann, 1975).

Robert M. Adams, *James Joyce: Common Sense and Beyond* (New York: Random House, 1966).

A. Owen Aldridge, *The Reemergence of World Literature: A Study of Asia and the West* (Newark: The University of Delaware Press, 1986).

J.W. Aldridge, *Time to Murder and Create: The Contemporary Novel in Crisis* (New York: McKay, 1966).

Walter Allen, *The English Novel: A Short Critical History* (Phoenix House, 1954)

_____. *Traditional and the Dream: The English and American Novel from the Thirties to Our Time* (Phoenix House, 1964).

_____. *Six Great Novelists: Defoe, Fielding, Scott, Dickents, Stevenson, Conrad* (Hamish Hamilton, 1965).

Miriam Allot, *Novelists on the Novel* (Routledge and Kegan Paul, 1959).

Robert Alter, *Partial Magic: The Novel as a Self-conscious Genre* (Berkeley: University of California Press, 1975).

Guy Armirthanayagan & S.C. Harrex, *Only Connect* (Adelaide: Centre for Research in the New Literatures, 1982).

Bill Ashcroft, et al, *The Empire Writes Back: Theory and Practice in Post-colonial Literatures* (Routledge, 1989)

Kofi Awoonor, *The Breast of the Earth: A Survey of the History and Literature of Africa South of the Sahara* (New York: Anchor Press/Doubleday, 1975).

Ernest Baker, *The History of the English Novel* (New York: Barnes, 1936).

Richard Bauman, *Verbal Art as Performance* (Massachusetts: Newbury House Publishers, 1977).

John Barley, *The Uses of Division: Unity and Disharmony in Literature* (Chatto and Windus, 1976).

Ulli Beier, ed., *Introduction to African Literature* (Longman, 1967).

Joan Bennet, *Virginia Woolf: Her Art as a Novelist* (Cambridge University Press, 1945).

Phyllis Bentley, *Some Observations on the Art of Narrative* (Home and Van Thal, 1946).

Richard Blackmur, ed., *Henry James: The Art of the Novel* (New York: Charles Scribner's Sons, 1934).

Bernard Blackstone, *Virginia Woolf: A Commentary* (New Hogarth Press, 1949).

Joseph Blotner, *The Modern American Political Novel 1900-1960* (Austin, Texas: University of Texas Press, 1966).

Morton W. Bloomfield, ed., *The Interpretation of Narrative: Theory and Practice* (Cambridge, Massachusetts: Harvard University Press, 1970).

Wayne Booth, *The Rhetoric of Fiction* (Chicago: University of Chicago Press, 1961).

Helmut Bonheim, *The Narrative Modes: Techniques of the Short Story* (Cambridge: D.S. Brewer, 1982).

Eugene Ted Boyle, *Symbol and Meaning in the Fiction of Joseph Conrad* (The Hague: Monton, 1965).

Malcolm Bradbury, *Possibilities: Essays on the State of the Novel* (Oxford: Clarendon Press, 1973).

Nicola Bradbury, *Henry James: The Later Novels* (Oxford: Clarendon Press, 1979).

Christine Brooke-Rose, *A Rhetoric of the Unreal: Studies in Narrative and Structure Especially of the Fantastic* (Cambridge: Cambridge University Press, 1981).

_____. *Grammar of Metaphor* (Cambridge: Cambridge University Press, 1958).

Cleanth Brooks, *William Faulkner: The Yoknapatawpha County* (New Haven Yale University Press, 1964).

_____. *William Faulkner: First Encounters* (New Haven: Yale University Press, 1983).

Cleanth Brook & R.B. Heilmer, *Understanding Drama* (New York: Henry Holt and Company, 1945).

Oscar Cargill, *The Novels of Henry James* (New York: Macmillan, 1961).

David Carrol, *Chinua Achebe* (New York: Twayne, 1970. Revised Macmillan, 1980).

Wilfred Cartey, *Whispers from a Continent* (New York: Random House, 1969).

Richard Chase, *The American Novel and its Traditions* (New York: Doubleday, 1957).

Seymour Chatman, *The Later Style of Henry James* (Oxford: Blackwell, 1972).

_____. *Story and Discourse: Narrative Structure in Fiction and Film* (Ithaca: Cornell University Press, 1978).

Dorrit Cohn, *Transparent Minds: Narrative Modes for Presentating Consciousness in Fiction* (Princeton: Princeton University Press, 1978).

David Cook & Michael Okenimkpe, *Ngugi Wa Thiong'o: An Exploration of His Writings* (Heinemann, 1983).

Malcolm Cowley, *The Faukner-Cowley File: Letters and memoirs 1944-62* (Chatto and Windus, 1966).

C.B. Cox, *Joseph Conrad: The Modern Imagination* (A. Deusch, 1974).

Jean B. Craige, *Literary Relativity: An Essay on Twentieth Century narrative* (Lewisburg: Bucknell University Press, 1982).

R.S. Crane, ed., *Critics and Criticism: Ancient and Modern* (Chicago: University of Chicago Press, 1957).

I.K. Crossman, *Metaphoric Narration: The Structure and Function of Metaphors in A La Recherche du Temps Perdu* (Chapel Hill: University of North Carolina Press, 1978).

Umberto Eco, *The Role of the Reader* (Hutchinson, 1979).

Leon Edel, *The Psychological Novel: 1900-1950* (Hart-Davis, 1974).

John M. Ellis, *Narration in the German Novelle: Theory and Interpretation* (Cambridge University Press, 1974).

_____. *The Theory of Literary Criticism: A Logical Analysis* (Berkeley: University of California Press, 1974).

Una Ellis-Fermor, *The Frontiers of Drama* (Methuen, 1964).

Ruth Finnegan, *Oral Literature in Africa* (Oxford: The Clarendon Press, 1970).

E.M. Forster, *Aspects of the Novel* (Arnold, 1927).

Robert Fraser, *The Novels of Ayi Kwei Armah* (Heinemann, 1980).

Ralph Freedman, *The Lyrical Novel: Studies in Herman Hesse, Andre Gide, and Virginia Woolf* (Oxford University Press, 1963).

Alan Warren Friedman, *Multivalence: The Moral Quality of Form in the Modern Novel* (Baton Rouge: Louisiana State University Press, 1978).

Melvin Friedman, *Stream of Consciousness: A Study in Literary Method* New Haven: Yale University Press, 1955).

Arthur S. Gakwandi, *The Novel and Contemporary Experience in Africa* (Heinemann, 1977).

Peter Garret, *Scene and Symbol from George Eliot to James Joyce* (New Haven University Press, 1969).

Gerard Genette, *Narrative Discourse* (Oxford: Basil Blackwell, 1980).

Simon Gikandi, *Reading the African Novel* (James Currey and Heinemann, 1987).

Peter Glassman, *Language and Being: Joseph Conrad and the Literature of Personality* (New York: Columbia University Press, 1976).

Judith Gleason, *This Africa: Novels by West Africans in English and French* (Evanston: Universityy of Illinois Press, 1965).

Joseph Gold, *William Faulkner: A Study in Humanism, from Metaphor to Discourse* (Norman: University of Oklahoma Press, 1966).

Arnord Goldman, *The Joyce Paradox: Form and Freedom in his Fiction* (Evanston: North Western University Press, 1966).

John Goode, ed., *The Air of Reality: New Essayys on Henry James* (Methuen, 1972).

Philip Grover, *Henry James and the French Novel: A Study in Inspiration* (Paul Elek, 1973).

Albert Guerard *Conrad the Novelist* (Cambridge, Massachusetts: Harvard University Press, 1958).

_____. *The Triumph of the Novel: Dickens, Dostoevsky, Faulkner* (New York: Oxford University Press, 1976).

Andrew Gurr & Angus Calder, eds., *Writers in East Africa: Papers from a Colloquium held att the University of Nairobi, June 1971* (Nairobi: East African Literature Bureau, 1974).

Andrew Gurr & Pio Zirimu, eds., *Black Aesthetics: Papers from a Colloquium held at the University of Nairobi, June 1971* (Nairobi: East African Literature Bureau, 1973).

Frederick Gwynn and Joseph Blotner, *Faulkner in the University* (Charlottsville: University of Virginia Press, 1959).

Paul Hansen, ed., *Visionaries and their Apocalypse* (SPCK, 1983).

Barbara Hardy, *The Appropriate Form: An Essay on the Novel* (The Athlone Press, 1964).

W.J. Harvey, *Character and the Novel* (Chatto and Windus, 1965).

Jeremy Hawthorn, *Joseph Conrad: Language and Fictional Self-Consciousness* (Lincoln: The University of Nebraska Press, 1979).

David Hayman & Eric Rabkin, *Form in Fiction: an Introduction to the analysis of Narrative Prose* (New York: St. Martins Press, 1974).

Paul Hernadi, *Beyond Genre: New Directions in Literary Classification* (Ithaca: Cornell University Press, 1972).

Frederick Hoffman, *William Faulkner* (New York: Twayne, 1961).

John Hollowayy, *Narrattive and Structure: Exploratory Essays* (New York: Cambridge University Press, 1979).

Irvin Howe, *William Faulkner: A Critical Study* (New York: Random House, 1962).

Robert Humphrey *Stream of Consciousness in the Modern Novel: A Study of James Joyce, Virginia Woolf, Dorothy Richardson, William Faulkner and others* (Berkeley: Universit of California Press, 1954).

Abiola Irele, *The African Experience in Literature and Ideology* (Heinemann, 1982).

Wolfgang Iser, *The Implied Reader: Patterns of Communication in Prose Fiction from Bunyan to Beckett* (Baltimore: Johns Hopkins University Press, 1974).

Walter Isle, *Experiments in Form: Henry James's Novels, 1896-1909* (Cambridge, Massachusetts: Harvard University Press 1968).

Janheinz Jahn, *Muntu: An Outline of Neo-African Culture* (Faber, 1961).

Abdul Jan Mohammed, *Manichean Aesthetics: The Politics of Literature in Colonial Africa* (Amherst: The University of Massachusetts Press, 1983).

Eldred Jones, *The Writings of Wole Soyinka* (Heinemann, 1973, revised 1983).

Donald Kartiganer, *The Fragile Thread: The Meaning of Form in Faulkner's Novels* (Amherst: The University of Massachusetts Press, 1979).

Graham Kenneth, *Henry James, The Drama of Fulfilment: An Approach to the Novels* (Oxford: Clarendon Press, 1975).

Frank Kermode, *Essays on Fiction: 1971-82* (Routledge and Kegan Paul, 1983).

Robert Kiely, *Beyond Egotism: The Fiction of James Joyce, Virginia Woolf and D.H. Lawrence* (Cambridge, Massachusetts: Harvard University Press, 1980).

G.D. Killam, *The Novels of Chinua Achebe* (Heinemann, 1969).

_____. *An Introduction to the Writings of Ngugi* (Heinemann, 1981).

Bruce King & Kolawole Ogungbesan, eds., *A Celebration of Black and African Writing* (Zaria and Oxford: Ahmadu Bello University Press and Oxford University Press, 1975).

Mark Kinkead-Weekes, *Samuel Richardson: Dramatic Novelist* (Methuen, 1973).

Paul Kirschner, *Conrad: The Psychologist as Artist* (Edinburgh: Oliver and Boyd, 1968).

Ira Konisberg, *Samuel Richardson and the Dramatic Novel* (Lexington: 1968).

Dorothea Krook, *The Ordeal of Consciousness in Henry James* (Cambridge: The University of Cambridge Press, 1967).

Shiv Kumar, *Bergson and the Stream-of-Consciousness Novel* (Glasgow: Blackie and Son Ltd., 1962).

Susan Sniader Lanser, *The Narrative Act: Point of View in Prose Fiction* (Princeton: Princeton University Press, 1981).

Charles Larson, *The Emergency of African Fiction* (Bloomington: Indiana University Press, 1971).

Margaret Laurence, *Long Drums and Cannons* (Macmillan, 1968).

Benjamin Lease, *Anglo-American Encounters: England and the Rise of American Literature* (New York: Cambridge University Press, 1982).

Mitchell Leaska, *Virginia Woolf's Lighthouse: A Study in Critical Method* (Hogarth, 1970).

F.R. Leavis, *The Great Tradition: George Eliot, Henry James and Joseph Conrad* (Chatto and Windus, 1948).

Hermion Lee, *The Novels of Virginia Woolf* (Methuen, 1977).

Harry Levin, *Joyce: A Critical Introduction* (Norfolk, Connecticut: University of Connecticut Press, 1941).

Bernth Lindfors, *Folklore in Nigerian Literature* (New York: Africana Publishing Company, 1973).

Bernth Lindfors & C.L. Innes, eds., *Critical Perspectives on Chinua Achebe* (Heinemann, 1979).

David Lodge, *Language of Fiction* (Routledge and Kegan Paul, 1966).

Percy Lubbock, *The Craft of Fiction* (New York: Charles Scribner's Sons, 1921).

M. Mahood, *The Colonial Encounter: A Reading of Six Novels* (Rex Collings, 1977).

Edris Makward, *Is There an African Approach to African Literature?* (Los Angeles: African Studies Centre, 1969).

Jay Martin, *Harvests of Change: American Literature 1865-1945* (New Jersey: Prentice-Hall, 1962).

Daniel Massa, *Individual and Community in Commonwealth Literature* (Malta: The University Press, 1979).

F.O. Mathieson, *Henry James: The Major Phase* (New York: Galaxy, 1963).

A.A. Mendilow, *Time and the Novel* (New York: The Humanities Press, 1972).

J. Merriwether & M. Millgate, eds., *Lion in the Garden* (Lincoln: University of Nebraska Press, 1968).

James Miller Jr., ed., *Theory of Fiction: Henry James* (Lincoln: University of Nebraska Press, 1972).

J. Hills Millers, *Fiction and Repetition* (Oxford: Basil Blackwell, 1982).

George Moore, *The Lake* (Heinemann), 1905).

Gerald Moore, *Wole Soyinka* (Evans, 1971)

_____. *Twelve African Writers* (Hutchinson, 1980).

Richard Moreland, *Faulkner and Modernism: Rereading and Rewriting* (Madison: The University of Wisconsin Press, 1990).

Thomas Moser, *Joseph Conrad: Achievement and Decline* (Connecticut: Archon Books, 1966).

Edwin Muir, *The Structure of the Novel* (Hogarth, 1928).

Peter Nazareth, *Literature and Society in Modern African* (Nairobi: East Africa Literature Bureau, 1973).

Elsa Nettels, *James and Conrad* (Athens: The University of Georgia Press, 1977).

Emmanuel Ngara, *Stylistic Criticism and the African Novel* (Heinemann, 1981).

Ngugi Wa Thiong'o, *Homecoming* (Heinemann, 1972)

_____. *Writers in Politics* (Heinemann, 1981).

_____. *Barrel of Pen: Resistance to Neo-Colonial Kenya* (New Beacon Books Ltd., 1983).

J.H. Nketia, *Funeral Dirges of the Akan People* (New York: Negro University Press, 1969).

Lewis Nkosi, *Tasks and Masks: Themes and Styles of African Literature* (Longman, 1981).

Emmanuel Obiechina, *Culture, Tradition and Society in the West African Novel* (Cambridge University Press, 1975).

Kolawole Ogungbesan, ed., *New West African Literature* (Heinemann, 1979).

Stein Haugom Olsen, *The Structure of Literary Understanding* (Cambridge: Cambridge University Press, 1978).

Kole Omotosho, *The Form of the African Novel* (Akure: Fagbamigbe Publishers, 1979).

Michael O'Toole, *Structure, Style and Interpretation in the Russian Short Story* (New Haven: Yale University Press, 1982).

Palaver: Interview with Five African Writers (Austin: African and Afro-American Research Institute, 1972).

Eustace Palmer, *An Introduction to the African Novel* (Heinemann, 1972).

Richard Poirer, *A World Elsewhere: The Place of Style in American Literature* (New York: Oxford University Press, 1966).

John Press, ed., *Commonwealth Literature: Unity and Diversity in a Common Culture* (Heinemann, 1965).

John Preston, *The Created Self: The Reader's Role in Eighteenth Century Fiction* (Heinemann, 1970).

Martin Price, *Forms of Life: Character and Moral Imagination in the Novel* (New Haven: Yale University Press, 1983).

V. Propp, *Morphology of the Folk Tale* (Austin: University of Texas Press, 1973).

Eric Rabkin, *Narrative Suspense* (Ann Arbor: The University of Michigan Press, 1973).

Arthur Ravenscroft, *Chinua Achebe* (Longman, 1969).

Joseph Reed Jr., *Faulkner's Narrative* (New Haven: Yale University Press, 1973).

William Riggan *Picaros, Madmen, Naifs, and Clowns: The Unreliable First-Person Narrator* (Norman: University of Oklahoma Press, 1981).

Harvena Ritcher, *Virginia Woolf: The Inward Voyage* (New Jersey: Princeton University Press, 1970).

Adrian Roscoe, *Mother is Gold* (Cambridge: Cambridge University Press, 1971).

Louis D. Rubin, Jr., *The Teller in the Tale* (Seattle: University of Washington Press, 1976).

Hugh Ruppersberg, *Voice and Eye in Faulkner's Fiction* (Athens: The University of Georgia Press, 1983).

Edward Said, *The World, The Text, and the Critic* (Faber and Faber, 1984).

Robert Scholes, *The Fabulators* (New York: Oxford University Press, 1967).

_____. *Fabulation and Metafiction* (Illinois: University of Illinois Press, 1979).

Robert Scholes & Robert Kellong, *The Nature of Narrative* (Oxford University Press, 1966).

Mark Schorer, *The World We Imagine* (Chatto and Windus, 1969).

William Schuette, ed., *Twentieth Century Interpretation of a Portrait of the Artist as a Young Man* (New Jersey: Prentice-Hall, 1968).

Sallie Sears, *The Negative Imagination: Form and Perspective in the Novels of Henry James* (New York: Cornell University Press, 1968).

Shlomith Rimmon-Kenan, *Narrative Fiction: Contemporary Poetics* (Methuen, 1983).

Robert Stallman, *The Art of Conrad: A Critical Symposium* (East Lansing: Michigan University Press, 1961).

Oladele Taiwo, *Culture and the Nigerian Novel* (Macmillan, 1976).

Tony Tanner, ed., *Henry James* (Macmillan, 1969).

Tzvetan Todorov, *The Poetics of Prose* (Oxford: Basil Blackwell, 1977).

Boris Uspensky, *A Poetics of Composition* (Berkeley: University of California Press, 1973).

Allan Wade, ed., *Henry James, The Scenic Art: Notes on Acting and Drama* (Rupert Hart-Davis, 1949).

Edward Wagenknecht, *Cavalcade of the American Novel, from the Birth of the Nation to the Middle of the Twentieth Century* (New York: Holt, Rinehart and Winston, 1967).

Ronald Wallace, *Henry James and the Comic Form* (Ann Arbor: University of Michigan Press, 1975).

William Walsh, *A Manifold Voice: Studies in Commonwealth Literature* (Chatto and Windus, 1969).

Joseph A. Ward, *The Search for Form: Studies in the Structure of James's Fiction* (Chapel Hill: University of North Carolina Press, 1967).

Robert Penn Warren, ed., *Faulkner: A Collection of Critical Essays* (New York: Prentice-Hall, 1962).

Claude Wauthier, *The Literature and Thought of Modern Africa* (Pall Mall, 1966).

Rene Wellek, *The Attack on Literature and Other Essays* (Brighton: The Haverster Press, 1982).

Virginia Woolf, *The Common Reader*, Second Series (Hogarth Press, 1965).

Robert M. Wren, *Achebe's World: The Historical and Cultural Context of the Novels of Chinua Achebe* (Longman, 1980).

Michael Wree & Donald M. Callen, *Monroe Beardsley: The Aesthetic Point of View, Selected Essays* (Ithaca: Cornell University Press, 1982).

Edgar Wright, *The Critical Evaluation of African Literature* (Heinemann, 1973).

Donald C. Yelton, *Mimesis and Metaphor: An Inquiry into the Genesis and Scope of Conrad's Symbolic Imagery* (Mouton: The Hague, 1967).

II ARTICLES

Chinua Achebe, 'An Image of Africa,' *Research in African Literatures,* 9:1 (1978), 1-15.

_____. 'Viewpoint,' *TLS*, February 1, 1980, 113.

Regina Amadi-Tshiwala, 'Critical Bearings in African Literature,' *Presence Africaine* 115 (1980), 148-155.

Ayi Kwei Armah, 'Larsony or Fiction as the Criticism of Fiction,' *Asemka* No. 4 (1976), 1-14.

_____. 'The Definitive Chaka,' *Chindaba* 50 (1974), 10-13).

_____. 'African Socialism: Utopian or Scientific?' *Presence Africaine* 64 (1967), 6-30.

Kofi Awoonor, The Poem, the Poet and the Human Condition, *Asemka* 5 (1979), 1-23.

_____. 'Come the Voyager at Last,' *Okike* 7 (1975) 31-56.

N.I. Bailey, 'Pragmatism in *The Ambassadors,' Dalhousie Review* LIII (1973), 143-148.

Warren Beck, 'Faulkner's Point of View,' *College English* II (1941), 736-749.

Joseph Blotner, 'Mythic Patterns in *To The Lighthouse*,' *PMLA*, 71 (1956), 547-562.

Lawrence Bowling, 'What is the Stream of Consciousness Technique?' *PMLA*, LXV (1950), 333-345.

Steven Cohan, 'Readable Character' in *Novel: A Forum on Fiction* 17: I (1983), 5-27.

Dorrit Cohn, 'Narrative Monologue: Definition of a Fictional Style,' *Comparative Literature*, 18 (1966), 97-112.

Thomas E. Connolly, 'Point of View in Faulkner's *Absalom, Absalom!*, *Modern Fiction Studies* 27:2 (1981), 255-272.

J.I. Cope, 'Joyce: Test Case for a Theory of Style,' *English Literary History* 21 (1954), 221-236.

Philip J. Egan, 'Embedded Story Structures in *Absalom, Absalom!*, *American Literature*' 55:2 (1983), 199-214.

Romanus Egudu, 'Criticism of Modern African Literature: The Question of Evaluation,' *World Literature Written in English* 21:1 (1982), 54-66.

Victor Emmett, Jr., 'The Aesthetics of Anti-Imperialism: Ironic Distortions of the Vergilian Epic Mode in Conrad's *Nostromo*,' *Studies in the Novel*, 4:3 (1972), 459-472.

Suzanne Ferguson, 'The Face in the Mirror: Authorial Presence in the Multiple Vision of Third-Person Impression-istic Narrative,' *Criticism*, 21:3 (1979), 230-250.

Joseph Frank, 'Spatial Form in Modern Literature,' Parts I-III, *Sewanee Review* 53 (1945), 221-240, 433-456, 643-653.

R.W. Franklin, 'Narrative Management in *As I Lay Dying*,' *Modern Fiction Studies* 13 (1958), 57-65.

Philip L. Greene, 'Point of View in *The Spoils of Poynton*,' *Nineteenth Century Fiction* XII (1967), 359-368.

Mark Goldman, 'Virginia Woolf and the Critic as Reader,' *PMLA*, 80 (1965), 275-284.

Susal Gorsky, 'The Central Shadow: Characterisation in *The Waves, Modern Fiction Studies*' 18:3 (1972), 449-465.

John Graham, 'Point of View in *The Waves*: Some Services of the Style,' *University of Toronto Quarterly* 39:iii (1970), 445-467.

Thomas A. Hale, 'Africa and the West: Close Encounters of a Literary Kind,' *Comparative Literature Studies* Vol. 20:3 (1983), 261-275.

Irene Hendry, 'Joyce's Epiphanies,' *Sewanee Review* 54 (1946), 445-467.

John A. Hodgson, 'Logical Sequence and Continuity: Some Observations on the Typographical and Structural Consistency of *Absalom Absalom!*' LIV (1946), 87-101.

Abiola Irele, 'The Season of a Mind: Wole Soyinka and the Nigerian Crisis,' *Benin Review* 1 (1974), 111-122.

Solomon Iyasere, 'Oral Tradition in the Criticism of African Literature,' *The Journal of Modern African Studies* 13:1 (1975), 107-119.

_____. 'Art, A Simulacrum of Reality Problems in the Criticism of African Literature,' *The Journal of Modern African Studies* XI:3 (1973), 447-455.

_____. 'Cultural Formalism and the Criticism of Modern African Literature,' *The Journal of Modern African Studies* XIV:2 (1976), 322-330.

_____. 'African Critics on African Literature: A Study in Misplaced Hostility,' *African Literature Today* 7 (1975), 20-27.

_____. 'Modern African Literature and Ideological Commitment,' *West African Journal of Modern Languages* 2 (1976), 5-9.

_____. 'Narrative Techniques in *Things Fall Apart*,' *Critical Perspectives on Chinua Achebe*, B. Lindfors and C.L. Innes op. cit., 92-110.

_____. 'Narrative Techniques in Okara's *The Voice*,' *African Literature Today* 12 (1982), 5-21.

D.S. Izevbaye, 'The State of Criticism in African Literature,' *African Literature Today* 7 (1975), 1-19.

_____. 'Issues in the Reassessment of the African Novel,' *African Literature Today* 10 (1979), 7-31.

_____. 'Time in the African Novel,' *The Journal of Commonwealth Literature* XVII:1 (1982), 74-89.

J.Z. Kronenfeld, 'The Communalistic African and the Individualistic Westerner: Some Comments on Misleading Generalisations in Western Criticism of Soyinka and Achebe,' *Research in African Literatures* 6:2 (1975), 199-225.

Isle D. Lind, 'The Design and Meaning of *Absalom, Absalom!, PMLA*' 70 (1955), 887-912.

Bernth Lindfors, 'Ambiguity and Intention in *Arrow of God*,' *Ba Shiru* V: 1 (1973), 43-48.

Edward Lobb, 'Armah's *Fragments* and the Vision of the Whole' *Ariel* X: 1 (1979), 25-38.

Juri Lotman, 'Point of View in a Text,' *New Literary History* 6: 2 (1975), 339-352.

W.R. Macnoughton, 'The First-Person Narrators of Henry James,' *Studies in American Fiction* 2 (1974) 145-164.

Michael Moloney, 'The Enigma of Time: Proust, Virginia Woolf and Faulkner,' *Thought* XXXII (1957), 69-85.

David Monoghan, 'The Single Narrator of *As I Lay Dying*,' *Modern Fiction Studies* 18 (1959), 213-220.

Sister Kristin Morrison, 'James's and Lubbock's Differing Points of View' *Nineteenth Century Fiction* XVI (1962), 245-255.

James Naremore, 'Style as Meaning in *A Portrait of the Artist as a Young Man*,' *James Joyce Quaterely* 4 (1967) 331-342.

Peter Nazareth, 'Is *A Grain of Wheat* a Socialist Novel?,' *Literature and Society in Modern Africa: Essays on Literature* (Nairobi: East Africa Literature Bureau, (1972), 128-154.

Charles Nnolim, 'The Form and Function of the Folk Tradition in Achebe's Novels,' *Ariel* 14: 1 (19883), 35-47.

Joyce Carol Oates, 'The Tragedy of *Nostromo, Novel: A Forum on Fiction*' 9: 1 (1975), 5-22.

Novel: A Forum on Fiction, Vol. 21, Nos. 2 and 3 (1988), Conference Issue.

E.N. Ibiechina, 'Transition from Oral to Literary Tradition,' *Presence Africaine* 63 (1967), 140-161.

E. Obumselu, '*A Grain of What:* Ngugi's Debt to Conrad,' *Benin Review* 1 (1975), 80-91.

Kolawole Ogungbesan, 'Simple Novels and Simplistic Criticism: The Problem of Style in the African Novel,' *Asemka* 5 (1979), 24-40.

Isidore Okpewho, 'Armah's *Two Thousand Seasons,*' *African Literature Today* 13 (1983), 1-23.

Richard Poirer, 'Strange Gods in Jefferson, Mississippi: Analysis of *Absalom, Absalom!,*' *Twentieth Century Interpretations of Absalom, Absalom!,* (New Jersey: Engleweed Cliffs, 1971), 14-27.

Richard Priebe, 'Kofi Awoonor's *This Earth, My Brother* as an African Dirge,' *Benin Review* 1 (1975), 95-111.

Felicity Riddy, 'Language as a Theme in *No Longer at Ease,*' *The Journal of Commonwealth Literature* 9 (1970), 38-47. Also in B. Lindfors and C.L. Innes, op. cit., 150-159.

Kenneth Schmitz, 'Community: The Elusive Unity,' *The Review of Metaphysics* XXXVII: 2 (1983), 243-264.

Mark Schorer, 'Technique as Discovery,' *The Theory of the Novel,* ed., Philip Stevick (New York: The Free Press, 1967), 65-84.

Austin Shelton, 'The Palm-oil of Language: Proverbs in Chinua Achebe's Novels,' *Modern Language Quaterely* 30 (1969), 86-111.

Bob Sherrington, 'Metaphor and Narrattive Meaning: Some African Examples,' *Essays and Monographs Series* 1 (Adelaide: Centre for Research in the New Literatures in English, 1982), 71-110.

R.W. Short, 'Some Critical Terms of Henry James,' *PMLA*, LXIX (1954), 1076-1084.

Jack Stewardt, 'Existence and Symbol in *The Waves, Modern Fiction Studies*' 18: 3 (1972), 433-447.

Wole Soyinka, 'From a Common Back-Cloth: A Reassessment of the African Literary Image,' *American Scholar* XXXII: 3 (1963), 387-396.

Peter Swiggart, 'Time in Faulkner's Novels,' *Modern Fiction Studies* 1 (1955), 25-29.

Helen Tiffin, 'Commonwealth Literature and Comparative Methodology,' *World Literature Written in English* 23: 1 (1984), 26-30.

Patricia Tobin, 'The Time of Myth and History in *Absalom, Absalom!,' American Literature* XLIII (1971-72), 97-101.

Edgar Wright, 'African Literature 1: Problems of Criticism,' *The Journal of Commonwealth Literature* 2 (1966), 103-112.

Karl Zink, 'William Faulkner: Form as Experience,' *South Atlanttic Quarterely* LIII (1954), 384-403.

Robert H. Zoellner, 'Faulkner's Prose Style in *Absalom, Absalom!,' American Literature* XXX (1959), 486-502.

INDEX

A

Abame 143
Abena 153
Abdulla 82; 83–84; 91–92; 94; 97; 98
Achebe, Chinua 1–2; 4; 12; 14–15;
    129; 131; 133–136; 138; 140; 142;
    143–150; 156; 157; 181; 183
        Things Fall Apart 1; 4; 12–
           13; 125–129; 134–135;
           141–142; 144–149; 156;
           181; 183–184
        No Longer at Ease 1, 183
        Arrow of God 13; 125; 132–
           135; 139–140; 145–146;
           148–149; 156; 181
Adisa 48; 57; 64
Affinity 11; 15; 76; 103
African dirge 73
African literary criticism 2
African mythology 39
Agnes, Lady 36
Akukalia 148
Akuebue 134
Alternative religion 154
Amamu 46–47; 49; 56–57; 63–64;
    70–71; 72
Amatu 164–165; 167; 168; 171–172;
    173–176; 177–178
Armah, Ayi Kwei 2–3; 7; 9–14; 102;
    104; 112; 121; 126; 150; 155–156;
    158; 163; 170; 173; 180; 182–183
        *The Beautyful Ones Are Not
          Yet Born* 2

Armah, Ayi Kwei *(continued)*
        Two Thousand Seasons 3;
          103–104; 109; 112–113;
          115; 118–121; 123–124
Armah's Simplicity 156
America 111; 184
American Modernist novel, British
    and 2
Anoa 150; 152; 153; 154; 158–160;
    161; 183
Anthology of wise sayings 139
Antonia Avellanos 80
Apostasy 17; 20–21; 27; 28; 32; 37–
    38
Authorial intervention 33
Awoonor, Kofi 6–7; 40–46; 48; 55–
    56; 64; 69; 73
        This Earth My Brother 7;
          40–41; 46–48; 55; 57–
          58; 70; 72–73
Azuera 89; 96; 100

B

Baker, Earnest 5
Bandele 19–22; 29; 34; 38
Battista, Gian 81
Bauman, Richard 161; 163
Beck, Warren 9
Beelzebub 108
Belvedere 67
Bentley, Phyllis: *Some Observations
    on the Art of the Narrative* 23

Bernard 44–46; 62; 68–70
Bethlehem 93
Biddy 31
Blood 92; 99; 107–108; 110
Bomey 158
Bon, Charles 104; 106–108; 114–115; 118; 122
Boyle, Eugene 78
Bradbury 2
Brisbane 68
British and American Modernist novels 2
Broken chronology 121
Burke 161
Businessmen 90; 93

C

Calvinistic images 114
Capataz of the Cargadores 76–77; 80; 88; 100
Caroll, David 132
Cateret, Charles 17–19; 26; 32–33; 36
Catholic priests 52
Characters 5–6; 13; 16–26; 29–30; 34; 37–38; 41; 45; 47; 54; 57–58; 61–62; 65; 67–69; 73; 75; 78; 81–90; 91; 93–94; 96–102; 104; 106; 108–109; 113; 114; 125–127; 131; 132; 134; 140–142; 151–152; 170; 173–174; 176; 180–181; 182–183
Character's point of view 40
Characteristics 30–31; 41–42; 152; 158
Characterisation 3; 6; 12–13; 17; 39; 41; 44; 48; 61; 65; 84; 113; 126; 133; 149; 150; 153; 181
Chief priest 131–133; 139–140; 145–148
Chinese eggs 9
Christian missionaries 130
Christian Pilgrim 57
Christmas dinner party 67
Chui, Msigo 85; 94
Clarke 134; 148
Classical attributes 3; 12
Clongowes 66–67

Collaborative expectancy 161
Coldfield, Rosa 104–106; 108–109; 114–117; 119; 122
Collective individual 128
Collective struggle 81
Colonialism 1; 184
Comic possibility 28
Communal ethic 151
Communal narrators 157
Communal objectives 168
Communal voice 134; 150; 156; 160
Communicative means 161
Community 3–4; 12; 73; 76; 82; 103–104; 125–142; 145–155; 157–158; 160; 162–163; 167–170; 173–181
Complex conception 3
Compson, Mr. 104–111; 114–119; 122
Conceptual constants of novels 86
Concomitant dramatic situations 17
Confusing stampede 38
Confusion and conflict 25
Congherian experience 111
Consciousness 9; 19; 50; 66; 71; 74; 103–104; 117–118; 120; 149
Contrasting relationships 21
Controlling fibres 130
Conviviality 146
Cosmic Communication 61
Costaguana 79; 87; 96; 100
Cultural background 4
Cultural purity 73

D

Dahomey 58
Dallow, Julia 17–19; 25–27; 36
Darkness 2; 60–61; 63; 87–89; 100; 175–176
Decoud, Martin 76–78; 80–81; 87; 88–89; 96; 100
Debt to Conrad 102
Dedalus household 42; 51
Dedalus, Stephen 41–44; 48–53; 58–61; 64; 65–67
Denunciatory tone 155

Densu 164
Derinola, Sir 22
Densely metaphoric texture 86
Despondency 72
Dialogue 6; 14; 17; 30–33; 35; 39;
    141
Discombobulation 3; 156
Distortion of vision 104
Dofu, Modin 109–112; 115–117;
    119–121; 123–124
Dominant substantiality 87
Dormer, Grace 31, 33
Dormer, Nick 17–19; 21; 24–26; 28;
    31; 32–33; 35–36
Dramatic conflict 31
Dramatic elements 14
Dramatic partnership 76
Dramatic relationships 21–22; 99
Dramatise personae 17
Dublin 64
Dumenyo, Paul 57

E

Eco, Umberto 75
Eden 158; 160
Edogo 148
Egwugwu 129, 138
Eileen 43; 60
Eliot, T. S.: "The Journey of the
    Magi" 1
Emancipation 3
Emma 43
Empire Writers 15
Enchanting and rhetorical 158–159
Eschatological vision 162
Esuba 158
Eternal renewal 54
Europe 184
Europeans of Sulaco 81
Evil Forest 143
Excrement of the clan 138
Existentialist country 2
Ex-Mau Mau fighter 82
Experimentation 1–3; 38; 150
Exploitative designs 93
Ezeudu 127

Ezeulu 125–126; 131–135; 139–141;
    145–147; 183

F

Failed revolutionary 110
Faseyi, Ayo 20; 22
Fate 106; 124
Fathers of Umuofia 137–138
Faulkner and Modernism 10–11
Faulkner's narrative technique 103
Faulkner, William 8–11; 14; 102;
    183
        As I Lay Dying 9; 104
        Absalom, Absalom! 103–
            104; 109; 112–113;
            117–123; 124; 131
Faustus 108
Fictional universe 3; 15
Fidanza, Captain 88
Fire 90–92; 97–98; 101
Fixed perspective 134
Form 31; 45
Forster, E. M. 35
Fowler, Roger 127
Fragmentation 29; 72
Fraser, Robert 111
Fulani 158

G

Gao 158
Garibaldino 78
Ghana 2
Gibbon, Lewis Grassic 126
Golder, Joe 20; 22; 38
Goodcountry, Mr. 135
Golgotha 71
Gorky, Susan 61
Gould, Charles 77–81; 89; 95
Gould Concession 87
Gould, Emilia 78; 79–81; 86–90; 95;
    96
Government house 148
Grammer of values, a 138
Great River 143
Griffiths, Gareth 141
Guerard, Albert 10

Gulf 87–88; 96
Guzman Bento 79

H

Hampton Court 62
Hardy 126
Harmonious relationship 55
Heaven 160
Henry 107
House of Commons 17
Humanising influence 78

I

Ibrahim 57–58
Idawa 153; 155–156
Idemili 133
Ideological system 127
Igbo cultural heritage 142
Ignorance of context 126
Ijele Mask 134
Ikemefuna 127; 144
Ilmorog 82; 84; 86; 92–93; 98; 99;
    101
Images 61–63; 73; 90–91; 94–96;
    106; 108; 115–116; 117; 159;
    164–165
Imaginative sharing of experience
    103
Inexorable law of the mental
    power, the 84
Inherent dramatic qualities 27
Inspector Godfrey 86
Integrity of art 6
Intellectutal board 42
Interpretation 12; 30; 55; 86; 91; 97;
    102; 104
Intimidating presence 72
Isanusi 152–154; 157; 160–161
Isolated consciousness 113
Izevbaye 150
Iyasere, Solomon 164

J

James, Henry 4–6; 14; 16–17; 19–26;
    30–31; 33–36; 38; 103

James, Henry (*continued*)
    The Tragic Muse 6; 17–21;
        24; 27–35
Jefferson, Mrs. 117
Jeremiah 152
Jesuits 51
Joseph 86
Jinny 44; 62; 69
Journey across America 153
Joyce, James 3; 6–7; 40; 46; 48; 55;
    64; 72–73
    *A Portrait of an Artist as a
        Young Man* 6; 40–41;
        46; 47; 48; 50–51; 53;
        55; 58–59; 61; 65; 68;
        71
Judith 108; 114; 119
Juxtaposition of features 21

K

Karega 83–86; 91–93; 97; 101
Kartiganer, Donald 108
Kedia 158
Kenya 84
Keta 64
Kimeria 94
Killman, Douglas 84
King Koranche 150; 152–153; 154;
    160
King of Sulaco 77
Kinkead-Weakes, Mark 16; 28; 37
Kinship and affinity 11
Kinship with Jesus 71
Kinship in method 76
Kola 19–21; 34; 38
Kole Omotoso 2

L

Laccryville 112
Language 2–3; 7; 13–14; 42; 52; 56;
    135; 139; 142; 154–156; 158–159;
    165; 169–172; 180–181
Lanser, Susan 4
Lasunwon 28
Lazarus 29–30; 33–34; 38
Leech, Geoffrey 163

Leeds 76
Light 60; 68; 87
Linda 81
Lindfors, Bernth 138
Linguistic mistake 86
Literary nationalists 15
Literary theory 4
Logical finish 24
London 26; 36; 64
Louis 44–46; 47, 48; 68
Lubbock, Percy 5
Lynch, Dr. 115

M

Mabel 43
Macfarlane 2
Manoeuverability 39
Masks 143
Materialism 78; 165
Marthiessen, F. O. 23
Mau Mau War 84
Mbaino 143
Mbanta 143
McEwan, Neil 136
Mercedes 43; 60; 68
Memory 7; 58–59; 60; 61–62; 63; 64;
     68; 71; 72
Mendilow 35
Methaphorical darkness 89
Metaphorical undercurrent 87
Metaphors 7; 9; 11; 13; 43–45; 89–
     95; 102; 112–117; 119; 132; 141;
     150; 166
Miscegenation 108; 115
Mitchell, Captain 76; 81; 84–85; 88;
     96, 100–101
Modern African novel 4
Modernism 1–2; 8–11; 14; 44; 184
Modernist God 44
Modernists interpreters 6
Modernist literary device 140
Modernist novels 6–7; 38; 42; 46;
     65; 76
Modernist rebellion 43
Modernist tradition 40
Modernist triumph 109
Monkey Nigger 107

Moral darkness 87
Moreland, Richard 10–11; 142
Monterists 76
Monygham, Dr. 78–80; 81; 96
Moore, George 7; 50
Moore, Gerald 84; 131
Moser, Thomas 8
Muir, Edwin 17
Munira 82; 83; 84–85; 90–94; 97; 98;
     101
Mythic dimensions 83

N

Nairobi 3
Naita 116
Narrator 3–4; 13; 31; 36; 59; 84; 109;
     112; 113; 118; 119; 127–128; 135;
     137–138; 144–148; 156; 157; 160;
     161; 163; 164; 171–173
Nash, Gabriel 6; 18–19; 21; 24; 25;
     29; 32; 36
Ndola 153
New Yam Feast 149
Neville 44–45; 62
Ngara, Emmanuel 153; 165
Ngugi Wa Thiong'o 7–9; 11; 14; 75–
     76; 84; 90; 93–94; 97–99; 101–
     102; 117
     A Grain of Wheat 76
     Petals of Blood 76; 81–82;
         84–85; 90–91; 97; 101–
         102
Neo-colonial Africa 11
Nicholas, Sir 36
Nigome 153
Nima 57; 63
Nineteenth century village 101
Nkonam, Solo 109–112; 115–117;
     119–121; 123–124
Nnolim, Charles 149
Noliwe 153
North 152
Nostromo 9; 77; 80–83; 87–90; 94–
     97; 100
Novels for the reader 75
Nwaka 132–134; 139–141
Nweke Ukpaka 141

Nwoye 131
Nyakinyua 91

O

Obiechina, Emmanuel 165
Obierika 130; 131; 142
Obika 148
Oduche 134
Ofoka 134; 140
Oguazors 20; 22; 30; 35
Ogungbesan, Kola 36
Okara, Gabriel 4; 14; 126; 133; 150;
    161; 164–165; 169–175; 177–181;
    183
        The Voice 4; 126; 133; 150;
            161–181; 183
Okolo 133; 164–169; 171–180
Okonkwo 125–132; 134; 136–138;
    142; 144–145; 147; 183
Okpewho, Isidore 153
Okperi 147
Orientation of the society 76

P

Palmer, Eustace 84; 150; 158; 165
Pan-Africanism 163
Parallelism 161–163
Paris 36
Participating narrator 146
Paternalistic terms 148
Percival 46; 62; 68–69; 72
Perspective 4; 7; 9; 14; 46; 50; 59; 65;
    75; 104; 112; 126; 131; 147–148;
    154; 163; 166; 180
        Commanding 131
        Communal 3–4; 11–12;
            104; 154; 156
        Inward 6–7; 14; 58–59; 65; 72
        Multiple 7; 9; 14; 75; 102;
            104; 112; 117
        Narrative 86; 103
        Primary 14
Poirer, Richard 10
Placido 87
Plastic values 20
Poano 158

Point of view 3–4; 6–7; 10; 12–13;
    14; 41; 75–76; 83; 86; 94; 99; 112;
    127; 130; 136; 148; 164; 181
Portuguese girl 116
Positive protest 111
Priebe, Richard 7
Priestess of Agbala 138
Protagonists 7; 12; 16; 37; 40; 48; 60,
    62; 67; 72; 125
Prawer, S. S.: *Comparative Literary
    Studies: An Introduction* 182

Q

Quentin 104; 108–109; ,110; 111;
    113; 115; 119–120; 121–123
Questionable solidarity 101

R

Racial War 152
Radcliffe 112
Reference point 61
Reitsch, Aimee 109; 112; 116–117;
    124
Relationship 6; 17–18; 20–22; 42; 82;
    86; 99; 154
Repetition 10–11; 14; 28; 37; 63; 85;
    94–99; 112; 117–118
Republic 80; 82; 87; 100
Retreat 51–53; 59
Revolutionary innovation 149
Rhoda 44–45; 62; 67; 69; 72
Rhythmic changes 148
Richardson 16
Romantic idealism 77; 78
Roth, Miriam 17–18; 24–26; 32; 36

S

Sagoe 19; 21–22; 28–29; 34; 38
San Tome mine 79
Schmitz 128
Schorer, Mark 11
Sekoni 19–20; 27–29; 33–34; 37–38
Sears, Sallie 5
Self-search 41
Sequence of actions 23

Sexual depravity 155
Shadow of memories 64
Shakespeare 68
Sheikh 33
Shreve 108–109; 114–115; 119, 120
Shrieking ghosts 89
Sherringham, Peter 18; 25; 32
Silver 86–87; 89–90; 94–98
Simpa 158
Siriana Secondary School 85; 98
Smith, Rev. 138; 141
Soliloquies 44; 47; 68
Sologa 164; 167
Soyinka, Wole 4–6; 16–17; 18; 19–
    20; 22–23; 27–30; 33; 35; 36–39
        The Interpreters 5–6; 18;
            19–22; 27–28; 33; 35–
            38
Spanish wife 107
Speculative narrators 104
Sphinx-like nature 83
Standards of criticism 3
Sterne: *Tristram Shandy* 65
Sulaco 77; 80–81; 87; 100
Style 6; 14; 38; 45; 86; 124
Susan 67–68; 72
Sutpen, Ellen 119
Sutpen, Thomas 104–107; 110; 113–
    115; 118; 119; 120; 122; 129; 130
Su Tsen 158
Symbolism 7; 14; 49; 53; 177

T

Tebeowei 169
Technique 4; 6; 10–11; 22; 24; 26–
    27; 50; 72; 76; 102; 115; 117–119;
    135; 154; 172; 181
        of alternation 24
Technical requirements 23
Temporary intelligibility 121
Texas 73
Theme 29; 101
Thengeta 93; 101
Thimaera, Witi 125
Time 35–37; 65–72; 99–101; 121–
    124; 127; 142
        Chronological 65; 72; 124

Time *(continued)*
        Circular 121
        Clock 65
        Mechanical 65; 70–71
        Mythical 99
Tradition 40; 168; 172; 174; 179; 184
        Communal 139
Trans-Africa Highway 93–94
Three
        The three Isabels 100
        The three villages 100
        The third of May 100
Throw away the burden 89
Toppling linguistic systems 149
Tortoise tale 136
Tuere 165; 170; 174–175; 176–178

U

Uchendu 129–130; 138; 142–143
Ulu 133
Umuaro 125–126; 132–134; 139–
        142; 144; 147–150; 183–184
Umuofia 125–128; 130; 131; 135–
        138; 142; 144; 150; 183–184
Umuru 143
Uncanny complementarity 112
Understanding human nature 8
United States 111
United States of Europe 65

V

Variation of the technique 9
Victim of material interest 85
Vincent, Theo 2

W

Wallace, Ronald 39
Wanja 82–84; 91–93; 97; 101
Wattie, Nelson 125–126
Way 7; 18; 54; 78; 81; 88; 93; 136;
        151; 155; 156; 158; 159; 162; 168
        Our 151
Web of relationship 7
Welleck, Rene 184–185
Week of peace 128

Weight 89; 94
Western criticism, conventional 7
Winterbottom, Captain 132; 134–
      135; 148–149
Woolf, Virginia 3; 6–7; 14; 40; 41;
      44–45; 61; 64; 70; 72; 75; 99; 121
            The Waves 6–7; 40; 41; 44–
                  46; 48, 49; 56; 57; 58;
                  61; 67–69; 71–73
World view 6; 56; 141

Y

Yaro 47
Yoruba god 38
Yoruba mythology 28
Yoknapatawpha County 126; 142

Z

Zink, Karl 103

James L. Hill, General Editor

Studies in African and African-American Culture

Studies in African and African-American Culture has the objective of presenting an outstanding series of original works which, in their critical appraisals and reappraisals of a wide variety of African/African-American topics, provide fresh and insightful analyses to broaden the contemporary point of view. With special emphasis on the basic traditions that are unique to African/African-American cultures, this series seeks to present studies from disciplines as diverse as literature, history and sociology, and in this thematic variety, reveal the richness and global nature of the black experience. Each volume of the series will be a book-length study of a selected African/African-American topic, employing the most recent scholarship and methods of inquiry to explore the subject.

For additional information about this series or for the submission of manuscripts, please contact:

Peter Lang Publishing, Inc.
Acquisitions Department
275 Seventh Avenue, 28th floor
New York, New York 10001